P9-CCL-814

*Divorce Doesn't Have
to Be That Way*

Publisher's Note

This publication is designed to provide accurate and authoritative information in regard to the subject matter covered. It is sold with the understanding that the publisher is not engaged in rendering psychological, medical, or other professional service.

Books in The Practical Therapist Series® *present authoritative answers to the question, "What-do-I-do-now-and-how-do-I-do-it?" in the practice of psychotherapy, bringing the wisdom and experience of expert mentors to the practicing therapist. A book, however, is no substitute for thorough professional training and adherence to ethical and legal standards. At minimum:*

- *The practitioner must be qualified to practice psychotherapy.*
- *Clients participate in psychotherapy only with informed consent.*
- *The practitioner must not "guarantee" a specific outcome.*
      — Robert E. Alberti, Ph.D., Publisher

Other titles in The Practical Therapist Series®

Anger Management

Anger Management Video Program

Creative Therapy with Children and Adolescents

Creative Therapy 2: Working with Parents

Defusing the High-Conflict Divorce

How To Fail as a Therapist

Integrative Brief Therapy

Meditative Therapy

Metaphor in Psychotherapy

Rational Emotive Behavior Therapy (Second Edition)

The Soul of Counseling

Divorce Doesn't Have to Be That Way

A Handbook for the Helping Professional

Jane Appell, Ph.D.

The Practical Therapist Series®

Impact Publishers®
ATASCADERO, CALIFORNIA

Copyright © 2006
Jane Appell

*All rights reserved under international and Pan-American Copyright
Conventions. No part of this book may be reproduced, stored in a retrieval system,
or transmitted in any form or by any means, digital, electronic, mechanical,
photocopying, recording or otherwise, without express written permission of the
author or publisher, except for brief quotations in critical reviews.*

ATTENTION ORGANIZATIONS AND CORPORATIONS:
This book is available at quantity discounts on bulk purchases for educational,
business, or sales promotional use. For further information, please contact
Impact Publishers, P.O. Box 6016, Atascadero, California 93423-6016. Phone:
805-466-5917, e-mail: info@impactpublishers.com

Library of Congress Cataloging-in-Publication Data
Appell, Jane.
Divorce doesn't have to be that way : a handbook for the helping professional / Jane Appell.
p. ; cm. — (The practical therapist series)
Includes bibliographical references and index.
ISBN 1-886230-71-4 (alk. paper)
1. Divorce. 2. Divorce counseling. 3. Divorce therapy. 4. Divorced people—Counseling of. I. Title.
HQ814.A58 2006
362.82'948—dc22
20060109859

Impact Publishers and colophon are registered trademarks of Impact
Publishers, Inc.

Cover design by Passion4Design, Templeton, California
Composition by UB Communications, Parsippany, New Jersey
Printed in the United States of America on acid-free, recycled paper
Published by **Impact** *Publishers*®
POST OFFICE BOX 6016
ATASCADERO, CALIFORNIA 93423-6016
www.impactpublishers.com

Dedication

To Melanie, Kenny and Steven for your love and all that you have taught me.

— Jane Appell

Contents

Acknowledgements

The challenge in listing acknowledgements for a book such as this lies in knowing where to stop. Every client who has stepped into my office and had the bravery to shine the light on his or her private pains and triumphs has had a hand in shaping this book. Every professor, every colleague, every professional friend has played a part. Hundreds of gifted authors and speakers over the years have helped to shape my thinking and bring me clarity. Bits of their wisdom, inspiration and teaching are inextricably woven throughout the fabric of this endeavor. Thank you to all of you.

Since I can't begin to acknowledge all of those who have really helped to mold this book, I will thank by name only the obvious few:

My husband, Steven Shapse, Ph.D., for his constant support, encouragement, critical eye and peer consultation. (Most of all, Steven, thank you for giving me time and space and your unending good will).

My publisher and editor Robert Alberti, Ph.D., for believing in the project right from the start, for his exceptional input, and for just being terrific to work with.

Andy Wolfendon, for his words and invaluable assistance.

The many trusted friends and colleagues who read various drafts and sections of this book and offered important insights, criticisms and suggestions. The book is substantially better for their help. My deepest thanks to Marsha Boumeil, J.D., John Fiske, J.D., Sheara Friend, J.D, Linda Taffet, J.D., Amy Tishelman, Ph.D., Ruth Whitney, MSW, and Robert Zibbell, Ph.D.

Finally, I would like to thank the board of directors and membership of Massachusetts Association of Guardians *Ad Litem* for their support, encouragement, and fellowship over many years. This group has been like a professional family to me and has provided much of the soil in which I, and the ideas in this book, have grown. I wish also to thank them for their ongoing efforts to bring to Massachusetts the best and brightest names in the divorce field to seed and fertilize professional learning in this area.

Introduction

We all know the divorce horror stories — the courtroom battles, the property seizures, the dueling restraining orders. Children being passed like hockey pucks between warring factions. We know about the long-term emotional damage that divorce can cause, especially to children. What we *don't* necessarily know is what *we* can do to change the picture. We in the helping professions actually wield quite a bit of power in the matter. Just as the flapping of the proverbial butterfly's wing can alter the course of a global weather system, our actions in the burgeoning "storm" of divorce can go a long way toward influencing how these swirling emotional forces play out. We have such power: power to make things better; power to help our clients see a divorce as a growth process; power to help produce an end result that is not a net loss, but at least a partial *net gain* for all parties; power to promote a peaceful, respectful divorce process and postdivorce environment; power to protect kids from the burden of unnecessary pain.

Most of us are committed to using that power in an intelligent and responsible manner. But a major impediment has been the lack of good training materials to guide us in how best to help people through the divorce process.

I have worked as a psychologist for thirty years and specialized in divorce for nearly twenty. I've taught a great many professional seminars and workshops on the topic. Divorce has played a leading role in my life, both personally and professionally. Over the course of my many years of work and personal experience, I have read, or at least skimmed, the bulk of the divorce literature that has been published. What has continually astounded me is that no truly practical guide has been written specifically for *helping professionals who want to give healthy support to their clients throughout the divorce process*. There have been many excellent theoretical and research-driven books, some good general readership books on the topic of divorce, some how-to guides on particular *aspects* of the divorce process from various angles and approaches, and several recent books on working with high-conflict divorce. Yet no one seems to have written a comprehensive *working guide* designed for the counseling professional to *help his or her client* navigate the minefield that is the twenty-first-century American divorce. Such a resource has been sorely needed.

In my various professional capacities as custody evaluator, parenting coordinator, mediator, and psychotherapist, I have seen that too often we in the helping professions think we are helping our divorcing clients when we're not. We unwittingly get drawn into advocacy roles, supporting what we believe to be our clients' best interests — winning custody of the children, keeping the house, securing restraining orders, avoiding nasty alimony judgments — without stepping back to look at the big picture. Because of our own personal agendas or our desire to form an alliance with our clients, we make assumptions that may not be entirely valid: "Women need to fight for their rights." "Divorce is a negative life event." "Divorce is a moral failure." "Empathy for the client is always the most important thing." "My client's point of view is objectively valid." These assumptions lead us to advocate certain positions.

Or sometimes our simple lack of awareness about the divorce process results in failure to help clients consider all their options. Every decision made during the divorce process has ripple effects that can reverberate in clients' lives for years, positively or negatively. Too often, our clients seek shortsighted solutions and take rash actions. Litigious lawyers are hired, spouses are cast as enemies, restraining orders are filed, assets are seized, and lives — especially those of the children — are spun out in painful trajectories.

Divorce doesn't have to be that way. What is needed is a holistic approach, a way to help individuals, couples, and families navigate the divorce process in a functional, growth-oriented, and rational manner. Because we in the helping professions *can* see the big picture — where the client often cannot — we are in a position to have an enormous healing effect on the process. We can help clients escape the trap of black-and-white, I win/you lose thinking that has poisoned the waters of modern divorce. There is a good deal of information out there, but we need guidance on how to apply it.

Thus, this book. Born of my decades of work on many sides of the divorce process, this book is a guide for helping professionals whose clients are already having marital problems and are contemplating divorce or who are already embroiled in the divorce process. There are many excellent resources out there for helping clients improve their communication and intimacy skills to avoid a marital crisis in the first place. Naturally, these approaches should be tried first. This book comes next. Yes, it will look at some strategies for improving communications and for assessing whether troubled relationships should indeed be terminated, but its main focus will be on helping clients for whom divorce is already "on the table."

The purpose of the book is twofold. First and foremost it is an attempt to give helping professionals — marriage and family therapists, psychologists, social workers, guidance counselors, physicians, clergy, and others — a means of helping our clients and ourselves maintain a sense of balance and objectivity. As we work with clients, it is natural to get drawn into seeing events from their points of view. But taking a "the customer is always right" approach to divorce may not be what is best in the long run. If I were a real estate agent and a customer came to me with a list of desired features for a new home, I could respond in one of two ways: (1) I could simply find a house that matched the customer's list and facilitate the purchase, believing that my role is to give the customer what he wants; or (2) I could do an assessment of the customer's housing needs. If I believed there were factors that the client was not taking into consideration — the tax rate, the school system, local conservation laws — I would then try to "re-educate" him and help him choose a house that was *truly* a match for his family.

I believe that, as helping professionals, it is often our duty to take the second approach. We are, after all, the "experts." As one would go to a real estate broker for his or her specialized knowledge of the housing market, clients come to *us* for our specialized knowledge of the social/psychological/emotional landscape. Therefore, we must, at least to some degree, play the part of educators. Let's say, for example, that a client wants to "slap a restraining order" on her controlling, type A husband. It is incumbent upon us to explore the likely results of such an action. Is it really a good idea? How would *you* react, we might ask our client, if you came home from work one day to find the police at *your* door with a legal order in hand banning *you* from setting foot in the house you purchased with your own money? Is it not logical to assume that your husband — especially given his personality — might react very badly to such an event? That he might decide to "fight fire with fire," call in the most litigious lawyer in town, and dedicate himself to the proposition of taking you down in flames, no matter what the cost? Is this really what you want? Is this a price you are willing to pay for the satisfaction of "getting even?" Will this really lead to the most peaceful, healthy long-term environment for your children?

Or what if the client is a recently separated man intent upon winning joint physical custody of his children? Perhaps the marriage broke up because of his wife's infidelity, so he feels victimized by the whole situation. He does not want to let her win by waltzing off with the kids while he gets stuck paying child support. While the client's hurt and anger may be justifiable, are the children really going to be served by a protracted court drama? Are there ways to help the client work through his pain and resentment and stay in the children's lives without making them pawns in their parents' game?

If the *child* is our client, how do we do what is best for him or her when both parents may be pressing the child (and us) with competing agendas? How do we balance what is best for the child against the legitimate needs of other family members? How do we best maintain a working relationship with both parents to facilitate a positive adjustment for the child?

Another purpose for this book is to protect *us*, the professionals, as we tap-dance through the highly charged and volatile arena of divorce. Working with divorcing clients can be ethically challenging, to say the least. The book will focus on such issues as being clear about our role and not rendering opinions, avoiding "entangling alliances," maintaining written records so as to minimize the likelihood of their being misused in legal proceedings, using the proper release forms, and knowing how and when to seek consultation. The goal is to keep us out of trouble, ethically, legally, and emotionally, as we try to do our very best for our clients and their families.

This book will also provide guidelines on how to work with divorcing couples or individuals and their children. It will look at the major issues for men and women in divorce. It will strive to provide tools for keeping clients at the maximum level of functioning through all of the ebbs and flows of the divorce process. Alternatives to conflict-provoking strategies will be offered, as will techniques for coping with the stresses of divorce. The book will highlight some of the common traps into which helpers often fall.

Divorce Doesn't Have to Be That Way will present divorce as a dynamic process, in which the type of feedback we give the client may differ depending on who the client is and in what stage of the divorce process he or she might be. There may, in fact, be times in which it is quite healthy and useful for a spouse to be assertive with the soon-to-be ex-mate. Anger may provide the necessary booster fuel to propel that client out of a potentially dangerous or "stuck" situation. However, once the partners have begun to disentangle themselves from an unhappy relationship, it is generally more fruitful to help our client view the ex-partner with some degree of compassion once again.

Finally, the book will offer a brief working overview of the nuts and bolts of the divorce system. We'll look at litigation and its alternatives, such as mediation and collaborative law. We will examine the roles and purposes of key players, such as attorneys, parenting coordinators, and guardians *ad litem*. We will examine the pros and cons of some typical divorce scenarios.

Philosophically, the book will take a stand against black-and-white, I win/you lose thinking. Its emphasis will be on maintaining a systems perspective, one that takes the entire family into consideration, whether the counselor is working with one or multiple members of the family. The family as a whole, I believe, is not usually well served by having a Divorce Winner and a Divorce Loser but by having all parties come out as favorably as possible. Being crowned victor is a hollow achievement if the runner-up is going to continue to bear a grudge and act out with hostility in the future.

I advocate the following notion: all parties can and should *grow* from a divorce. Once divorce has been determined as the road of choice, it can and *must* be viewed as an opening, an opportunity. A win/win divorce is not always possible, but it should certainly be our goal. It is possible far more often than we think it is.

I will not pretend in this book to offer a complete and comprehensive handbook for working with the divorcing client in a single volume, but I will focus on what I see as the most important points, based on my own years of experience "in the trenches." My goal is that all professionals reading this book will be moved to view their own client communications and interventions with a wider lens. I hope this book will help everyone to resist the divorce-as-warfare mentality that pervades our culture and legal system. Divorce can be a devastating, draining, and demoralizing process. *But divorce doesn't have to be that way.*

How Might Things Have Gone Differently?

The process of a divorce evolves like a weather system: add a little moisture here, feed in a little hot air there, throw in a change of pressure, and suddenly you can have a full-blown tempest. But alter a few conditions by just a small degree and fairer weather may be on the horizon. As we review the case histories of the most painful divorces, we notice what I call Critical Entry Points along the way. These are key decision points at which helpers or other outside parties did, or might have, become involved and at which the quality of their input might have spun "the storm" in a completely different direction, or perhaps diffused it entirely.

Before proceeding to the substance of this book — an exploration of the issues, principles, and dynamics of the divorce process and how to deal with them in our work — I would like to stress the importance of Critical Entry Points. These "on-ramps" along the road to divorce are our biggest, and sometimes our only, chances to make a difference. A Critical Entry Point is simply a junction in the road, a place where the client is on the verge of making a key decision and looks to a helping professional for input or support. When these opportunities arise, we can try to make sure that all decisive actions the client takes serve his or her highest goals for the whole family system.

Mapping out mature and appropriate goals with a client is crucial, even if we see that client only one time. If you ask almost any divorcing person to describe an ideal vision of life two years down the road, very few would consciously choose interpersonal acrimony, legal warfare, psychological trauma for their children, and financial stress. That is not the destination at which a rational client wants to arrive.

Then why do so many end up there? Often, they do not have a good map or they lose sight of their route and take bad turns along the way, driven by the exigencies of the moment. In many cases, they are encouraged by "helpers" to take actions that cannot possibly steer them to a desirable destination. Or they are "unconditionally supported" by helpers to stay on an ill-chosen road rather than select a better one.

We in helping professions can be the "holders of the map." We can imagine a rational vision of the future for the client and for the family as a whole. We can encourage the divorcing individual to embrace and internalize this vision. Then we can provide the tools, information, and counseling to help the client get there.

If a divorcing client has the equanimity and maturity to step back from the cauldron of emotion that divorce stirs up, then his or her vision for the future will probably include such elements as a peaceful and workable relationship with the ex-partner, maximum individual happiness for both parties, a fair and reasonable settlement of property issues, and a low-stress family life for the children. If the needs of any of the parties are trampled or ignored during the process, then this vision will not unfold. Too often, helpers lose sight of the family system as a whole and encourage actions that they *think* will help the client gain an advantage in the battle. But every action has an equal and opposite reaction. Any act of aggression, subversion, or one-upmanship during the divorce process will usually spark a counterattack of some sort against the client. This, in turn, triggers an even bigger *counter*-counterattack, and so on. The storm builds. However, every action made with a mature, loving intention (if not toward the ex-partner, then at least toward the children and/or the self) may calm the ripples and lay the groundwork for a rational solution to unfold.

Because we in the helping professions have some objectivity in the matter, we are often the only ones capable of holding the map of the rational vision and advocating for it, especially when the going gets rough. We can remind clients of the desired end result and then consider each decision in the light of whether it will move them *toward* this destination or steer them away from it. As Critical Entry Points arise we can seize these as opportunities to look at the map afresh.

In this chapter we will follow one couple's story. It's a story with many "typical" plot points. I don't mean to suggest that there is a "typical divorce." But there are all-too-familiar scenarios that play out again and again, often spurred by the intervention, or lack thereof, that one or both of the partners receives. We will follow events from the first signs of serious trouble in the marriage to the state of affairs two-plus years after the divorce.

The particular case presented here is an amalgam of many cases with which I have been involved. Naturally, specific details have been changed in the interest of privacy, but the core events and dynamics have real-life origins. As the story unfolds, we will stop at Critical Entry Points along the way to consider what might have happened if the helpers had offered different support or feedback. Remember that the client who is caught up in the storm is far too emotionally charged to see clearly — it is up to the helping professional to provide the broader perspective. If we fail to do so, we fail the client and we fail the family.

The story of John and Marian, in pencil-sketch form:

John and Marian have been married for thirteen years. They have two children, Kim, 10, and Greg, 8. John is a physician, the chief of his department at a well-respected hospital. Marian is a stay-at-home mother who willingly gave up her career as a lab technician after the children were born. John and Marian met when he was a young resident at the hospital. She was attracted by his confidence and his "strong, silent" demeanor; he liked her wholesome good looks and desire for a white-picket-fence family life. They were wed in a grand church ceremony.

Now, thirteen years into the marriage, John's "strong and silent" character has devolved into "controlling and uncommunicative" in Marian's eyes. John is, in many ways, the classic high-achieving, type A male. Driven and professionally focused, he pours most of his attention into work. He routinely logs sixty-hour weeks in the name of providing stability and financial security for the family. Dinner and a movie once a month or so and a two-week vacation every summer add up, in his mind, to giving his wife and children plenty of attention. John makes all the major money decisions in the household. He keeps a close eye on the family finances. If asked about his relationship with Marian, he would say, "Everything's great!"

Marian, on the other hand, finds herself becoming more and more restless and empty as the years pass. Since the kids started school she has felt vaguely dissatisfied and depressed. She attributes her nagging sense of emptiness to the marriage, though she still likes the comfort and stability it provides. Relationships with female friends provide the only real intimacy in her life. Her attempts to get John to talk about the marriage are rarely productive. When she initiates a discussion about family activities, he perceives her as complaining and demanding and retreats to his basement office to read online medical journals and catch up on cases.

Finally Marian gets into therapy. As she begins to explore her own inner terrain, her dissatisfaction with her life situation becomes more acute. Feeling "empowered" by therapy, she begins to see the need to take some kind of concrete action. Encouraged by her therapist, she starts to openly complain about the marriage and to challenge John to change. He reacts defensively. John and Marian start to have prolonged arguments, often in front of the children.

Critical Entry Point #1: Marian starts therapy

Marian's therapist focuses on Marian's "empowerment" but does not focus on the impact of Marian's own behaviors on the dynamics of the marriage. Marian's confrontational behavior, misconstrued as empowerment, comes across to John as a nebulous sort of anger, from which he retreats further. What is Marian hoping to accomplish by lashing out at him? Does she want to be closer to him or farther apart? Her therapist could help her clarify this. Either way, is yelling and accusing a good means for getting there? Is there a more productive method of asserting herself?

Helpers are wise to consider the impact of their advice on the family system. Perhaps the therapist could have worked with Marian to better understand John — his cognitive and communicative styles — so as to find ways to approach him that would not trigger his defenses. Marian may temporarily feel empowered by behaving in a challenging manner, but real empowerment consists of having an idea about what one is trying to accomplish and feeling capable of taking the steps to realistically get there. Open conflict with her husband is frightening the children and turning John into The Enemy. Is Marian's behavior effectively moving her toward making the changes she desires?

Growing increasingly unhappy in the marriage, Marian invites John to come to therapy with her. He declines, largely because talking about emotional matters seems alien, even threatening, to him. Over a period of weeks, Marian remains insistent and John grudgingly joins her for a therapy appointment. The three parties meet, but John's experience, from the moment they start, is that Marian and the therapist are already "allied." Uncomfortable and angry throughout the session, he decides that therapy is "not for him."

Critical Entry Point #2: Bringing John to therapy

Was attempting to see the couple together the wisest course of action for Marian's therapist? Doing so involves a change in role for the individual therapist. Assuming therapist and client decided that this was indeed the desired course, what might the therapist have done to help John feel less defensive on their first encounter? John already believes that the therapist and Marian are allied against him — after all, his wife only started "getting ideas" after she got into therapy. What if instead of seeing the couple together the first time, the therapist had seen John alone and presented an open, empathetic front to him? What if the therapist had begun by listening to his concerns without Marian in the room?

Instead, the therapist brings John into "enemy terrain," John retreats into defensiveness, and a critical opportunity to engage him in couple therapy is lost, probably for good. Couple therapy might have saved the marriage.

John steadfastly refuses to go back to couple therapy. This is the last straw for Marian. If her husband won't try therapy, then obviously he does not have any investment in the marriage. At her next therapy session, she announces that she intends to leave the marriage. She is not ready to tell her husband yet but decides that she will begin to work on that.

Critical Entry Point #3: Marian decides the marriage is over

Marian sees John's refusal to attend therapy as a key turning point. Does the therapist, a strong believer in therapy herself, unthinkingly support Marian's conclusion that the marriage is now "officially over," or does the therapist objectively help Marian assess the pros and cons of her decision? Are there further steps that can be taken to save the marriage even if John does not want to attend therapy with Marian's therapist?

Now that Marian has openly acknowledged to herself and her therapist a desire to be out of the marriage, she begins to slip into depression, a natural stage in the divorce process. In therapy she begins to realize that she has always carried around an idealized, fairy tale notion of marriage. Loss of the marriage will mean the loss of this ideal. Such a loss is extremely painful to Marian. Her entire sense of identity has been tied to the idea of marriage since she was a girl. Who will she be without it? She begins withdrawing, not only from her husband, but from her kids. She stops going to therapy. Finally, at the insistence of a friend, Marian enrolls in a women's group run by an assistant minister at her church. After a few weeks, she starts to turn the corner on her depression. She decides that the time has come. "I'm going to do it; I'm going to leave the marriage."

In the women's group sessions, Marian has indicated that she feels particularly disempowered around money. So the group, implicitly sanctioned by the minister, gives Marian a "homework assignment" of opening her own bank account. Marian opens her own bank account and, without telling John, moves a large chunk of money from their joint account into her own.

Critical Entry Point #4: The group's recommendation

The minister/group leader might have encouraged Marian to weigh the pros and cons of her actions first. Before encouraging an individual to take a potentially hostile action, the likely reaction from the spouse should be thoroughly considered. Methods of accomplishing the goal of financial empowerment without "guerilla tactics" could have been explored. If the group facilitator had taken more time to understand John's personality, she could have predicted that he would react very badly to Marian's secret money maneuvering.

Many of the most dramatic problems that occur during divorce happen because one party is simply *unprepared* for a sudden action that the other party takes. Such actions — wiping out bank accounts, walking out of the home, having an affair, hiring an attorney — seem to "come out of left field." Most people tend to get confused and defensive when these kinds of surprises occur. They then revert to primitive modes of defense — fighting, name-calling, counterattacks, etc. — and seek to re-establish power and control.

John discovers the money missing from the joint account and feels angered and betrayed. He confronts Marian. A screaming match ensues. John punches a wall. Marian spills the emotional beans. She tells him she is "finished" with the marriage. She tells him how disempowered she has always felt, what a lousy lover he is. He in turn reminds her how easy she has it, how she is nothing but a complainer. She announces that she is going to divorce him. John tells her that if she leaves him, he will see to it that she regrets it for the rest of her life. Marian picks up a plate and takes aim at John. He grabs her hand to stop her and calm her down. Marian reacts like a trapped animal. She springs from his grip and calls the police, telling them she has been threatened and assaulted. The police show up and arrest John. The court issues a restraining order and John is ordered to stay away from the house.

Later that evening, still shaking and sick to her stomach, Marian calls a battered women's help line. She tells the phone counselor that her husband punched the wall and twisted her arm. The phone counselor, knowing very little about the case, accepts Marian's account of the evening's events at face value and advises Marian to seek out a lawyer immediately and to file a restraining order against John. Marian does not know any attorneys and does not want to just pick one out of the phone book. The phone counselor happens to have on hand the name of a lawyer who has helped several women "deal" with an abusive husband. She gives the name to Marian.

Critical Entry Point #5: The phone counselor's advice

The counselor probably did not ask the right questions to ascertain whether there was serious domestic abuse. What was the context of the incident? Might this have been a mutual physical exchange? Was this a one-time incident? Conversely, could there have been an *even more serious* assault than Marian is reporting? Instead, the counselor immediately assumed that there must be abuse of a substantive nature and referred her to an adversarial attorney. She did not present Marian with more than one lawyer's name or offer alternatives for dispute resolution that might have been appropriate for her situation.

As we will see in a later chapter, some of the biggest decisions a person can make during a divorce are choosing a lawyer and choosing a divorce process. Some lawyers are extremely aggressive, while others are more conciliatory. Some like to take charge of their clients, while others play a supportive role. Helpers would do well to know that the choice of a lawyer can have a huge effect on the course of a divorce. Marian might have been advised to choose an attorney who shared her highest vision for the family and would help her get there. Latching onto a domineering, aggressive lawyer, even one who claims to be working for her best interests, may not really empower her or help her achieve a desirable outcome.

For many clients, alternative forms of dispute resolution, such as mediation and collaborative law, may be viable options.

Marian goes to the lawyer. Let's call him Bob Foster. Bob, it turns out, has a reputation as a "shark." He's a strong-arm type who believes in zeroing in on what you want and seizing it — the best defense is a good offense. Marian is not aware that there are other types of lawyers available. Bob wastes no time; he asks Marian a series of pointed questions aimed at getting her to state categorically what she wants to "get" out of the divorce. What are the deal-breakers, the things she can't do without? Though it makes her squirm to put it in cold material terms, Marian acknowledges that if indeed the divorce goes through, she would want to keep the house and the custody of the children. "If you want the house," Bob tells her, "then we need to get him out of there permanently. We need to set a precedent by which you are the primary caregiver and homemaker." Marian is thrown by this, but decides that she will follow her lawyer's advice. After all, he's the expert.

Meanwhile, a shell-shocked John has gone to stay with a buddy. The buddy has been through a costly and painful divorce of his own. He recommends John to a local fathers' support group. A few days later, John attends the group. It is led by a zealous pro-father activist. John gathers some ammunition he can use in his fight against Marian, plus the name of the number one litigious attorney in the entire county. John wastes no time in contacting him.

Critical Entry Point #6: John goes to a father's group

Just as Marian's choice of a lawyer might have been different if she had been given more information, so might John's. His seeking out the support group was really his first voluntary attempt at reaching out for anyone in the helping professions. If the group leader had been less focused on a personal campaign for fathers' rights and more focused on trying to help this individual father, he might have taken the time to talk to John about his ultimate goals. Rather than heaping fuel on the fire, John might have been able to stop and evaluate his alternatives.

A few days later the parties find themselves in family court with their attorneys at their sides. Marian's head is spinning as Attorney Foster ticks off his motions to the judge. John is dazed and numb. There's a "shark feeding frenzy" as motions are filed. The restraining order is renewed for six months and the family's financial assets are frozen. Score Round One for Marian.

John and Marian now find themselves in all-out war. John is feeling bitterly victimized. He's living in an apartment and can only see the kids two weekends a month. His life feels greatly diminished. Marian, on the other hand, is driving the new SUV and living large on "his" money. When he is not angry, he's dejected and misses his children and the security of family life. The children, not surprisingly, are having trouble sleeping and doing poorly in school. They miss their father and are not sure what to expect next.

Because the kids' grades have started slipping, Marian now decides that they need an educational evaluation, which she requests from the school. She does not mention the evaluation meeting to John, nor does she initially divulge to the educational team the level of family infighting that has been going on. The end result is that the team finds that both of the kids do indeed have educational "special needs" and draws up educational plans. "Hey, we didn't talk about this," protests John, who refuses to sign the educational plan because he was never notified of the meeting. Marian hauls him back into court, claiming that he is not acting in the best interests of the children. The court decides that the educational plan shall go into effect. Score Round Two for Marian.

Marian returns to the school with the court order in hand. She tells the counselor how abusive and inattentive to the needs of the family John has been. She reports years of verbal abuse and recounts the "shoving and hitting" incident. The school counselor accepts Marian's version of the story. Opting to be safe rather than sorry, the counselor files a report with the Department of Social Services.

Critical Entry Point #7: The school team

The school personnel could have made stronger efforts to communicate with John and to get him involved in the educational evaluation. Since mothers are usually the main family contact with school personnel, there is often a passive prejudice in favor of the mother and a failure to reach out to fathers. If the educational team had learned more about the details of the kids' family life, they might not have leapt to a finding of learning disabilities but might have focused more on making recommendations for family therapeutic intervention. They would also have included John in the team meeting. If they had heard his version of the story, it is questionable that they would have felt compelled to file the Social Services report.

The Department of Social Services reviews the case and eventually closes it without a finding. But John feels that he has been vilified.

John is now growing worried about the influence Marian is having on the children. When he calls them, they never seem available to talk on the phone. And Marian seems to be excluding him from their lives. When the children get sick, she takes them to the doctor but does not tell him. This is particularly irksome to John who, as a doctor himself, has always been involved with the children's medical needs. Marian also takes the children to a therapist, but John does not find out until he receives an insurance statement for six therapy sessions.

John feels out of control. He doesn't talk to anyone about this — that's not his M.O. Instead he devises a strategy by which he can win back more control. As head of his hospital department, he rearranges his work schedule to have more time at home. Citing his increased home hours and his ability to better help the "special needs" kids with their schoolwork than Mom, he goes back to court, pleads his case, and is awarded a more generous visitation schedule. John wins Round Three.

John next goes to talk to the children's therapist. Unfortunately, John's reputation, as reported by Marian, has preceded him. The therapist already "knows" the family story. John feels that the therapist does not really listen to his point of view. He believes that he is already perceived as the villain. Convinced that this therapist won't believe anything he has to say, he comes across in a belligerent manner and the therapist reacts defensively. It is not a productive conversation. John later calls the therapist and tells her that he refuses to allow the children to continue in treatment.

Critical Entry Point #8: The children go to psychotherapy

Once again, a colossal, but not uncommon, professional blunder occurs. The children's new therapist unquestioningly accepts Marian's version of the events and does not contact John. This would-be helper has become so swept up in the drama, she has passed up an opportunity to step back and view the case with fresh eyes. Because she does not solicit the father's input into the therapy process from the beginning, she is not able to gain his trust. She loses the ability to gather important input about the children and misses the opportunity to provide guidance to the father about how to help the children through the divorce process. The result is that the therapist has compromised her ability to help the children at a time when they sorely need the support.

Marian learns that John has fired the therapist. She asks the therapist to write a letter to the court. The therapist agrees. She also asks the children's physician to write a letter stating that Marian is an abused wife and that the children do indeed suffer serious emotional symptoms. The pediatrician states in writing a belief that the kids' symptoms are psychosomatic in origin due to the father's abuse and the resultant divorce.

Critical Entry Point #9: The therapist and physician write letters to the court

---

Sometimes intelligent, well-meaning professionals who are not sensitized to the ways in which information can be misused are coaxed into issuing ill-advised written opinion statements. These statements are then used as weapons by one party or the other. It would have been a wiser decision for both helping professionals to refrain from giving written opinions, at least without gathering all the facts first. Not only do the therapist and pediatrician unwittingly fuel the fire, but they also now run the risk of ethics complaints and of having to appear in court as witnesses in the ensuing battle. A neutral, well-trained third party probably would have wanted to take a closer look at both sides and would have thought about how to calm the growing tensions.

Marian takes the letters to court. At the hearing, both Marian and the children's therapist characterize John as hostile toward therapy and toward the kids' medical treatment. Mother asks for full legal custody, that is, the right to make all medical and educational decisions about the children. She also motions the court to once again limit father's contact with the children. The letter from the kids' physician is cited. A child custody evaluator is now appointed by the court to evaluate the children's safety and well-being. The judge, based on reams of "documentation" from the mother, recommends a temporary cutback in the father's visitation rights, to be reviewed after the evaluator submits a report that may take as long as six months. Score Round Four for Marian.

Meanwhile, John's and Marian's attorneys are staging World War III over money and property issues. Rumors about John's psychological well-being are starting to swirl around the hospital where he works. The kids are turning solidly against him. John starts to buckle under the strain. For the first time in his life his work performance begins to slip. Teetering emotionally, John finally seeks out a therapist for himself. He chooses one recommended by a member of the father's rights group that he still sporadically attends. John's new therapist, seeing this defeated, deflated man walk through his door, offers immediate emergency counsel to John: you must fight back — it's the only way you're going to regain your motivation and self-respect.

John decides to fight back via his computer keyboard. He begins to write lengthy documents, citing minute details about Marian's behavior dating back to long before the marital troubles even began. He sends these diatribes to his attorney and to Marian herself. John's writings read as vaguely threatening and contain pages of obsessively detailed justifications of his "case." Marian happily turns these documents over to the child custody evaluator, who forms the opinion that John has, at minimum, an anger problem.

Critical Entry Point #10: John starts therapy

John's therapist might have focused on getting John *healthy and functional first* and probably should not have advocated *any* action on John's part until that step had been accomplished. It is one of the therapist's jobs to recognize that productive decisions are not made when people are under great emotional stress. Instead of offering reflexive advice, helping professionals can advocate for a sane, peaceful *end result*, which often means counseling clients *not* to take the action that may seem the most emotionally rewarding at the moment.

The child custody evaluator suggests that John enroll in an anger management program and that the parties hire a parenting coordinator, a neutral professional whose role is to help parents communicate and solve problems, ideally in a better way than they have so far.

On and on goes the story of John and Marian. John gets a new girlfriend and Marian takes him to court to prevent the girlfriend from spending any time with the kids. You get the picture. By now, it is too late to go back and untangle the web that's been woven here. It has been two and a half years since the divorce began, and the children have become deeply

*dysfunctional. There are constant school meetings to adjust the
special education plans, frequent court dates, endless meetings
with the custody evaluator and the parenting coordinator,
a plundering of the former couple's assets to pay the busy
attorneys, and on and on and on . . .*

Cases as sad as this one are playing themselves out in countless
families. They cry out for a third party with wisdom and awareness
to step in and make a difference. I pointed out only a few of the
Critical Entry Points at which this kind of input might have
occurred in John and Marian's case. There were undoubtedly
many more.

Many powerful forces work to feed the "gathering storm" of
divorce — an adversarial legal system, attorneys who frame
arguments in black-and-white terms to win quick settlements for
their clients, participants who lapse into primitive defensive modes
when they feel threatened, friends and family members who
encourage decisive action at the worst possible moments. There
may not be much we can do to fight some of these forces, but we
can recognize the tremendous opportunity that presents itself
when a Critical Entry Point arises and *our input* is sought. We can
do a great deal to prepare ourselves for such opportunities so that
we can maximize the contribution we are able to make when they
do occur.

It takes courage and awareness to stand as the voice of reason
in the midst of the hurricane. But we in the counseling
professions have that privilege. Since we have nothing personal or
financial at stake in the divorce, we have the opportunity to stand
as spokespersons for the big picture, for the rational vision, for a
divorce process that promotes maturity and growth. We owe it to
our clients, their children, and society in general to play this role
with wisdom and equanimity and not get swept up in the storm.
Divorce is all around us. The more we increase our awareness
about its manifold complexities and our power to influence them,
the more we can help our clients do the same.

Divorce Is a Process

Let's assume that a Critical Entry Point has arisen. You are called upon to counsel a client who is either going through a divorce or actively considering one. Divorce has been placed on your professional table. How do you start off on the right foot with this client? What do you need to know, right from the start, to help make the divorce process as productive and positive as possible?

In my decades of divorce-related counseling, I have learned that there is a two-part foundation upon which professional helpers can build from the very start. We will refer to the two parts of this foundation as *process* and *principles*. We will cover them in this chapter and the next. This two-part foundation can serve to underlie and support everything we do with the client. Laying a good foundation requires only a relatively minor investment of time and understanding. But failure to do so accounts, in large measure, for why many therapists and other helpers add fuel to the fire of divorce rather than help to promote peace and growth.

The first part of our foundation is the firm understanding that divorce is not a discrete event, but a *process*. Dynamic *inter-* and *intra*personal changes occur from one phase to another. What is true for the client today, psychologically speaking, may not be true tomorrow. Staying fluid and responsive with the kind of support we offer is vital. The divorce process usually extends over a lengthy period of time (typically one to three years).

The second part of our foundation, *principles*, is a core cluster of helpful approaches and strategies helpers can incorporate into our thinking if we wish to be of the highest service to the client and his or her family. If you only read two chapters in this book, I recommend this and the next one.

❖ *Understanding That Divorce Is a Process*

Again, for emphasis: *divorce is a process.* A process is a course of development that unfolds over time and through and by which a person changes dynamically. The client's emotions, outlooks, attitudes, and motivations are *qualitatively different* at various stages in the divorce process. Unless we understand what part of the process our client is currently experiencing, our support and advice will miss the mark. Attitudes and actions that are appropriate for the client at one stage will probably not be appropriate at another. For example, very assertive — even angry — actions and attitudes may be necessary for a client who needs to break free from a controlling, domineering, or abusive partner. The client may need a sharp, decisive kind of energy at this stage of the process. This same kind of uncompromising urgency can be harmful a few months later when the ex-partners are negotiating delicate issues such as visitation rights with the children. We best help the client when we are not locked into any one treatment strategy or form of advice but change adaptively with the client's needs.

Being overly focused on concrete *goals*, such as winning custody of the children or getting a big financial settlement, we fail to see where the client "is at" in the here and now. When we focus too much on such goals, we and our clients can become rigid. The goals become more important than the client's present state of being. What does the client need to do *today* to function more healthily on an emotional, mental, and interpersonal level? What actions *today* will best serve the overall adjustment of the family? Goals are best held in the background to help inform thoughts and actions, rather than used to dictate specific moves in the immediacy of the moment. The client cannot always see that he or she is in an unfolding process, but *we* can. Helping clients transition productively through the various stages of divorce is our overall goal.

Generally, we can speak of three *types* of processes when it comes to divorce: (1) the individual process, (2) the *family* process, and, on a more macrocosmic level, (3) the *societal* process. The *individual* process is the series of personal emotional adjustments that the individual undergoes as divorce unfolds in his or her life. The *family* process describes the practical, chronological stages that play out for the whole family system. The *societal* process is the global background for all of this: the ever-changing face of divorce as a societal phenomenon. What could comfortably be said of divorce twenty or fifty years ago can no longer be said. Divorce is being dynamically redefined and repositioned in our culture in ways that affect our clients in the here and now. The divorce process is affected by evolving ways of defining male/female roles, the place of children in society, what constitutes economic fairness, etc.

Of course, every client and every family is unique. No two families or individuals go through the same stages of divorce in the same order, at the same times, and in the same ways. The purpose of discussing process here is not to focus too heavily on any particular process *model* — though we will look at a few — but simply to acknowledge that divorce is a process, not a discrete event. Only by seeing it as such will we be able to recognize when a client is stuck somewhere within that process and how to help that client move on.

❖ *The Individual Process*

Divorce may be the most traumatic and life-altering event, short of death itself, that many people will experience in a lifetime. It can represent a "death of the familiar" as well as a death of one's hopes, fantasies, self-image, plans, and investments (both financial and emotional). It is crucial for helpers to recognize the enormity of stress and strain that divorce represents. Divorce is deeply challenging on many levels. Human beings are not wired to adjust to change of this magnitude easily and quickly. One cannot digest a two-pound steak in one bite; neither can one digest divorce in a single day or week or month. *A course of emotional adjustment is necessary.*

Some theorists have described this adjustment process in terms of definable *stages;* others have taken a more cyclical approach.

But whichever model we use, it is clear that clients are in very different *states of being* at various points along the road. Our job as helpers is twofold: (1) to help normalize the feelings that the client is experiencing at any part of the process, so that he or she feels less anxious; and (2) to foster a healthy transition from one part of the process to the next to help the client constructively move on with her life.

❖ Stages of Divorce

Let's look at a couple of the most popular *stage* models that can be applied to the divorce process. As we do so, let's remember that models are just that: models. Each has its limits and should not be taken too concretely. But they can all be helpful in their own ways.

Since divorce is indeed a death-like loss to many people, it is not surprising that its stages often parallel the emotional stages we pass through when dealing with biological death. Kubler-Ross's (1969) five-stage framework for mourning and loss is the best-known model of this type. This "classic" model can be observed, to varying degrees, when we're working with divorcing individuals. Though most of us are probably familiar with these five stages from the popular literature, I will list them again as a reminder: Denial, Anger, Bargaining, Depression, and Acceptance.

We should not assume that every client will go through all five in the above order. Nor should we assume that the stages progress neatly and discretely. Clients backtrack. Stages overlap. One day a client may be in Depression; the next day he or she may flip back to Anger or Denial. But these five stages do seem to occur, to one degree or another, for the majority of divorcing individuals. One stage can last for days, weeks, or months, depending upon the person. (In a mired process, one stage can drag on for *years*.) Each stage serves an important emotional purpose, which we would do well not to miss.

Denial. Denial makes its appearance in nearly every troubled relationship. During this stage, which can last for years, the couple may carry on in a dead-end relationship, going through the motions and superficially behaving as if everything were fine, or at least relatively fine. One scorned woman, whom I shall call Leila, told me, "I didn't see it coming. I knew he was working more, but he never said anything was wrong." In retrospect, however, the signs were there to be seen.

Once the topic of divorce is actually broached, there is sometimes a gap in which neither party mentions it again for a while, as if hoping that the marital problems will just fix themselves. When an unsuspecting partner is confronted with the real possibility of divorce, there is often a period of adjustment — long or short — in which the seriousness of the situation doesn't filter through to conscious awareness.

It is easy to forget that denial can serve a useful purpose. That is, it can protect the individual from falling apart in the face of overwhelmingly negative news. Denial can allow partners to soldier on with life for the time being as they start to subtly prepare themselves for potentially devastating upcoming changes. It is the mind's way of saying, "I will have my crisis in due time; as for now, I will carry on."

Anger. The Anger stage, when facing *actual* death, is characterized by a "shaking one's fist" at God or at the world. Why is this happening to *me*? In divorce, the fist tends to be shaken at one's *spouse*. Once denial runs its course, an angry confrontation sometimes occurs in the marriage. Blame, rage, and resentment toward the partner can pour out in torrents. The anger often acquires a personal focus and the partner can become the enemy, at least for a time. When Leila's husband told her the relationship was over, she furiously confronted him in front of the children and hired a lawyer to "take him for all he was worth."

Anger is often a necessary and important step in pulling one partner away from another emotionally. It can propel individuals to take difficult, but necessary steps such as moving out or filing papers. Without the energy fueled by anger, these steps might never be taken. However, helpers can influence how clients channel the energy of anger into productive action that will not have negative consequences down the road.

Bargaining. When dealing with bodily death, individuals may bargain with God or the universe; when dealing with divorce they also tend to bargain with each other. The Bargaining stage is often literal as well as emotional. Many couples suddenly begin to employ desperate, last-ditch measures to salvage the marriage. She tries becoming more sexual. He tries buying flowers. He begs, she pleads. Leila asked, "If I stop my compulsive shopping and lose twenty pounds, will you stay with me?" Sometimes the bargaining can pay dividends, at least temporarily. The couple gives the marriage another try. Occasionally this is successful. Bargaining can be important psychologically because it signals an effort — for some people a *first* effort — to assume some responsibility for correcting what went wrong in the marriage. It also helps provide the sense that no matter how things turn out, "I did everything I could."

Depression. Once the bargaining efforts have all been exhausted, the reality of the relationship's demise hits home. "My marriage failed. I'm getting divorced. This is real." Depression hits. Life may seem hopeless and meaningless, and there can be a sense that one will never be happy again. Clients often fluctuate between anger and depression for at least part of the divorce process. Taking vengeful action, such as Leila's hiring of an aggressive attorney, can have the effect of helping ward off depression, at least temporarily.

A period of depression or intense sadness is appropriate and useful in divorce, just as a grieving period serves a healthy purpose following the death of a loved one. It helps to cement the sense of finality. It also provides a dramatic "low" that eventually motivates a person to want to move on.

Acceptance. Acceptance occurs when the *attachment* to the partner finally dissolves. The more passionate the relationship, the harder it usually is to reach the acceptance stage. But there comes a point at which, even if the client is the involuntary "dumpee" (Fisher & Alberti, 2000), he or she awakens one morning and realizes that it is time to move on. He or she has let go. There is no longer an intense connection to the partner, nor is there an attachment to the dream, the fantasy, or the illusion of the marriage.

Detachment from the partner involves forgiveness in the sense of letting go of the energy of the relationship. Enright (2001), using the concept of forgiveness conceptualized by North (1987), describes forgiveness in the following way:

> When unjustly hurt by another, we forgive when we overcome the resentment toward the offender, not by denying our right to the resentment, but instead by trying to offer the wrongdoer compassion, benevolence, and love; as we give these, we as forgivers realize that the offender does not necessarily have a right to such gifts. (p. 25)

In other words, the individual detaches from the rage, anger, and hurt and is thus able to treat the ex-partner in a respectful manner.

Detaching from the *dynamics* and *ideals* of the marriage can take a good deal longer than detaching from the actual partner. This can involve facing the fact that there are no Prince Charmings out there. Or that a wife is not a substitute mother. Of course, many people do not take the crucial step of detaching from the dynamics. Such was the case for Leila, who immediately found a new partner with whom she tried to replicate the same maladaptive patterns that existed in the marriage. Eventually, Leila found a therapist who helped her accept the loss of certain unrealistic ideals and enabled her to move onto a new stage of her life with increased wisdom.

Acceptance implies an honest surrender to the reality of the divorce, including the personal failings that may have contributed to it. Once this type of healthy surrender occurs, the present moment takes on new possibilities and life may go on again in a fresh, invigorated way.

Another well-respected stage model for the loss/mourning process is one proposed by John Bowlby (1980). It has many areas of overlap with Kubler-Ross's stage model. Again, these phases are not clear-cut, but represent a *general trend* of inner movement: Numbing, Yearning and Searching, Disorganization and Despair, and Reorganization.

Numbing. This phase has some parallels with the Denial stage of Kubler-Ross. The individual is stunned by the tidings of divorce and goes through a period of feeling "this isn't real." The person may carry on with life as normal, but there is a tension and apprehensiveness below the surface. Raw emotion may bubble up at any time. The numbing stage tends to be more acute when dealing with actual death, especially unexpected death. But it certainly occurs in divorce as well. Some divorces, like some deaths, seem to come out of nowhere. One spouse thinks everything is fine until the other announces, "I've fallen in love with our neighbor and I want a divorce." By contrast some divorces, like some deaths, are not surprising at all. Generally, the more unexpected the event, the more intense the numbing phase.

Yearning and searching. When the reality of the loss hits home, there is a period of intense longing and distress. When we are talking about actual death of a spouse "...there is great restlessness, insomnia, preoccupation with thoughts of the lost husband combined often with a sense of his actual presence, and a marked tendency to interpret signals or sounds as indicating that he has now returned" (Bowlby, 1980, p. 86). In divorce, we may not see such a literal searching, but we may see clients rather desperately "looking for signs" that the relationship is still there or that it can be reborn. They may behave as if the ex-partner were still a presence in their lives in some way or another. This phase of the loss process is often marked by considerable anger, blame, and disappointment that the searching is not bearing fruit. It overlaps Kubler-Ross's Anger and Bargaining stages.

Disorganization and despair. Only by enduring the pain of the previous stage, says Bowlby, does the individual "come gradually to recognize and accept that the loss is in truth permanent and that his life must be shaped anew" and "register that his old patterns of behavior have become redundant and have therefore to be dismantled" (Bowlby, 1980, p. 93). And this is exactly what the person does — he or she dismantles the old life, the old persona. As the client begins to take on new and unfamiliar roles and to abandon former feelings and behaviors, there comes a sense of despair that perhaps no part of the old life can be salvaged. "Was my life until now a total waste?" This phase overlaps Kubler-Ross's Depression stage in many respects.

Reorganization. In this final phase, the person rebuilds a new life amid the ashes of the old. The chaos of the previous stage is reshaped into a new order. There is a "redefinition of self and situation" (Bowlby, 1980, p. 94). With this reorganization usually comes the recognition of the irreversibility of events that marks the Acceptance stage described above.

Fisher and Alberti (2000) describe a nineteen-step model of the tasks involved in individual recovery after the breakup of a relationship These steps generally occur over a one- or two-year period following the separation but may take longer depending on the circumstances of the individual, the family, and the divorce process. Other stage-based models, such as the seven-stage model of Kessler (1975), can be found in the literature. Of course, not all theorists favor stage-driven models. That is because stage models tend to be sequential — one stage following another. Though neither Bowlby nor Kubler-Ross would claim that their stages unfurl with unfailing predictability, there is still a neatness and *chronological progression* to them. This is partly due to the fact that these models were created primarily to illustrate adjustment to biological death. Death is irreversible. Divorce, however, does not carry the same literal and absolute finality. There remains the *possibility*, if only extremely remote, that the divorce could be reversed and that the partners might remarry. In addition, ongoing contact with the living ex-spouse can reignite various stages of the loss process, unpredictably, at any time. Thus the process of adjustment to divorce tends to be marked by more lability and emotional complexity than the adjustment to death.

Robert Emery (1994), for one, has suggested that we therefore need a more *cyclical* model for understanding divorce. People who are going through divorce tend to cycle back and forth among several states in a somewhat haphazard manner, rather than proceeding neatly from one "stage" to another. A linear order is not necessarily typical.

We need not explore all of the dimensions of Emery's model here, but its central points are noteworthy. His model revolves primarily around *emotions*, rather than stages. Emery believes that there are three strong emotions that together comprise the grief of divorce: Love, Anger, and Sadness. The client can and will experience all three in hefty doses. Love has a very general meaning here and includes the full range of emotions that draw one person to another — affection, sexual attraction, guilt, protectiveness, hope. Anger, by contrast, includes the full range of "negative" feelings toward another person and carries a repellant type of energy. Sadness encompasses the negative emotions that we direct *toward ourselves*. At is worst, sadness can include feelings that closely approximate physical pain.

Emery's model suggests that people dealing with loss should fluctuate among all three of these emotions. This is a healthy thing, as all three emotions must be experienced in reasonably equal measure. When working with a client, if we see one emotion predominating we seek balance with the other two. For the client who expresses only rage, for example, we help him to get in touch with the sadness and the love that underlie it. Because humans can generally experience only one strong emotion at a time, the only way for the client to fully experience all three is to cycle back and forth among them. Over time, in a healthy process, the cycling becomes less frequent, less extreme, and less all-consuming. The three emotions begin to form a more intimate weave. Emotional life starts to find a kind of settled manageability.

All of these models can give us some insight, but the most important point to remember is simply that at any given point in the process, the client will be dominated by *one particular emotional state, attitude, or motivation*. An awareness of the client's dominant emotional state will assist the professional to determine what the client needs to do to "complete" this stage and move on. The models can provide guidance on how to do that. But the greatest guide will be the client herself.

A major mistake that helping professionals sometimes make is giving support that is appropriate to the wrong part of the process. Clearly, if the client is in Denial, then our efforts are best geared toward helping the client see the situation more realistically. It would be counterproductive to encourage her to become more confrontational or to discuss action steps with her when she still believes there are no problems in her marriage. She has not even accepted the reality of the failed relationship! Our attention needs to be focused on getting her to come to that realization and to strengthen her inner resources. Similarly, it is poor strategy to try to move a client to a place of acceptance if the client is in an angry stage but does not know how to manage his or her emotions. What the client really needs is to learn to manage the anger so she can take appropriate and productive action.

Each part of the process has a function, but each must also give way, in its proper time, to the next stage. This means that we should take care not to provide one-dimensional support that enables the client to "wallow" or "dig in" at any particular place in the process. Our role is to facilitate *movement*. This can be particularly difficult for helpers who carry a personal or professional agenda of some kind. Someone who runs a women's shelter, for example, and sees mostly women who come from abusive relationships may find it very difficult to accept a bargaining stage of any kind. Similarly, some attorneys may be prone to fanning the flames of conflict and keeping the Anger stage locked in place far longer than desirable. When warring attorneys and/or aligned therapists become involved in a case, the Anger stage can persist literally for years.

❖ *Everyone Is at a Different Place in the Process*

Each individual in the couple/family will go through the emotional stages of adjustment at different times and in different ways. What is emotionally true for one member of the family today may not be true for another. We can recognize this truth and help our clients to see it as well.

Often conflict is exacerbated by the egocentric thinking of one party who fails to see that the other party is at a different place in the adjustment process. The party who initiates a divorce, for instance, is usually the one who has been thinking about it for a longer time. He or she may have already dealt with most of the mourning stages and is ready to move on. However, the partner may now need to go through his or her own lengthy Denial and mourning process. Engaging in displays of Anger with a person who is in Denial will only bring frustration and escalation. Trying to Bargain with someone who is deep in Anger can produce disastrous results.

Children can take longer to pass through the stages of adjustment than adults and must be treated with delicacy, respect, and insight. In some divorce cases, the parents may have been talking about divorce for quite some time — months, even years — before they decide tell the children. Once the children have been told, the parents immediately begin to mobilize — *they* are ready to take action. One or the other parent moves out, etc. *But the kids are not ready for this.* They have had little or no time to adjust to the idea. Parents are often mystified when a child's Anger stage kicks in many weeks or months after a new living arrangement has been initiated. Often that is because the child has not yet had sufficient time to adjust to the divorce.

We can help families to see that each member needs to have time to adjust and that the duration of the adjustment phase may be different for everyone. Patience and empathy can be encouraged. We can also educate parents about the general emotional stages through which they can expect to see their children pass. This will go a long way toward helping the parents understand their kids' moods and behaviors. A family in crisis benefits from the neutral eyes of professionals to help them to understand what is happening with other family members.

It is important to remember that certain events can serve as triggers that "reactivate" earlier stages. When an ex-spouse starts dating or when the custody litigation is filed, emotions are likely to flare up and a certain period of regression can be expected. Anticipating and normalizing these setbacks can help make them shorter and less painful.

❖ The Family Process

The members of the couple or family not only go through their own *individual* adjustment processes but, as noted earlier, undergo a group process together. Abigail Trafford (1982), in her book *Crazy Time*, describes the main chronological stages of this process as Crisis, "Crazy Time," and Recovery. Bogolub (1995) and Kaslow and Schwartz (1987) also identify three major divorce stages for the family. Bogulub terms these stages "Predivorce,"

"Divorce Transition," and "Postdivorce." Whatever we choose to call the stages, there seem to be three more-or-less distinct stages that the family as a group typically experiences. Interestingly, these correspond roughly to what dramatists call Act One, Act Two, and Act Three.

Stage 1 (Crisis — The Beginning — Act One). In Stage 1 the "drama" begins. The bomb is dropped. The idea of divorce is introduced into a stable or relatively stable family environment. Crisis is ignited. Sometimes a catalyzing event triggers this — a parent has an affair or perhaps there is an instance of abuse. Other times a more gradual decision has been reached by the two adults. And now that decision is finally communicated to the whole family. Extreme emotions fly — tears, rage, panic.

Life-changing decisions are made in Stage 1 and tend to happen more quickly than most of the parties would wish. A parent moves out. Living arrangements are altered. Children suddenly find themselves staying half-time in a strange apartment with a parent whose rules and routines are foreign. Parents lose familiar roles or inherit hosts of new responsibilities. Everything changes.

During Stage 1, clients typically feel frightened, confused, panicky, heartbroken, desperate, unsafe, and/or enraged as uncertainty arises for the family.

Stage 2 ("Crazy Time" — The Middle — Act Two). In drama, the second act is the period during which the conflict plays itself out. Characters adjust to strange new sets of circumstances. Complications and unexpected obstacles arise. Friends of both parties may suddenly take sides. Children may act up. New strategies are tried. New plans are laid.

"Crazy Time" is an often-chaotic time in the divorce process during which family members are forced by circumstance to try out all kinds of unfamiliar arrangements. Some work, some don't. But the old, comfortable patterns most definitely change. Everything seems strange and unsettled. Disorganization and Reorganization (Bowlby) are the dominant dynamics. The parents and the kids are forced to accommodate new elements, such as Dad's new girlfriend or Mom's tiny new apartment. Unpredictable alliances and conflicts arise. Everything seems new, scary, and unresolved. But slowly adaptation takes place.

During Stage 2, clients typically feel angry, anxious, resentful, bitter, regretful, depressed, disoriented, and/or "crazy" as the family restructures.

Stage 3 (Recovery — The End — Act Three). The third act, in drama, is that in which characters cross the point of no return and move toward a resolution of the chaos and conflict. Family members begin to accept, consciously or otherwise, that life is never going to return to its former state. Rather than looking backward to what once was, vision now shifts to a forward-looking mode. The present and future become more important than the past. New arrangements are endorsed emotionally, at least to some extent, and the parties can begin to truly appreciate what this new life has to offer.

If the process has been healthy, there is also a sense of growth. The children adjust to the changes in lifestyle, and fights between the parents are probably no longer daily or weekly occurrences. New friendships may have been established. A *new definition of family* has been established. There is freedom for the individual members to grow anew separately and together.

During Stage 3, clients typically begin to feel safer, more relaxed, optimistic, appreciative, and/or settled as new family structures solidify.

By recognizing the collective family process, we, as helpers, can again fulfill our two main roles with our clients. That is, we can normalize the process for them and help make sure that they do not become stuck anywhere along the way.

Normalizing the process means that we communicate to the client that what he or she is experiencing is to be expected, even if it is very painful and difficult. One of the main causes of anxiety during any crisis is the sense that something is wrong with oneself and that the world is falling apart. Simply assuring the client that his experiences are par for the course can help to alleviate anxiety. It also gives the client permission to fully experience the negative feelings that he may be trying to push away because he senses they are "wrong" or unacceptable. The more fully and readily the client can *live and cope with* the anger, the panic, and the resentment, the more fluidly he can move through it. The helping professional, in articulating and normalizing the stages of the divorce process, holds out assurance that "this too shall pass." When the client knows that the pain and craziness he is experiencing is likely, within a reasonable timeframe, to give way to more positive, grounded feelings, he gains at least a measure of hope that mitigates the pain.

Keeping the client from getting stuck in the process can be a delicate matter. Every client and family moves at its own speed. There is no preset "healthy" length of time for Crisis or Crazy Time to last. We need to use our intuition, along with intelligent questioning of the client, to determine whether the family has reached an impasse. "Crazy Time" is the stage where families are most likely to become stuck. If this stage goes on for an inordinately long time, it may signal that the client or a family member is not accepting the reality of the divorce. The individual may be treading water, unable to return to the old life, unable to move on to a new one. She may be stuck in reactive mode, reeling from the blow of the divorce and unable to adopt a proactive stance. Or the client may have become addicted to the drama and chaos and is unconsciously carving a new identity for himself based on this — Angry Jilted Husband, Heroic Single Mom, Long-Suffering Saint.

As a very general rule, we can say that the divorce process — from pain to productivity — takes about one to three years. If a client seems to be fully adjusted within a five-month period, this may signal that all of the emotional work has not yet been done. If a client is still unable to move on to a new life after three years, then there's a very good chance that she is stuck somewhere.

❖ The Societal Process

In order for us to better understand our clients and help them through the divorce process, it is helpful to understand the larger societal context of divorce. We cannot view our clients as separate from their culture. In the past century Western society has seen a radical shifting of thought, from a system in which women and children were essentially viewed as a man's property through the feminist era to today's pendulum-swing toward fathers' rights. Society is actively redefining gender roles, economic and property issues, legal principles, children's rights, and marriage as an institution. We and our clients are an integral part of this process.

Let's take a very brief and admittedly oversimplified look at the history of divorce in America. *Gender politics* and corresponding changes in the *legal system* can be seen as the two main drivers that have been redefining divorce in our culture over the past century.

From the Colonial period until not much more than a century ago, the husband was the head of the family and was deemed to have certain ownership rights to the wife and children. A family was, in effect, a man's property. The mother worked in the home, performing maternal duties and domestic labor. Children worked in the fields and thus were valuable economic producers. Farmers had as many children as they could. With the advent of the Industrial Revolution, fathers began leaving home to work and mothers' roles became more consolidated as caretakers. Children were in the home or at school now rather than on the farm, and so a more intense focus on child rearing emerged. Children shifted from being economic assets to economic responsibilities. Childbirth rates went down.

Toward the end of the nineteenth century, the legal system began to view children less as parental property and more as individuals with basic rights. The so-called Tender Years Doctrine was adopted. Courts took the position that children's welfare was primary and adopted the psychoanalytic view that the bond between mother and child, especially the young child, was vital to proper development. A bias toward mothers as primary parents became entrenched in the case law of most states by the 1920s. Fathers were now viewed as economic providers rather than primary physical custodians.

The predominance of mothers as primary caretakers, along with a relative infrequency of divorce cases, continued until after WWII.

In the 1950s and 1960s, however, society became increasingly mobile and restless. People had money, moveable jobs, cars, airplane tickets, and the freedom to explore themselves and the world. In the late 1960s the so-called Sexual Revolution and Women's Movement began to take root as self-actualization (Maslow, 1970) became a dominant theme in society. The institution of marriage itself was questioned. The number of couples living together in unmarried relationships increased exponentially. As a culture, Americans developed an impatience with relationships that did not serve them individually and pressed for divorce to be easier and fairer. The concept of no-fault divorce was born and the divorce rate increased.

Meanwhile gender roles were being placed in the metaphorical blender, a blender that continues to whir even today. Women began to seek more economic power via equality in the workplace. Men were suddenly being asked to share in the responsibilities at home while also being forced to compete with women at work. In response, many men began to become more active parents and to develop their "feminine sides." At the same time, many men also began to feel that their role in society had been usurped. The increase in prosecuted domestic violence and sexual crimes over the last forty years can be seen, at least in part, as some men's misdirected attempt to reclaim their lost power, as well as women's attempt to fight back against perceived victimization.

In the 1970s and 1980s, as more women entered the workforce, family norms about parenting and wage earning began to be redefined. At the same time, a new definition of women's psychology started to develop. (Belenky, Clinchy, Goldberger, & Tarule, 1986; Chodorow, 1978; Miller, 1976). In this new model, some of the traditional characteristics of women began to be redefined as strengths. Women's "connectedness," inner resources, and relationship-building skills began to be consciously honored. The power of these traditional feminine qualities was being touted at the same time the women's movement was encouraging women to assert their power in more traditionally masculine ways. Women started feeling the stress of balancing ambitious career goals with traditional home responsibilities, all in the name of "being all they could be."

In reaction to the women's movement, men in the 1980s and 1990s began to redefine and reaffirm themselves. There was a reconnection with some of the traditional qualities of masculinity along with an incorporation of less traditional ones (Bly, 1990). A plethora of books began to appear, advocating a new understanding of men's psyches and proposing redefined roles that allow for emotional growth while preserving outer-directed male energy. Corresponding research stressed the importance of fathers in the raising of children — not fathers who, in effect, mimic mothers but fathers who play a key role in the development of the child's sense of competence in the world (Braver & O'Connell, 1988; Lamb, 1986, 1997).

Though the belief in mothers as the best natural caretakers of children remains pervasive, laws have begun to move toward more egalitarian models. In the 1970s, courts across the United States started adopting the standard of "best interest" of children as the deciding factor in all custody and guardianship actions. It was no longer a legal given that children were best served by being in their mothers' care. In some cases working mothers found themselves faced with the prospect of losing custody of their children. As the men's movement grew, the courts accordingly began extending greater visitation and custody rights to fathers. The recent guidelines for child custody developed by the Massachusetts chapter of the Association of Family and Conciliation Courts (2004), for one state's example, recommend an expanded range of postdivorce roles for fathers.

Over the last thirty years, custody of children has become linked to the *qualifications*, rather than the gender, of the parents. And distribution of the finances after the divorce has become tied in large part to the distribution of the children. The result is that men now scramble to prove that they can be just as capable parents as women. While women have "infiltrated" the workplace, men are now "infiltrating" the home and competing with women to win victories in custody actions. Money and children are both up for grabs as the battle for parental status and economic advantage plays itself out in the divorcing family. The salient point in all of this, for today's helping professional, is that *both men and women feel disempowered*. Women, who still earn less than men, feel disenfranchised in the workplace and economically disadvantaged in the family. Men, who still face a maternal bias in the courts, feel disenfranchised as parents and exploited financially. Equality and power remain huge gender issues in the early twenty-first century as parental rights interweave and sometimes compete with children's "best interests." This power struggle plays itself out in dramatic and complex ways in the courts. Prenuptial agreements are becoming commonplace. Property and custody questions abound. Who owns what? Who owes what to whom? Who gets the kids and how much money goes along with that? It is no surprise that divorcing clients react with confusion to the onslaught of mixed messages society and the courts send them.

Nowhere are rights and roles more ill-defined and confusing than in same-sex marriages and unions. With no identified "mother" and "father," what roles do the partners legally play? How will the legislature and the courts recognize their parental rights?

Given the complexities of today's gender politics, it is no wonder that five to ten percent of divorces are considered "high-conflict." We can only hope that as the pendulum of gender roles finds some sort of balance, the legal system will find better ways to address the balancing of economics and parental roles in divorce.

As helpers, we cannot ignore this larger political/historical context when dealing with clients. It is within the context of murky and ever-changing power dynamics that our clients must negotiate their divorces. How disempowered does the client feel? What is the client's general *understanding* of personal power, especially as it relates to gender, and how is that manifested in his interactions with his ex-spouse? We do best not to make assumptions or peddle our own agendas but to find out where the client stands.

❖ ### *Where People Get Stuck*

"Stuckness" is a general problem for clients who are going through divorce and one that we frequently address in our practices. Somewhere within the client's multidimensional divorce process, she becomes mired in a nonproductive and self-sustaining pattern that she cannot seem to break out of on her own. For a closer examination of where people get stuck in the divorce process, we will look to the respected work of Janet Johnson. In *Impasses of Divorce*, she points to three main sources of divorce impasse: the Intrapsychic level, the Interactional level, and the External/Social level.

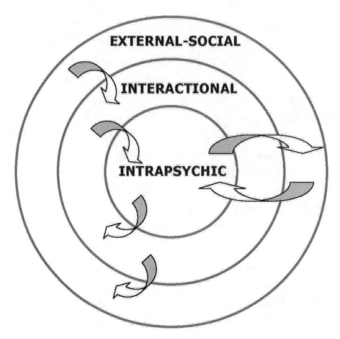

[This figure is adapted from training material developed by Janet R. Johnston. Reproduced by permission of the author. A full explanation can be found in the book, *Impasses of divorce: The dynamics and resolution of family conflict*, by J.R. Johnston and L.E.G. Campbell. The Free Press, 1988.]

The Intrapsychic level. The Intrapsychic level encompasses all of the factors that are internal to the individual. Johnson identifies three major emotional "quicksand areas," so to speak, that tend to grab people and hold them back from further growth. These will be discussed in greater detail later in the book (Helping the Individual) but are mentioned briefly here. They are Vulnerability (Helplessness, Fear/Uncertainty, Loss), Anger, and Shame (Low Self-Esteem, Self-Blame, Narcissism, Paranoia). Note that there is a great deal of overlap with Emery's "big three" emotions of Love, Anger, and Sadness as he broadly defines those emotions. Identifying which strong emotion may be locking our clients into inaction or counterproductive action is extremely fruitful. Part of the solution usually involves putting the client in touch with one or both of the other two major emotions.

Chapter 5 will discuss some techniques and approaches for helping clients move out of these stuck spots.

The Interactional Level. The interactional level entails factors inherent to the way the couple interacts. It is well known that many couples have "blind spots" or unconscious, repetitive patterns that prevent healthy growth from occurring. The partners get locked into "automatic" responses to one another. Open thinking breaks down and growth cannot proceed. When working with *couples together* in our office, helping professionals can try to observe these patterns first hand. When working with *individuals*, we can try to elicit data to recreate conversations and interactions with the partner so that we can try to identify the patterns.

To root out an Interactional-level "stuck spot," it is helpful to get a good history of the relationship. How did the partners meet? Was the relationship based on passion or friendship? Was either partner trying to fill a neurotic need by entering the relationship?

At the same time, it is equally useful (though often overlooked) to get a thorough and meaningful history of the *marital breakdown.* How people come apart is quite telling and important. When did the problems start? What else was going on around that time? Often marital problems arise in conjunction with other major life events, though the clients may not see any connection.

Are there any repetitive patterns in the relationship? What have been the common themes for arguments? If there was infidelity, what were the circumstances surrounding it for both parties and for the couple as a whole? The helper tries to establish a *context* for any meaningful event. If clients do not get better insight into their interactional patterns, they cannot take responsibility for changing and will likely duplicate the same patterns in any new relationships.

The book will look in greater detail at how to help break logjams at the Interactional level in chapter 4, Uncoupling.

The External/Social Level. The External/Social level includes influences from the client's extended family, community, and society itself. Under ideal circumstances, family, friends, and community would serve as supports and catalysts for a healthy divorce process. Quite often, however, these external influences can undermine a person's or couple's ability to move forward productively. They can include extended family; friends; professional, political, or social affiliations; mental health professionals; religious advisors; attorneys; financial planners; the family court; the criminal-justice system; and other social service agencies.

External forces tend to pull at the divorcing partners according to *their own*, not the couple's, agendas. Parents or friends, for example, may strongly like or dislike a loved one's spouse and try to push for a marital resolution in line with that feeling. This may or may not be what the client needs. Because such external forces can exert a great deal of influence, the client may second-guess her own instincts and lose the ability to make the right decision for herself and her family.

In some families or social circles, divorce may be frowned upon (or advocated). Pressure may be exerted on the client to make a decision that does not break any social taboos or that represents the wishes of the family member. If our client has strong conformity and acceptance needs, these "tribal" influences can be quite powerful. Many people stay in miserable marriages because they have not wanted to upset family members. Others whose relationships end act on the advice of family or friends without a proper assessment about whether the advice makes sense for their situation.

Religious advisors can serve as invaluable resources, but they can sometimes take a narrow and rigid stance when it comes to resolving marital issues. Because the client fears moral failure or a fall from grace, he may go along with religious advice he does not truly believe but also does not feel comfortable refusing.

Attorneys, of course, can be a major cause of impasse. Though some are conciliatory and responsive to their clients' truest desires, others take the position of advocates who are deeply invested in having their clients "win." At times when the client should ideally be working on acceptance and perhaps forgiveness, the attorney is still planning war strategies and gathering ammunition for a battle.

Therapists and other counselors often unknowingly play a detrimental role in the process. By advocating too strongly for perceived client needs or their own political agendas, they can lose sight of the big picture, i.e., the whole family system. They may fail to balance, for example, advice for the client to behave more assertively with an honest appraisal of how that new behavior may affect other members of the family. By trying to correct one area of "stuckness," they may end up creating new ones.

Helping professionals have a dual role in this regard: First, we can find out what the client's external influences are and help her deal with them. We can ask questions to ferret out all of the overt and hidden persuaders that are weighing on her — family, friends, faith. What is the client's view of gender roles and power issues and where did these come from? During the process we remain particularly alert to any statements of concern that the client seems to be "parroting" rather than expressing organically: "A good father doesn't break up his family," "Divorce is a moral failure." Do these statements come from the client himself or do they seem to be inherited from somewhere else? Once *we* have identified some of the client's external influences, we can work with the client to consciously recognize them. How does the client feel about each external influence? Is the influence a productive, positive one? Does it echo a genuine *internal* concern, one that the client truly shares? Or is the outside influence one that the client would do better to reject? If so, we can explore with the client ways in which he might comfortably "extricate" himself from any unwanted influence.

Second, we take care not to *become* an unhealthy external influence ourselves. This can happen when we lose sight of the big picture, the whole family system. It is not uncommon for divorcing partners to engage in the War of the Therapists. "My therapist tells me I need to do [*x*]." "Oh really? Well, *my* therapist says I should do [*y*]." Our potential negative influence is greater than we may imagine and often goes beyond the mere problem of providing lopsided advice. Sometimes we are called upon to give written opinions or to advise other professionals or testify in court. So we often find clients "playing to the helper," trying to create a favorable impression with us so that we will render the desired opinion when the time comes. Allowing ourselves to be used in this way runs counter to a healthy therapeutic relationship.

What are some ways we can ensure that we are serving as a healthy influence in the overall divorce process? We will address that question in the next chapter.

Chapter Two Key Points:

- ❖ Acknowledge that divorce is a *process*.
- ❖ Know where your client is in the divorce process.
- ❖ Provide feedback and interventions accordingly.
- ❖ Recognize that family members may be at various places in the process.
- ❖ Allow clients and family members to proceed at their own speed.
- ❖ Do not get locked into any one particular strategy, goal, or approach.
- ❖ Recognize where the client may be stuck and provide appropriate interventions.

LAYING THE GROUNDWORK, PART 2

Helping Principles

The second part of laying a solid foundation for working with divorcing clients is to adopt a sound set of core helping principles. Chapters 4-8 will discuss specific techniques to employ in specific instances with couples, individuals, parents, and children. For now, however, we will look at *general* principles that can guide our work with virtually all clients in divorcing families. Adopting these principles will help prevent us from falling into common traps and missing important opportunities to promote healing and growth.

Enhancing Functioning ("How Is My Client Doing?")

One of the most important questions we can ask at the beginning of our involvement in a case, and continually thereafter, is simply, "How is my client functioning right now?" It is a question that can easily be forgotten amid the emergent drama of divorce.

Divorce presents huge moral and emotional dilemmas for our clients and forces them into making difficult, life-changing decisions. Oftentimes clients seek our help initially because they need support in making such decisions or taking critical actions. At such Critical Entry Points, before we proceed with a client, before we address any particular course of action, such as divorce, we are well-advised to ask ourselves what shape the client is in *right now*, mentally and emotionally. A client may be too much of a "mess" at the moment to be able to think straight. His or her mental and emotional health may be in crisis. He or she may be leaning on the wrong people for support and may be vulnerable to making catastrophic decisions.

So, right from the start, instead of focusing on major, concrete decisions such as what kind of lawyer to hire or whether to pursue physical custody of the children, we may need to focus on more immediate issues relative to getting the client *functional. Then* we can address other matters. Our initial work with a client often entails putting on the brakes, stepping out of the drama, and assessing the client's present-moment mental health landscape. We may then find ourselves practicing a form of psychosocial *triage*, addressing the most pressing needs first. We will want to ask questions such as the following:

What kinds of supports does the client have right now? Does the client have a good emotional support system or is she going it alone? If the latter is true, we might need to "circle the wagons" and make sure that friends, relatives, and perhaps social service agencies become involved immediately. Is there a wide enough *range* of supports in place or is all the client's support coming from one source? If a client has moved back in with her mother, for example, she may be getting plenty of support, but it may not be the kind of well-rounded adult support that will ultimately best serve her and her family. The client may not be able to make healthy decisions until she broadens her support system.

Where is the client living and how? Are there immediate housing issues? Is she living with the kids in a battered women's shelter? Is he living in a walk-in closet in a friend's apartment? If so, then before making any decisions about the future, we will want to address present housing needs. Stabilization becomes our priority. Is the client in crisis financially? Does he or she have immediate critical issues with child care or employment? Is the client in *danger* — should a restraining order be filed? In our triage system, these issues take primacy. The rule of thumb is remove the *immediate* sources of stress, then start to tackle the long-term sources.

What professional services might the client need in order to cope? Would he benefit from regularly scheduled therapy? Parent coaching? A support group? Is the client seriously depressed or anxiety ridden or losing sleep? Then perhaps a medication consult is indicated. If the client is in any kind of mental/emotional crisis, then that is the first focus of our work. Divorce decisions get put on hold.

What self-help strategies might be employed? If the client is having anxiety problems, could she perhaps be encouraged to meditate? Are there other relaxation, breathing, or creative visualization techniques that might be appropriate? Can we recommend any books or audiotapes that we think our clients would respond to? How about exercise, sports, or other forms of stress release? Recreational or creative outlets?

What interventions can we provide to improve functioning? What are some immediate interventions that can be used in the office with the client? If the client is locked into overwhelmingly negative perceptions, might cognitive restructuring help him start seeing things in a new way? Perhaps some ego-building techniques are immediately needed to get the client in shape to weather the divorce process and make tough decisions. Until the client has the necessary ego strength, we may need to serve as the observing ego, helping him sort out what is real, right, and important from what is not.

We will talk more about techniques in the next several chapters — the important thing to remember for now is to ask the question, "How is my client functioning?" And to ask it often. Until the client is thinking straight, he will not be able to use support in a healthy way.

Maintaining Neutrality

Neutrality *is perhaps the most important working attitude* that any of us who deal with divorcing clients can adopt. Neutrality is a cornerstone of the mediation profession. For mediators, neutrality means that (1) the professional has no prior relationships with either side that predispose her to choose one side or the other; and (2) the professional remains impartial; that is, she keeps an open mind as to the "rightness" of one position or another in a conflict (Moore, 1996). As counselors, both forms of neutrality are important though it is the second of these standards that is usually more challenging to meet.

Maintaining neutrality is one of the most central points in this book. Its importance cannot be stressed enough. The largest number of helper-created problems that I have witnessed over the years — and I have seen many — have stemmed, in one way or another, from helpers failing to maintain neutrality regarding the divorce.

It is easy to see how neutrality is lost. The instincts and training of many helpers tell us to ally with our client, to be his or her champion. This is particularly the case for those who are trained to work with individuals as opposed to those with family therapy training. But *advocacy* alone is not the best long-term approach when it comes to divorce. Advocacy means we try to *win* for the client because the client is, in effect, our "employer." We accept the client's point of view as right, almost the way a defense attorney would. *Neutrality*, on the other hand, calls for us to try to see the divorce picture from many points of view and not to become unduly slanted toward one side or the other, even our own client's. It means becoming an advocate for the *whole family system*, not just one member. In the end, trying to protect the needs of all of the family members will produce the balanced long-term results that work best for everyone, including the client.

Of course, true and absolute neutrality may not be possible. We may form private opinions as to who is right and who is wrong. The behavior of one member of the family may indeed seem more "blameworthy" than that of others. But we can still adopt a *neutral stance*. That is, we can gather information from all sides, give equal time and attention to all parties (when we're seeing the couple or the whole family together), give fair "airplay" to all points of view, and consciously avoid championing one side over the other. The principles of systemic family therapy remind us of these points. In the family systems literature we are encouraged to "keep in mind the perspective of all family members in relative and relational terms" and to maintain neutrality with regard to our "hypothesis regarding the family game." (Selvini Palazzoli, Boscolo, Cecchin, & Prata, 1980). In other words, we try not to assign absolute rightness/wrongness. We avoid, to the greatest extent possible, looking for heroes and victims.

Empathy is important when working with clients, but too often empathy translates into listening to our client in a way that reinforces our client as "right" at the expense of others in the family who are not our clients. While it is helpful for clients to feel that they are validated by the active listening of a counselor, it is important for counselors to be careful about how they respond. One-sided empathy can actually be harmful if it is construed by the client as a validation of the correctness of his viewpoint and actions. Championing one family member over another can serve to polarize the family. It is preferable, and possible, to maintain empathy and support for our client while still remaining neutral as to who is to blame and who is ultimately "right."

It is relatively easy to establish neutrality when we are seeing multiple members of the family together in the office. In these cases we can use fair-play techniques to make sure that everyone has a say and that everyone tries to listen to everyone else. It is more difficult to be neutral when we are seeing only one individual client. Then we must rely on the client to supply the "truth" about the partner and the family. Frequently in these cases we end up adopting a point of view that is at least somewhat prejudicial in favor of the client. We can get pulled into the advocacy game.

And so it is useful, especially when seeing only an individual, to make extra efforts to elicit information about what the other members of the family do, think, feel, and say. We can prompt the client with questions in this regard. Why did the other partner behave as she or he did? What action *on the client's part* preceded the partner's action in any given situation? What was our *client's* role in the conflict? Broader questions are important as well, about both the past and present. Did the two partners communicate well? Did they enjoy doing things together? How was their sex life? What needs were not being met in the marriage for either or both of them?

Let's say, for example, that a client comes to us complaining of an "absentee" husband whom she is considering divorcing. She characterizes the man as an insensitive workaholic who is emotionally distant from his family. She suspects him of having an affair. We can either accept the story at full face value, or we can dig. We can try to determine whether the children have an alliance with one parent or the other. We can try to get a picture of the family's habits and customs by asking about what kinds of things the family does when the father is out working. We can ascertain whether the family is split around certain issues and how this polarization plays out in day-to-day life.

Perhaps with sufficient prodding a fuller picture will emerge. We may discover, for example, as I did in a recent case, that the children have a strong alliance with the mother, an alliance that she has done nothing to discourage. When the father is absent, the mother's "culture" dominates the household and the family engages in many bonding rituals together. When father comes home, wanting to be part of the family, he has a hard time breaking in. He doesn't understand the in-jokes that the others share and has a different set of expectations and preferences. His attempts to "join" the family come across as awkward and obtrusive. The rest of the family responds to his awkwardness by alienating him, subtly or overtly. Feeling excluded, he pulls away and pours himself back into his work again, which further feeds the family's image of him as absentee father. This father loves his family but can't find a way in. Perhaps he eventually does have an affair.

It is important to try to understand this husband's motivations, even if he remains an offstage player, even if we're only seeing the wife as a client. There is a big difference between a serial adulterer who is genuinely neglectful of his family and a father who simply feels unaccepted and unloved. The only way to find out which of these we're dealing with is to consciously maintain some neutrality.

Once we have uncovered enough information about the father to glimpse some understandable human motivations, the mother's initial point of view no longer has total dominance. We can create some balance in the picture. It becomes possible to give some voice to the father's point of view. This doesn't "excuse" an affair, if one indeed occurred, but it does give us a way to more fairly examine the way the family system works. Only then can an intelligent decision be made as to whether or not to end the marriage.

In general we are more likely to maintain neutrality if we have the opportunity to spend some time with all of the involved parties. Thus, when working with a child, we would do well to try to meet both parents. When working with an individual, we might ask to have at least one or two sessions with both partners (or ex-partners) together in the same room, provided this is feasible and acceptable to the client. In lieu of that, we can ask questions such as those mentioned above or ask the client to role-play the ex-spouse to bring the other person's view into the room *in absentia*.

One potent indicator that we have lost our neutrality in a case is that we start thinking and talking in terms of good partner vs. bad partner, right partner vs. wrong one.

❖ *Promoting Healthy Empowerment*

Healthy empowerment is the next core principle of divorce work. It dovetails another cornerstone concept of mediation, *balance of power* (Haynes, 1988; Kelly, 1995; Moore, 1996; Neumann, 1992), but applies to all helping relationships with divorcing couples.

Healthy empowerment revolves around promoting a fair power balance in the relationship. It is difficult to counsel couples through a healthy divorce process if one party holds all the cards. Therefore the helper works to try to ensure that *both* parties in a divorcing couple feel a roughly equal sense of power as the divorce proceeds. In an immediate sense, this means that when a couple sits in our office, both parties feel they can assert their point of view and be heard. The power in the room is not unduly weighted to one side or the other. Often an imbalance of power can be felt as a palpable reality when both parties are present. As with neutrality, balance is a more difficult principle to promote when seeing only one divorcing party as the client. In such cases, the professional can help the client not only empower herself, but also give her the tools to provide her ex with some sense of empowerment. By communicating her own position clearly and then giving equal credence to the ex-partner's position, clients can develop power strategies that work for the entire family.

Balance of power, of course, extends beyond what occurs in the helper's office. Some indicators of healthy, balanced empowerment include the following:

❖ **Both parties have equal knowledge and information.**
Power is imbalanced when one party has access to important information that the other does not have. In many older and more "traditional" marriages, for example, the husband alone may possess detailed knowledge about the family's monetary resources. He holds all the financial cards. There cannot be a balance of power here until the wife gets an objective reporting of where all the money is, who has access to it, and how. Knowledge is power.

I recently counseled a couple where the husband was a lawyer and the wife knew relatively little about the law. She felt completely disempowered when the three of us would discuss divorce, despite her husband's earnest attempts to correct this. The couple made the decision to have her attorney attend some of our sessions so as to address the power imbalance and move the parties toward resolution of their divorce.

Many subtle areas of knowledge can tip the balance of power. The primary caregiver to the children, for example, often knows many things about the children's needs, rhythms, and preferences that the other partner does not know. By withholding this knowledge from the spouse, the caregiver partner may be able to hang onto a greater degree of power when it comes to discussing parenting issues. The helper remains sensitive to key areas of informational imbalance, calls them to both parties' attention, and attempts to take steps to remedy them.

❖ **Both parties can assert themselves.** In a marriage, often one party is more assertive about his or her needs than the other. This may be an arrangement that, until now, both parties have unconsciously endorsed. During a divorce, however, it is crucial that this type of imbalance be redressed. The old "rules" of the marriage no longer apply. We, as helpers, can provide the structure and encouragement by which the less assertive member gains equal voice. A shy and nonverbal person needs to become accustomed to stating personal desires and preferences aloud. Part of our job is to make sure this is happening and take steps to correct it when it isn't.

❖ *Both parties have confidence that their needs will be addressed.* If we are dealing with a couple, both parties will want to know that they're not simply being "heard" but that protections are in place to ensure that their needs will not be trampled in the outer world. If one party, for example, has a high-powered attorney, a high-profile public persona, and strong community supports but the other does not, this can create an imbalance of confidence. Helpers can bring this kind of imbalance to the attention of clients and help them figure out ways to address it.

❖ *Both parties have realistic goals and know how to accomplish them.* Real empowerment comes from having goals that can be attained *in reality* and a clear sense about how to accomplish them. Grand goals that are fantasy based have no power behind them. The goal of achieving "total victory" in a divorce, for example, is unrealistic. Realistic goals should address the ex-partner's needs and the needs of the whole family and should be built on an understanding that perfect solutions are not always possible.

Of course, the most realistic goals in the world remain unrealistic unless the client has the real-world ability to attain them. Part of the helper's job is to inventory the client's skills, tools, and resources and make sure that these are adequate for reaching any agreed-upon goals. In whatever area the client may need help — finances, parenting skills, job skills, legal support — the counseling professional should encourage him to seek support and provide appropriate referrals where needed.

A crucial aspect of *healthy* empowerment is that it is not driven by conflict, aggression, or provocation. Very often clients falsely believe that empowerment means the ability to boldly confront others, particularly one's ex-spouse. Sadly, many therapists and other helpers do nothing to discourage this misunderstanding. David Hawkins (1995), in his book *Power vs. Force*, draws a useful distinction. Power, he maintains, is a quiet self-assurance that comes from being fully grounded as a human being. It proceeds from a deep knowledge of who one is at one's core and a confidence that no one else can threaten that core. It includes a pointed *lack* of aggressiveness and defensiveness. Though power includes speaking up for one's own needs, it does not include attacking others. True power is not the kind of energy that provokes counterattacks.

Force, on the other hand, is a more superficial kind of energy. It is all about aggression, confrontation, manipulation, and strategies of victory and one-upmanship. Force has a "push-back" effect; it always causes others to react against it in one way or another. Use/abuse of force is responsible for many of the problems that arise in divorce. Exercising authentic power, on the other hand, is generally curative.

❖ *Avoiding Triangulation*

Family therapists trained in the theories of Bowen (1976) are familiar with the concept of triangulation. *Three* seems to be a magic number in the world of human relationships. When two people are at odds with one another or have issues that they cannot deal with openly, a third party often gets drawn into the conflict. The two original parties may vie for the allegiance of the third in order to tip the balance of power. Or the third party can become a "false opponent," externalizing some of the internal forces that are pulling at the two main "combatants." The third party — a child, for example — can often say or do things that the other two are constrained from saying and doing.

Kerr and Bowen (1988) also make the point that the "involvement of a third person decreases anxiety in the twosome by spreading it through three relationships. The formation of three *interconnected* relationships can contain more anxiety than is possible in three separate relationships because pathways are in place that allow the shifting of anxiety around the system. This shifting reduces the possibility of any one relationship emotionally 'overheating'" (p. 135). To some extent, it is normal for helping professionals to play a diffusing "point in the triangle" when we counsel a couple. It becomes unhealthy only when our third-party role becomes rigidified, when the couple begins to use *us* to evade personal responsibility or to focus blame.

When we work with divorcing parties, we may see frequent attempts to cast us in such a triangulated role. One or both members of the couple may try to use a helper as a chess piece in their struggle with one another. Forming an alliance with the helper can give one of them a stronger sense of power. Or, having the helper provide advice or make decisions may allow an individual to sidestep confrontation and avoid being held accountable for his or her opinion. If the professional says A is the right thing to do, then A can be treated as an objective goal, rather than one's own personal agenda. Frequently there is an attempt to get the third party helper to take sides in the divorce struggle.

The unmindful helper can end up being used as a messenger or go-between for the opposed parties. Some helpers actually encourage this type of dependency, in a subtle way, because it makes them feel meaningfully needed. It is important that we avoid being cast in such a position, except when it is our clearly defined and agreed-upon role. All attempts at triangulation, in the end, are ways for clients to avoid taking complete personal responsibility for their decisions, desires, and actions. Whenever we allow clients to get away with triangulating us, we are enabling them to dodge growth and, in some cases, nourishing the flames of growing conflict.

We may also wish to take measures to help *others* avoid being used as unwitting third parties and to help the couple *avoid using* others this way. Anyone who crosses the path of a divorcing couple — friends, family members, priests, neighbors, children's teachers — is susceptible to being pulled into an alliance in the conflict.

The children themselves are very commonly used in this way. Children love both of their parents and can easily be drawn into echoing whatever opinion one of the parents wants them to have. In my practice I sometimes get phone calls from children of divorce and can immediately tell which parent's home they are calling from, based on the concerns they are voicing. For instance, in one family the children when staying with their father called to tell me that they want more time with him. When staying with their mother, they called to report that their father was late to pick them up. Parents often fool themselves into believing they are protecting their kids' interests, when they are in fact *projecting* their own interests onto the child.

To summarize, helpers are wise to guard against being drawn into triangulation themselves and to watch out for its occurring elsewhere in the family system. Most especially, helpers can urge clients to avoid triangulating their children into the parents' battle.

❖ *Understanding Circularity*

One of the most useful principles for both diagnosing problem patterns in a relationship and helping clients to *break* those patterns is Circularity (Selvini Palazzoli et al., 1980). The principle of Circularity allows the helping professional to see a chain of causality in relationships that is more predictable and repetitive than a strictly linear *A causes B* formula. Circularity reveals a pattern more like *A causes B, which causes C, which causes D, which causes A*. A cycle, rather than a linear progression, is observed. The cycle feeds itself, often growing stronger with each loop.

As an example of circularity, consider the case of an ex-husband who tends to be a bit scattered and disorganized. This sometimes causes him to be late dropping the kids off and meeting other obligations. The ex-wife's reaction to this is to become belittling and controlling toward him. He then loses self-confidence, which in turn causes him to become even *more* disorganized. As he becomes more disorganized he has an *even harder* time staying on schedule and drops the kids off even later. She then becomes *even angrier* and insulting, which causes his self-confidence to further erode, thus perpetuating the cycle.

In the case of the "absentee father" mentioned earlier, a similar kind of circular pattern emerges. The wife and kids perceive Dad as uninvolved so they form a bond among themselves. Dad comes home and cannot find a way to interject himself in the bonded unit, so he goes away. This causes Mom and the kids to further conclude that he's emotionally unavailable, which makes them close off to him even more. The next time Dad tries to "break in," the reaction he receives is even more hostile, which causes him to make even less of an effort to break in, which further feeds the perception that he doesn't want to be part of the family. And on and on.

Great strides can sometimes be made in fixing "broken" family patterns when the helper can get one or more of the parties to recognize circularity. Sometimes, just *watching* a familiar pattern unfold along a predictable trajectory several times is enough to make the client begin to change her behavior. Spontaneously, she may try to make a better choice. But old habits can be hard to break. If an individual cannot change on her own, then we can suggest some appropriate pattern-breaking behaviors. For example, a simple act of *kindness* or understanding can be astonishingly effective when used in place of predictable defensive reactions. Almost any positive act inserted into a destructive cycle can start to unravel the old pattern. Sometimes, however, it may take years of conscious practice and a lot of falling down and trying again to break a powerful interpersonal cycle. It may not be possible to break the cycle until the parties have worked their way to resolution of the divorce process.

One way to help discover circularity patterns in a marriage or postmarriage situation is inspired by Watzlawick, Weakland, and Fisch (1974). It involves prompting a client with the phrase, "the more ___, the more ___." As in, "the more I do A, the more he or she does B." For instance, "The more I yell at him, the more withdrawn he gets. The more withdrawn he gets, the angrier I become." If we can get our client to make some key "the more, the more" statements about the relationship, they are well on their way to uncovering some of its circularity. Clients can then take the first steps toward breaking the spiraling patterns by applying conscious attention.

❖ *Seeing the Big Picture*

As helpers, we remain advocates for the big picture. Helping clients see outside the box of their own immediate needs and constricted emotions is crucial if we wish to promote a growth-oriented divorce process for everyone in the family. This is more than any one particular technique; it's a general approach we need to take. Clients who are in pain often become myopic and reactive. They regress, both cognitively and emotionally. They can only perceive their own needs and cannot think in a broader context. It is an important part of our work to help them consider the big picture — how their actions may affect everyone in the family in the long run. In order to accomplish this, we may first need to open up *our own* vision.

As mentioned earlier, this is not always easy to do, especially when the counselor is seeing an individual client alone. The client may be in crisis and may have acute needs to which we indeed must respond immediately. If a client is in a domestic situation of escalating verbal abuse and conflict, for example, then good triage dictates that we deal with this crisis first — perhaps facilitate a temporary separation or put other protective measures in place. Once the immediate problem is resolved, though, we may not wish to buy into the client's one-sided view that the spouse is "the bad guy." Accepting this point of view might mean that we would advocate a reduction in the spouse's contact with the children. But is this the best course of action for the whole family system? If the spouse is a repeat physical abuser, then probably yes. But what if the "abuse" in this case turns out to be a cycle of escalating, *mutual* yelling, throwing objects, and pushing? Then is the big picture best served by depriving the children of one parent on a long-term basis? The client may be too angry and embittered to consider this. It is our role to pull the camera back for a wider shot.

Often clients simply get locked into their own story, their own set of meanings, and their own point of view. They may need a trained pair of eyes to help them look at things from a different perspective. The concept of "reframing" became an integral part of systemic family therapy in the 1980s (Weeks & L'Abate, 1982). It has since found its way into mediation work as a way of helping clients to see situations with fresh eyes. Benjamin (2003) adapts family therapy techniques to the process of conflict resolution and compares a mediator to a "trickster" who "takes the communication of a party and . . . alters and redirects that meaning to allow more constructive use in the settlement process" (p. 116). Reframing involves altering the context of a situation by altering its meaning.

Consider a woman who has a history of alcohol abuse but is working on her sobriety. She believes that her ex-husband holds complete disdain for her and is trying to turn the children against her. So when the children, ages 12 and 14, stay at her place and fail to help with the dishes, she becomes convinced that her ex-husband is coaching them against her. Her therapist might try out some alternate explanations for the children's behavior. It might be an eye opener for this client to realize that it is perfectly normal for young teens to test their parents' authority and rebel around household chores. She may be forced to admit that she has been thinking so lowly *of herself* as a parent that it never occurred to her that she might actually possess some legitimate parental authority against which the kids would try to rebel. Seeing the situation from a new perspective, she may be able to consider new strategies for setting limits with the children.

Mutual Perspective-Taking (Selman, 1980) is a goal we aim for in counseling. Selman describes the ability to view situations from the perspective of others as a developmental stage that occurs during normal maturation. But during crisis, such as divorce, regression often takes place. Clients can lose the ability to take a sophisticated view of a situation, one that includes others' points of view. They can become extremely self-absorbed and nearsighted. By simply coaching clients to view conflicts and disagreements from the perspective of the ex-spouse, the helper can go a long way toward defusing potential bombs.

A client of mine recently complained about his ex-wife's "controlling attitude" toward him. "Every time it's my turn to take the kids, she spends ten minutes on the phone haranguing me to get them to call her every night. Like she's convinced I'm going to screw it up. And she's so controlling about it, she needs them to call at the *same time* every night. Exactly 7:30." When he was able to step out of his own cognitive framework and momentarily into hers, he came to see that maybe his ex-wife just missed the kids tremendously when they were gone and didn't really know how to handle their absence. She was not used to letting go. Her insistence about having the kids call every night at 7:30 was perhaps more about quelling her own anxiety than trying to control *him*. The next time he spoke to his ex-wife about visitation, he took a reassuring attitude, rather than a defensive one. Not surprisingly, she instantly stopped "trying to control" him.

❖ ### *Establishing Clear Rules and Boundaries*

Last, but certainly not least, of our core helping principles is the idea of enforcing and supporting clear rules and boundaries. This involves two approaches for helpers: (1) keeping a watchful eye on the whole family system and recognizing when rules between family members are in need of being established or clarified, and (2) establishing clear rules and boundaries between the helper and the client. We will talk in greater detail about the first of these approaches in the next chapter. In this section we will deal only with the second.

As helpers we are well-advised to establish firm, clear rules and boundaries in relation to our clients. Members of the board of registration of psychologists in my state (Massachusetts) tell me that the majority of professional ethics complaints they receive stem from boundary violations between therapists and families in high-conflict divorces. The therapist goes too far in playing advocate or friend or makes ill-advised recommendations based on limited evidence. He gets pulled into the drama and loses neutrality and objectivity.

As helpers we want to be very clear about our role definition and about *communicating that role* to clients. Some basic questions we can ask ourselves in order to clarify that role are

- ❖ What things will we do for the client and what things must the client do for him or herself? These can include making referrals, communicating with other professionals, and tracking down resources.
- ❖ How far are we willing to go in playing a mediator or messenger role between the divorcing parties?

❖ What kind of stance do we plan to take regarding advocacy and neutrality?
❖ How much communication from the client — letters, emails, phone calls — will we accept and respond to?
❖ Can the client call us in an emergency?
❖ Under what conditions will we or will we not speak to other family members?
❖ Will we be available to see other family members in our office?
❖ Will we ever offer verbal and/or written opinions about the case to third parties? If so, under what conditions?
❖ Will we offer expert testimony on behalf of the client and, if so, what will be our fee structure for providing this service?
❖ Will we offer advice to the client or not?
Some of these issues will be further addressed in chapter 10.

Clients, particularly those who have never been in counseling, come to us with many conscious and unconscious assumptions — that we will be their advocate, judge, friend, advisor, mediator, teammate, coconspirator. The more clearly we explain our actual role, the fewer boundary problems we will have. We spell out to the client, up front, how we see our role and make sure the client understands it and is willing to work with us under the restrictions that the role implies. Then we assiduously stick to the role as we've described it. Putting such an agreement in writing is a good idea, especially if we get a sense that the client may be a boundary tester. Then whenever the client approaches us in a way that sets off our boundary alarms, we can remind her again of our initial understanding. If we have established a very clear and specific agreement, verbal or written, then this task becomes much easier.

If we do not establish clarity about our role at the beginning of our work, it becomes harder to introduce restrictions later, when trust is beginning to develop. It is likelier that lines will become blurred. Just as a teacher who sets clear rules on the first day of class has an easier time maintaining order than one who plays it more loosely, the counselor who sets clear rules up front has an easier time enforcing boundaries than one who does not.

Firm rules and boundaries help provide a sense of containment and make the client feel less anxious. Divorce is a chaotic time. Clients' own roles and the roles of the people closest to them are being rewritten day by day. Confusion reigns. Clarity around our own role can serve as an anchor during this time, whereas indecisiveness from us will ultimately only add to the confusion.

There are, of course, many, many other useful principles that helping professionals can adopt, but I believe that the above seven constitute an excellent foundation. Now, armed with these fundamental strategies, we are ready to press onward. In the next chapter we will take a look at the delicate art of "uncoupling."

Chapter Three Key Points:

- ❖ Reinforce healthy functioning.
- ❖ Maintain neutrality.
- ❖ Encourage healthy empowerment.
- ❖ Avoid triangulation.
- ❖ Recognize the circularity of interactions — "the more . . . the more."
- ❖ Help clients look at the Big Picture.
- ❖ Clarify and enforce healthy rules and boundaries.

4 ❖

Uncoupling

The art of *un*coupling is at least as delicate and fraught with hazards as the art of coupling. Many couples pour a great deal of thoughtful work into preserving a marriage, but once the decision to end the relationship has been reached, they "wing it" in a haphazard or misguided manner. Separating an intimate union is one of the most difficult emotional and practical challenges that many people will ever face. And yet our culture offers few good models as to how to do it sanely. The only exemplars for divorce that many clients have seen are the bitter and explosive dramas that are played out in the media. We can help our clients do better. We can help them to see that uncoupling can be done in a humane, healthy, and peaceful manner.

❖ The Decision to Divorce

As we set out to help a client in marital crisis, the first thing we need to focus on is the decision to divorce. Has the client made a clear decision? If so, how did it come about? Is it a realistic decision? Is it what the client truly, deeply wants? Our assessment of whether the decision to divorce seems well grounded will shape our treatment approach. We need to be sure that the *client* is sure. Only then can we determine what the client's main treatment issue(s) will be.

Clients in relationship trouble come to us with a wide variety of attitudes. One may be adamant about divorce but unable to take action while another may be deeply unhappy but reluctant to consider divorce as a solution. Others may be confused, reactionary, depressed, shocked, or in denial. Whatever the presenting state of the client, we need to help her make a realistic assessment of her marital situation. It is important to explore whether divorce, *right now*, is indeed the best option. Often the helping professional is the only person standing between the client and a precipitous bad decision.

Let's take a look at two clients. We'll call Client A *Margot*. When she first walked into my office a few years ago, she reported that she had been wanting a divorce for some time, though she had not yet taken any action in that regard. She felt that there was no hope for happiness in her present marriage and that she no longer loved her husband. Couple counseling had been tried without success. The husband, Kent, had decided not to continue with it. Kent seemed completely unwilling to explore her feelings or his own in the relationship.

Complicating the situation were the husband's medical issues — a stroke had left Kent partially disabled. Margot had assumed a caregiver role in the relationship from the start, and Kent had always depended on her. After the stroke, this dependency deepened; he became unwilling to make even minor efforts to help himself or overcome his disabilities. As one example of this, she told me that he was capable of tying his own shoes (though it was a bit difficult for him), but constantly asked her to do it. There were many such examples, from folding his laundry to turning the pages of his newspaper. Margot cooked all the meals and did all the household chores. Guilt was one of Margot's main emotional issues when she considered divorce. She would feel wrong "abandoning" her "patient."

The other issues for Margot were financial and social. Margot was an artist who did not make a lot of money. Nor did she have much of a social circle or professional network. So leaving her husband, who brought in most of the limited household income through disability insurance and a few small investments, was going to be a major practical hurdle.

After carefully sifting through the relationship's history for a few sessions, Margot concluded that she had thoroughly explored the decision to divorce. It seemed to be a sound, mature one that was not impulsive. The essential treatment issue for Margot, then, was one of getting herself ready emotionally and financially to take the step. That was where we needed to focus our attention.

Let's call Client B *Lillian*. Like Margot, Lillian stepped into my office stating that she wanted a divorce. Lillian had quite a tale to tell. Lillian and her family had faced enormous health challenges over the past several years. Both she and her husband had battled cancer, with many dramatic ups and downs. Each had provided care for the other at various times, but Lillian's illness had been more prolonged and more serious. She had been facing a dire prognosis when a new form of chemotherapy was introduced. This treatment had had a near-miraculous effect on her health.

This couple also had a son with substantial learning issues that required constant attention and monitoring. For the past five years this family had essentially *lived* at clinics and hospitals. In the midst of all this, Greg had somehow managed to have an affair. Lillian was shocked and wounded by the betrayal. The son was enraged. Given the apparent callousness of Greg's actions amid the strong emotional needs of his own family, divorce seemed to Lillian like the logical and only option.

As we explored the situation over the next session or two, though, the portrait of her husband that emerged was one of a man in tremendous turmoil himself. Greg seemed to be going through an acute midlife crisis triggered by a brush with not only his own mortality, but that of his wife. His successful law career, which had always provided his main source of identity, was in serious jeopardy due to the time and energy involved in attending to all of his and his family's medical issues. He had been keeping strange hours, sleeping in hospital rooms four or five nights a week and this had played havoc on his biological rhythms. He was, rather understandably, an emotional mess. Did this mean it was okay for him to have an affair? No. But was the affair an act of callousness or one of emotional desperation? It seemed to be the latter. I asked Lillian if she could imagine forgiving Greg. She wasn't sure. Did she really, deeply want to divorce him? She wasn't sure. She wasn't sure about anything. Lillian, I came to believe, did not necessarily want the marriage to end but simply did not know what else to do.

Lillian's case was quite different from Margot's. In Margot's case a rational and clearly thought-out decision had been made. In Lillian's case, she and her family were emotionally confused. Divorce *seemed* like the natural choice, but was it the best one?

What really lay at the heart of Margot's dilemma was a search for the self. Margot, the artist, had never really "found herself," had not learned who she was apart from her husband and what her place and purpose in the world might be. And so the treatment goal for her became one of aiding her self-development so that she could rise to the task of leaving Kent. Therapy not only provided support but allowed her to develop several ego-building techniques and practical strategies. Slowly, bit by bit, Margot began to prepare for the decision that lay on the horizon. She began getting her artwork out into the world, learning how to "package" and exhibit it. She taught herself how to make prints so that she could sell more pieces. She spoke to attorneys and financial planners and put together an economic strategy. She started setting limits on her husband: stopped tying his shoes, required him to cook for himself two nights a week while she went out and took classes, and spent some time marketing her art. Margot is finally at the place now, two years later, where she is ready to take the actual step of getting the divorce. It has been a long journey of adult growth.

In Lillian's case, an entirely different approach was needed. What this client and her family needed to do was step on the brakes. Lillian had plenty of career and financial skills — that wasn't her issue. She could survive on her own emotionally as long as her health remained intact. The issue here was that this family was in tremendous crisis and had been for some time. Crisis time is a very poor time to make a major decision, such as divorce, that will only trigger exponentially more crises. Even if divorce was the best idea, it needed to wait. What everyone in this family needed to do was STOP, take a collective deep breath, and give themselves an emotional "time out" to gain perspective on the situation. It was not my place to recommend *for* or *against* divorce. But, as the therapist, what I did need to do was to get my client and her family to calm down and take a sober look at the options.

Lillian and Greg decided on a trial separation. He went into individual therapy to better understand his own behavior. The couple agreed to talk together with a couples therapist for a limited number of sessions to try to understand the issues that had affected the marriage. Lillian began meeting with a financial planner and an attorney for informational purposes. Father and son are now working through their respective anger and are talking to one another about what happened.

Neither party is filing for divorce at this point. If divorce turns out to be the best course of action, it can be undertaken six months or a year down the line. Now that the pressure is off, the husband and wife are communicating — sharing their sense of fear with one another. They are also beginning to look at the marriage dynamics that were problematic before and during the turmoil of the last few years. It is unclear whether this marriage will end, but if it does it will at least end with a broader understanding of the reasons. Husband and wife will be less likely to repeat the same problem dynamics in a new relationship. If my approach had been simply to accept Lillian's decision to divorce as a "done deal" and recommend an attorney, this case would have taken a very different turn. When any client, new or old, announces an intention to divorce, we can regard this as a Critical Entry Point, where our intervention can make a crucial difference.

Understanding the Marital Context

It is useful to obtain a thorough marital history from the client(s) in order to understand the *context* of the current crisis. When helping professionals understand how and why the partners came together initially, what their life together was like *before* the troubles started, and how the crisis began, they can help clients evaluate whether divorce is really the best solution. Clients can make a realistic assessment of the value of the marriage and then decide, based on that assessment, whether or not to work on the relationship.

Let's take, for example, a couple that loses a child in a car accident. Couples who suffer such a tragedy commonly experience marital difficulties in the ensuing months and years. To assess whether this couple should stay together or end the marriage, it is important to understand the history and dynamics of the marriage. Was the marriage sound to begin with? Did the partners initially come together for healthy reasons or was some neurotic or immature need being filled? Did the couple enjoy a rewarding adult relationship before the child was born? Before the child died? If so, then perhaps the issue is that one or both of the partners is stuck somewhere in the grieving process. Communication may have broken down because of the enormous emotional weight of the death, creating a marital crisis. In this case, the marriage can probably be saved once the personal grieving work is done and the communications wounds healed.

If, on the other hand, the marriage seemed to originate out of immature or neurotic needs, the story might be very different. Perhaps the couple was already experiencing a void in their relationship and had a child as a way to "fix" it. When the child was alive, the partners may have diverted their attention to the child as a means of ignoring the void in their own relationship. With the child gone, the basic flaws in the marriage are now revealed in stark relief. In this case it is far less likely that the marriage can and should endure.

Helping professionals can ask themselves and their clients the following questions in order to clarify the context of the present marital discord:

- ❖ **Does the desire to divorce stem from a particular action or event?** Did this event "happen" to the couple, as in the case of a death, or was it precipitated by the actions of one partner, as in the case of infidelity?
- ❖ **What seemingly unrelated events occurred around the same time as the marital breakdown?** Such events may include a major job change, a move to a new home, an illness in the family, the death of a parent, an in-law moving in, or the birth of a child. Clients may not connect these events with their relationship problems, but, upon closer examination, they may come to see them as underlying causes of marital stress.

❖ **Is this the couple's first marital crisis or one of many within the context of dysfunctional marital dynamics?** Clients often cite a single event as the reason to break up a relationship. Often the event in question happened within a context that the client or couple may not have fully understood. Questions that expose any circularity in the couples' interactions can help clarify the context in which events occurred and reveal whether there is hope for change and growth.

❖ **What measures have been tried to save the marriage?** Has the couple tried counseling, trial separation, spiritual guidance, etc.? Which measures have helped and which haven't? How willing have both parties been to genuinely work on the marriage?

❖ **Did the marriage break down because it was *based on unhealthy needs?*** An examination of how and why a couple came together can shed light on this question. Sometimes, a marriage may break down as the needs of one individual change. Margot, for instance, had assumed a caretaker role in her marriage from the start. This had allowed her to avoid looking at her own needs. As her husband's dependence on her grew, Margot became increasingly aware of her own unfulfilled needs.

❖ **Did one spouse outgrow the relationship?** Are *both* partners committed to growth or only one? Are the partners growing in authentically different directions? Sometimes individuals like Margot desperately need change and that change cannot be supported within the marriage.

❖ **What is the couple's sexual history?** Was sexual attraction a prime motive for the marriage? What role does sex serve in the marriage? Does the couple still have an active sex life? When did it stop being so and why? Does one partner withhold sex from the other or did they mutually grow apart?

❖ How mature/insightful is the couple/client? Is the decision to divorce a reflexive reaction to emotional pain?

An attempt to cause the partner pain? Do the partners have a good working understanding of healthy relationship dynamics? Of the art of commitment?

❖ Do the partners still love one another? Are they still friends? Is there a spiritual connection between the partners?

At bottom is this question: Does the marriage have the potential to encourage the growth and development of both partners or does it function as an impediment to growth? If the latter is the case, then divorce is often a viable choice.

❖ Assessing Short-Term Goals

As clients try to determine whether divorce is the best choice, counseling professionals can help them consider whether either or both parties are *ready* to separate. In Margot's case, the decision seemed sound but she was far from ready to take the step.

Clients often need to focus on short-term personal goals. These can be as varied as clients themselves. Margot, for example, began to focus on her career and on developing a social network. A client in an abusive situation may need to make an immediate physical move out of the house, contact an attorney, and begin intensive therapy sessions. Another client may need to begin couple therapy and start to work on assertiveness and communications skills. Yet another might need to contact a financial planner and take a job training course.

As clients work on short-term goals, they may wish to pursue living arrangements that offer alternatives to immediate divorce. These nondivorce options can buy the client time for a reasoned decision-making process. It is not our job to *advocate* for any particular alternative but to help clients consider possibilities. Alternatives to an immediate divorce process might be

❖ **A marital "vacation."** The partners might informally take a few weeks away from one another. One of them could stay with a friend or rent a cottage or a short-term apartment. Calling it a "vacation" takes the immediate pressure off and gives the clients time to think.

❖ **An open-ended "trial separation."** The partners separate temporarily — perhaps staying with family or friends — but remain in some degree of contact. Neither seeks a permanent new home. They agree to remain apart until such time as they mutually agree to get back together, or not.

❖ **A time-limited "trial separation."** The partners might try a three-month or six-month separation (or whatever length of time seems appropriate). The separation lasts for a predetermined period of time, during which clearly defined limited contact is maintained. After the set period of time living apart, the couple reassesses its status.

❖ **An "in-house separation."** Some couples are able to remain under the same roof but to live separate lives for a certain period of time. During this time they avoid sexual contact and limit the routine rituals they once did together. This can be stressful, however, and is ill-advised for clients who are in active conflict, especially if they have children.

❖ **A prolonged or "predivorce separation."** The partners move to separate households and live completely apart, as a divorced couple would. Perhaps they even date other people. The couple really gets to experience divorced life without the finality of signing the papers. A separation of this type can last indefinitely or until one or both parties decide to move toward legal divorce.

Achieving clarity about whether to divorce or stay together is a major milestone. It can take many weeks or months or, in some cases, can be accomplished fairly quickly.

❖ *Saying Yes to Divorce*

Once all of the analyzing, processing, and experimenting has run its course, a decision must ultimately be made. The following choices are among those that can be made regarding a troubled marriage:

1. The partners stay together and try to save the relationship.

2. The partners stay together temporarily while one or both of them prepare for later divorce. This type of decision may not be overt or mutual. Often it is made in private by one partner who intends to leave the other at some later date.

3. The partners stay together temporarily as they try **to decide** *whether to save the marriage.* Perhaps they experiment with some form of trial separation or go into couple counseling.

4. The partners stay together but do not try to "fix" the relationship. The couple does not get divorced but one or both parties resign themselves to the idea that the marriage is probably never going to be fulfilling. This type of "decision" may be made passively by default or may be an active decision when a client feels that splitting up is the more difficult option financially and/or emotionally.

5. The couple proceeds with a divorce. Once a client is clear that this is the way to go, then the first step is *telling the spouse.* When working with an individual, we can strategize with him as to when and how this should occur. Often there is no perfect time; the client just needs to find the most *realistic* time. We can help the client anticipate the most likely reaction(s) from the spouse and rehearse a response. When counseling both partners, the telling may come naturally as both clients come to realize that the dynamics of their relationship are not working. But often one spouse reaches a "breaking point." She has come to see the bigger picture and realizes that the relationship no longer provides satisfaction and that salvaging it will require more work than she is willing to put into it.

❖ The Rules of Disengagement

Failure to save a marriage is not necessarily a failure in the counseling process; rather, it is often the case that counseling served to clarify the decision to divorce. Unfortunately, couples who have been in counseling together often stop coming to sessions as soon as the decision to divorce is made. But counselors are often in a unique position to stay involved to help a couple disengage in a healthy way. The beginning of the divorce process is a Critical Entry Point that can have an enormous effect on the way events unfold.

In reality, though, helpers frequently do not have this opportunity. Often our first contact with a client is when the individual is in crisis because his or her spouse has initiated a divorce. But whether we have been working with the couple for some time or this is our first introduction, we still have the ability to influence the process. We can help our clients feel in charge of the process and make informed *choices* about how they break up. In so doing, we can assist them to define their "Rules of Disengagement."

General Rules of Disengagement

There are a few general rules we can encourage our clients to follow as the divorce process moves forward:

Move slowly. Making precipitous decisions based on raw emotion is extremely unwise. Think twice — three, four, five times — before taking any action. The need to "do something NOW" is usually a response to emotional pain and uncertainty. In the long term, moving slowly and carefully is generally the best strategy except in cases of emergency.

Avoid surprise attacks. Unanticipated "hostile" actions, such as taking out a restraining order, should be avoided whenever possible. As we saw with John in chapter 1, no one responds well to coming home and finding the police at their door or their bank account halved. A surprise attack causes people to react defensively and can be the catalyst for a high-conflict divorce process that generates pain for years to come.

Establish boundaries and "ground rules" as clearly and as early as possible. Clients frequently need to set firm boundaries with their spouses and others. Misunderstanding of unwritten rules by one party or the other is a major source of postdivorce friction. When families and couples are intact, they often operate by a great many *im*plicit rules that do not necessarily need to be made explicit. During the divorce process, however, the rules change. Not only does it help to clarify the old, *im*plicit rules, but a host of *new rules* need to be developed. It is useful if they can be achieved by mutual agreement.

Establishing new rules often is one of the thorniest and most uncomfortable processes for a divorcing couple/family. In fact, in some cases, the predominant role of the helping professional can be to help the ex-couple/family establish these rules and boundaries. In the postdivorce environment, *the more explicit the rules, the better* so as to head off possible conflicts down the road.

❖ *Getting the Story Straight*

One of the first rules the soon-to-be ex-couple needs to discuss is how they intend to tell friends and family members about the divorce. Can they agree on a single story, at least for the sake of the children? Some couples can, others can't. If Partner A has had an affair, for example, Partner B may insist upon this fact being openly acknowledged. Partner B may not be willing to play along with a neutral "we just grew in different directions" type of explanation. He or she may require that Partner A be seen as primarily responsible for the break-up. With a bit of coaching, infidelity can be framed in a way that does not overly demonize Partner A. Clients wishing to claim moral high ground by making the partner look bad can to be reminded of the practical consequences of turning people against the ex-spouse. Acting with blame and self-righteousness will likely create a counterreaction from the ex-spouse and his or her "camp" that will escalate conflict down the road.

If the two ex-partners cannot agree on a story, can they at least agree to present their two points of view in a way that does not triangulate others by making them take sides? One way to accomplish this is to state, "My version of the story is A, her version is B. I guess we see it differently."

Once the partners have agreed on how the story is to be presented, new questions must be answered. Who will be the one to tell others? Who will say what to whom? How are the children to be informed? (See more on this in Divorce and Children in chapter 8.) What will we say when people ask [x]? The more prepared the two partners are, the lower the anxiety and the less fuel for conflict as they go forward.

As difficult as it may be for the ex-partners to agree on the story and the rules for telling others about the breakup, doing so thoughtfully and maturely — in a way that avoids demonizing anyone — can set a civil, workable tone for the entire divorce process.

❖ *The Parameters of the Separation*

A second priority for the separating couple is the question of how to physically move apart.

Can the two stay in the same home until they work out long-range plans or not? If not, who moves out? Lawyers may advise clients *not* to move out because the partner remaining in the house tends to be viewed as the primary resident when custody and property issues are considered and the individual who moves may be seen as "abandoning" the marriage and the family. However, there may be ways to resolve this problem. Both parties might, for example, sign a letter of agreement stating that this is a short-term arrangement and that it will have no bearing on the divorce negotiations.

It is important to remind clients that *they* should be the drivers of the legal process, not their attorneys. Often attorneys make a recommendation, such as to remain in the family house, as a legal strategy. Such a strategy, however, may not be the most practical solution and may not be aligned with the client's goals for future family relationships.

Clients can be encouraged to find practical short-term solutions without committing to their permanency. For example, one partner may be able to move in with his or her parents or temporarily rent an apartment until both partners figure out how to divide the assets. In the case of Lillian, her husband wished to remain in the home until he could buy a suitable new house for himself. Greg had contributed the bulk of the couple's financial worth and felt that he was entitled to find himself a respectable new home before moving out. Lillian, however, was so angry with him that she could not bear to have him under the same roof. Once they both agreed that it would take time to determine their ultimate fate, they were able to consider the pros and cons of various plans and agreed that he should obtain a house rental for the short term.

If the partners have children, they need to set rules as to how far apart physically they may choose to live. If physical custody is being shared or if frequent visitations are planned, then practicality dictates that the ex-partners should not live too many miles apart. As the divorcing partners move toward developing a separation agreement, they would do well to establish specific rules about proximity. What if one partner gets a job transfer or promotion to another state? Are there any conditions under which a major relocation would be tolerated?

Specific rules about where and how the children will live need to be established. Again, it is useful for clear agreements to be made. Will the children have any say in where they live? Will the partners experiment with what works best for the kids or agree on a plan up front and stick to it? Will the partners allow any flexibility with one another in terms of time spent with the children or will they "play it by the book?" The couple should ask and answer a host of questions such as these. A discussion, rather than a fight, about these delicate questions is more likely when ex-partners have a mechanism for productive communication. This is one of the reasons staying in counseling through the uncoupling phase makes sense.

We will discuss parenting plans in more detail in the Parenting chapter (chapter 6). The important point here is that concrete rules can be adopted, but may take time to negotiate. In the immediacy of a separation, the establishment of short-term structures and solutions can maintain family stability while negotiations about the future proceed. Short-term solutions can provide security and clarity for everyone in the family but may change as the couple's circumstances change and the new family constellation unfolds.

❖ *Defining the Postdivorce Relationship*

It is useful to help separating couples to *define* their postdivorce relationship, at least for the immediate future. Some couples wish to remain friends but to remove all sexual overtones from the relationship. Others actually continue to "date" each other occasionally after a divorce/separation. Some may seek a merely cordial relationship in which the parties occasionally sit together at events for the children but otherwise have limited contact. Still others prefer a distant, even inimical, arrangement in which no attempts at contact are made by either party except when absolutely necessary. There are many possible permutations and variations of the above.

For couples who choose to retain a degree of friendship and/or romantic interest in one another after the divorce, some delicate questions should be addressed. Will they still have sex occasionally? How often or under what conditions? Will they ever sleep at the other's house? If so, how will they explain this to the kids? Sometimes couples go through phases of progressively less intimacy over time and these questions will repeatedly need to be readdressed as the family realigns.

In general, the least messy and problematic type of relationship to maintain in a postdivorce environment is a *businesslike* one. This businesslike relationship can be "warm" or "cool" — cordial or distant — depending upon the wishes of the ex-partners. In either case, though, the ex-partners must take a conscious giant step backward from the intimacy and familiarity of their former relationship. No matter how they may *feel*, they must now *behave* toward one another with the respect, restraint, and consideration that they would show to a business associate. That means the ex-husband no longer buys the ex-wife flowers, shows up unannounced at her house, or hurls insults when he runs into her. That means the ex-wife no longer calls the ex-husband to berate him, invites him to the house at night because she's feeling scared, or calls him up just to chat. Whether positive or negative, all of these are familiar, intimate behaviors that are no longer appropriate after the break-up. The client can be taught a simple test question: would I do [x behavior] to a business associate? If the answer is no, then the client should reconsider.

Communication

Communication missteps are an extremely common cause of postdivorce conflict. Helpers can encourage clients to develop a communication plan up front. Though it will seem awkward and unnatural for two people who have lived in an intimate relationship to suddenly adopt a set of formal rules regarding communication, doing so can remove much of the guesswork and awkwardness that create anxiety.

Ex-partners need to agree upon

* ❖ *How* **they will communicate.** What method(s) will be used? Phone? Email only? Will there be direct communication or will all communication be handled through third parties, such as lawyers, therapists, mediators, or parenting coordinators? (We will discuss some of these professional roles in chapter 9.)
* ❖ **How often they will communicate.** The ex-partners may wish to set artificial limits on how often they will communicate. This is especially necessary if one partner is attempting to either rekindle the relationship or harass the other.
* ❖ **Subject matter about which they will communicate.** Will they restrict themselves to speaking only of the children? Will they communicate with one another regarding other relationships? Are there any special topics about which they may freely communicate? What are these? Are there any special conditions under which the two will communicate?

❖ *In-Person Contact*

In line with the above, the dissolving partners can also state how they will handle any future in-person contacts. What if they see each other at a party or a restaurant? How will they behave? Anticipating potentially awkward situations and talking about them ahead of time can arm the partners with comfort and confidence when the situation actually occurs.

In-person contact rules are particularly important if there are children. Will the parents both go to the same events involving the kids? Will they attend school conferences together or separately? What about kids' sporting events, practices, or performances? Will both parents attend or will they alternate? How will they handle situations where both are present at the same event? Will they sit together or separately? Say a polite hello? Have a conversation? Ignore each other?

In one family, the two formerly married parents go to most of their children's games but always sit at opposite ends of the bleachers and avoid contact with one another. The children feel free to talk to each parent before and after the game and the child goes home with whichever parent is in charge on a particular date. Because the parents maintain the rules consistently, the children are not troubled by this arrangement. The more clarity the exes have about in-person parameters, the less likelihood of emotional flare-ups and public "scenes."

One of the most frequent questions that arises for a freshly separated couple is, How will holidays and special occasions be handled? Will the exes still attend holiday functions with the extended families? Will both parents attend birthday parties for the kids or will separate parties be held? Ex-partners need to make an early decision about these matters so that they can plan what they are going to tell the children. These rules may later need to be reexamined when there is more emotional separation between the partners and/or one or both of the ex-partners becomes involved in a new relationship.

Clear rules and expectations also need to be established regarding whether the exes will ever go to one another's homes and under what conditions. Only when transferring the children? For any other reasons?

❖ *Rules Involving Other Relationships*

Relationships with family and mutual friends also must be considered. Ex-partners need to decide what kinds of relationships they will maintain. Will they both continue to associate with *all* of their mutual friends or will he see some while she sees others — a "my friends/your friends" division of some kind? Regarding family, how will each relate to the in-laws and other members of the extended families? Often close bonds have been created between partners and their in-law families. Will all of these bonds now be severed? If not, how will the ex-partners manage them? If there are children, how will grandparent relations be handled? May each parent have direct contact with the children's grandparents on the other side or not?

Turning a formerly romantic relationship into a more businesslike one is not an easy transition. It is rife with potential hotspots. For many clients, the Rules of Disengagement must be re-examined on a frequent basis. Examination and re-examination of the rules may comprise the bulk of the work that divorcing couples do when they decide to continue working together with a therapist.

❖ *Rules May Change over Time*

Different rules and different *types* of rules will be needed at various points in the divorce process. When couples first separate, it might be most important to help them establish simple rules about how much time the children spend at each house, how far away either ex-partner is allowed to live, and how communications will be handled. Later, more complex subjects will need to be addressed, such as how new partners will be introduced into the family scheme and whether the former partners will try to have any kind of relationship with their ex-spouse's new partners. The primary concerns for the helping professional at any point in the process is to facilitate rules that are clear and to encourage appropriate boundaries between the ex-spouses.

❖ *Coaching/Refereeing*

If we are working with both partners during the divorce (and, to some extent, even if we're working only with one), we can help civilize the process by providing coaching, modeling, and/or "refereeing." We observe the communication styles and habits of the partners and, by direct or indirect intervention, try to help them improve their skills. Unlike in couples therapy, where the therapist aims at ameliorating the marriage, the overriding goal during the early stage of divorce is to help improve the couple's interactions and allow for the clearest and least hurtful communications possible as the divorce proceeds. The following interventions can be useful toward this goal:

Identifying triggers. What are the things one partner says or does that trigger an automatic emotional, verbal, or physical reaction in the other? Helping couples recognize their anger triggers goes a long way toward helping them gain control of reflexive, hurtful behavior. Some common triggers are a particular tone or volume of voice, physical postures or gestures, "hot" topics, accusations and *you* statements, facial expressions, lapsing into tears, or passive-aggressive behaviors such as refusing to answer a question. If we can get clients to recognize what the partner does to "set them off," we can help them avoid escalating the conflict by lapsing into conditioned responses. There are several strategies clients can use to avoid predictable, destructive reactions. We will discuss these in more detail in the next chapter.

Helpers can also work with clients to identify the words and behaviors they themselves use that trigger the *other* person's anger and to learn new behaviors and approaches that are less provocative.

Stopping the action. The helper needs to be alert to circularity patterns in the couple's relationship. When an interaction is spiraling out of control in a meeting with both parties, the helper simply calls a halt to it and asks the client(s) to try a new approach, say something in a different way, or perhaps take a time-out. In essence, we "stop the tape and rewind." Ideally couples can learn to recognize their own destructive communication patterns and to exercise control over them.

Teaching New Behaviors. When working with separating couples, counselors must occasionally play the role of teacher. Sometimes the ex-partners must be shown and taught new ways of behaving that lie outside their current repertoire. Tone of voice, body language, and verbal styles can be retrained via the modeling of an impartial observer. Clients may be unaware that their loud voice is seen as a sign of hostility or that folded arms and a knitted brow signify that one is not listening with an open mind.

Communications skills can be greatly improved by using some well-established methods. For example, it is sometimes possible to coach the client(s) to use "I" statements, rather than "you" statements, which tend to sound accusatory. Framing statements so that the speaker owns his or her own feelings rather than communicating a *"you make me* feel this way" message is a major step toward better communications. Avoiding global generalities, such as *we always, you never,* and *every time you,* is another. Some clients can be trained to repeat back and paraphrase their ex-partners' feeling statements, so that it is clear that the other has been heard and understood. Most mental health professionals are already familiar with these types of techniques (and we will talk about them a little more in the next chapter).

❖ *Forgiveness and Termination Rituals*

When divorcing couples have progressed through the psychological stages of grieving and have begun to let go of the relationship, there is still a further step they can take on the path to healthy adult advancement: forgiveness. Forgiveness is not about whitewashing bad behavior or pretending anger away, it is about making a clean emotional break with the past. It is about releasing one's emotional investment in hurt or angry feelings toward another. It is about saying to oneself or aloud to the ex-partner, "I no longer permit myself to be emotionally controlled by negative reactions to your past behavior. I let you go, fully and entirely. I give both of us permission to live our lives."

Saying goodbye is an important part of forgiveness and leaving the emotional past behind. Counselors can encourage clients to say goodbye to one another in a formal, deeply felt, and meaningful way. Saying goodbye effectively can often involve recognizing good qualities about the ex-spouse and genuinely wishing the other well. Ford (2001) urges individuals to look at one's marriage "through the lens of gratitude" (p. 151), appreciating the life lessons that one learned from the relationship with one's mate. She asks ex-partners to list and name for one another the gifts that they received from their relationship.

Cloke (2001) urges couples to communicate the positives about the relationship to one another through such exercises as the following:

❖ Ask the two people to sit opposite each other, or imagine the other person in front of them, and complete the following phrases:
  ❖ I fondly remember [x about you].
  ❖ I regret [x for myself].
  ❖ I wish you [x in the future].

❖ Ask each person to complete these sentences:
  ❖ I forgive you for [x].
  ❖ I forgive myself for [x].

One of the best ways helpers can aid clients in saying goodbye and fully ending a relationship is to encourage the use of rituals. It is fascinating that, although about half of all marriages in the United States end in divorce, there are few socially acceptable rituals for *ending* a marriage. Many couples spend months planning wedding rites down to the finest detail; however, they have little grounding in tradition for dealing with divorce. Thus for many, a court appearance before a judge has become the default ceremony of undoing a marriage.

Rituals can provide a mechanism by which one names and solidifies inner changes that otherwise might remain vague and undefined. Divorce qualifies as a major life passage fully deserving of ritual closure. Some religious or spiritual practices have ceremonies for the breakup of a marriage. In traditional Judaism, for example, a couple can receive a "Get," or Jewish divorce in which a rabbi grants a divorce under Jewish law and a scribe produces a legal certificate that undoes the union. The Wiccan tradition has a hand parting ceremony, which is a ceremonial undoing of the hand fastening marriage ritual.

For clients who have undergone no meaningful divorce rituals, we can assist them to design their own. Whiting (1988) believes that the most helpful rituals for letting go of an emotional connection are generally ones that involve using symbols such as photographs, symbolic objects, or angry feelings listed on file cards. "Letting go" actions involve a cleansing or healing process, such as burning, burying, flushing, or releasing something into the air or water. Sometimes releasing actions need to be paired with some form of holding on, particularly for those who are not yet ready to fully sever their emotional connection to a partner. For instance, listing hurts on separate pieces of paper and locking them in a box can be a useful way to provide a container for angry feelings. Pulling out each piece one by one when ready to let it go provides a mechanism for releasing hurts slowly. One can then perform a letting go action such as burning it, floating it in the ocean, or sending it up in a helium balloon. Giving and receiving are also ways of ritualizing the dual nature of both saying goodbye to a failed relationship and receiving a farewell from the other.

Cloke (2005) has culled the wisdom of several practitioners concerning ritual and offers the following ideas for creating rituals for divorce:

❖ *Symbolize* the transformation. What physical objects can you find, create, or buy to represent what you most want to end or bring into existence?

❖ Create the right time and place for the ritual.

❖ Reinforce the ritual with a witness.

❖ Incorporate personal stories in the ritual.

❖ Include food and friendship. Make it a celebration of positive changes.

❖ Ask each person to buy the other a gift symbolizing something that the recipient does not see or value in him or herself.

❖ Ask the two partners to say to each other whatever they need to say to finally and completely let go of the relationship.

❖ Encourage ceremonies of undoing using symbols from their relationship, i.e., cutting their rings in half or burying them.

Helpers can transform the nature of the breakup by assisting clients to find concrete ways to symbolize the end of the relationship.

In one recent case, for example, a couple was particularly acrimonious regarding the distribution of several joint items such as camping equipment, children's Halloween costumes, etc. With assistance, they agreed on a formula to split the goods and a time for the two of them to go through the marital home. When I asked them to describe the meaning of the disputed items to one another, their acrimony turned to shared sadness. They eagerly accepted the suggestion of providing one another with a symbolic present to be bestowed on one another on the day of their splitting the remaining household items.

As helpers, we can play a crucial role in humanizing, civilizing, and normalizing the way that many couples come apart. We can temper the panic and turn down the volume on conflict. We can also assist couples in saying goodbye to the relationship. In so doing, we can have a profound positive effect on the mental health of all family members.

Chapter 4 Key Points:

❖ Explore and question the decision to divorce.

❖ Help clients "put on the brakes" and avoid precipitous decisions.

❖ Encourage clients to remain in therapy through the uncoupling phase.

❖ Help couples define their "Rules of Disengagement."

❖ Clarify the boundaries of the postdivorce relationship.

❖ Coach clients to communicate in a "business-like" style with their ex-spouse.

❖ Facilitate forgiveness and letting go through the use of rituals.

5 ❖

Helping the Individual

W orking with a divorcing *individual* — as opposed to a
couple or a family — presents a unique set of challenges.
Extracting reliable information about the family system can be
difficult when we are talking to only one person. The client in
crisis often sees the world through a distorted lens of pain and
anger and presents the helper with a skewed picture. In addition,
every individual, whether in crisis or not, tends to have blind spots
regarding relationships, elements he is simply not capable of
seeing, given his psychological makeup and current level of
awareness and functioning. It is often these very blind spots that
have contributed to the breakdown of the relationship. So it falls
upon us, as helpers, to do a little detective work in order to
establish an objective and balanced view of the divorce scenario.

❖ *Helping Clients Move through the Divorce Process*

Our main job when working with individual clients is to usher
them through the divorce process with the minimal amount of
unnecessary pain. Fortunately for us, the process unfolds according
to its own exigencies. We do not need to drive the process; it happens
on its own. We merely act as facilitators. Preventing "stuckness"
is our chief aim. We strive to help the client move through the
process with the greatest possible fluidity and responsiveness.

As mentioned in chapter 2, there are three main arenas in which
clients get stuck during the divorce process — the Intrapsychic, the
Interactional, and the External/Social level (Johnston & Campbell,
1988). In this chapter, since we are focusing on the individual, we
will place our attention on the Intrapsychic arena.

Within the Intrapsychic arena there are several major emotional trouble spots. Various theorists, such as Johnston and Campbell (1988), Emery (1994), and Fisher and Alberti (2000) have elaborated on these key emotions that tend to ensnare clients and prevent them from moving on. I will borrow from these theorists, but with a slightly reframed perspective.

First this chapter will look at emotions of *vulnerability* — the hurt, wounded, and raw feelings that arise during times of crisis. These emotions could arguably be named differently, but let us call them Fear, Helplessness, Grief, and Shame. They are not always experienced discretely and distinctly, but as overlapping and commingling with one another. For the sake of clarity, though, we will look at each one separately.

After looking at the "vulnerable" emotions, we will look at the fifth emotional hot spot — Anger. Anger can be viewed both as a primary emotion and a secondary one. When clients become *stuck* in Anger, it is sometimes because one or more of the primary vulnerable emotions above is being felt but not acknowledged. Because of this, Anger will be examined last.

As clients make their way through the divorce process, helpers need to pay attention to these major emotional "planets," each of which has its own gravitational pull. Around which one does the client tend to orbit? What are the client's main emotional tendencies? Helping professionals must allow and encourage the client to *experience* most or all of these big emotions, but they must also be on the alert for signs that the client is stuck in an orbit and finding it difficult to move on. Then the task is to help him find the emotional fuel needed to pull away from that orbit and complete his individual journey.

As this chapter outlines specific ways to help the client with each of these major emotions, it will refer to many techniques that are already familiar to practicing therapists. In so doing, it may mention several points that seem obvious. Please forgive this. The presentation of these techniques is intended to be a reminder, not necessarily revelatory information. It is easy to get lost in the complexity and drama of a divorcing client's story and to forget to use basic therapeutic techniques or to teach key skills. During the divorce process, it is generally not sufficient for clients to understand the dynamics of their own behavior; they need skills with which to cope.

Fear

Fear is a primal human emotion — fear of immediate danger, fear of the unknown. For clients facing a separation or divorce, the latter is far more prevalent. This fear springs from the subjective sense that conditions are going to arise for which they will be unprepared and that they may not be capable of handling.

Fear usually accompanies any upheaval in a person's life. Divorce of course, being a *major* upheaval, engenders *major* feelings of fear. Divorce imposes more kinds of change on a person *simultaneously* than most other crises in life. Death of a loved one, major illness, natural disaster, or loss of a job — some of life's other catastrophes — do not usually entail all of the following at the same time: the break-up of one's family, the loss of one's home, the halving of one's financial worth, the need to face deep personal "failings," the death of one's hopes and dreams, and a sudden change of social roles and status. Divorce often means all of the above. For many people going through divorce, it feels as if the future has been torn open. Old hopes and dreams about home and family no longer stand. Life plans must be rewritten. Anxiety can permeate every aspect of life. "Fear of fear itself," in the words of Franklin Roosevelt, exacerbates the problem — clients feel anxiety and then fear that something is wrong with them for feeling this way.

Yet another kind of fear is prevalent in the divorce process. We might call this fear of betrayal, the fear that formerly trusted people (i.e., ex-spouse and other family and friends) may now be "against me." It is easy to see how this kind of fear takes root, especially if the client's spouse has an extramarital affair or suddenly tries to take away the house and the children. Sometimes however fear of betrayal, which may be at least partially grounded in reality, becomes exaggerated, generalized, and irrational during divorce. A sort of paranoia about the ex-spouse can creep into everyday life. The client may start reading dark personal intent into every interaction. If the children are presenting a discipline problem, for example, or a mutual friend cancels a dinner engagement, the client can leap to the conclusion that the ex is turning people against him.

How to Help

Helpers need to be sensitive to the magnitude and multitude of changes that the client is facing. It is safe to assume, when dealing with a divorcing client, that fear is a major emotional theme even if the client is not acknowledging it. In response, we should offer as much reassurance and structure as we can. It is important to let the client know that feeling anxious is normal and that it will pass in due time. Normalizing the feeling of fear helps to contain it and prevent it from magnifying.

When clients are in the grip of fear, thinking becomes highly charged with emotion. Dread and worry expand. "What if" thinking replaces peace of mind. Feelings become globalized and generalized ("I'll never be happy," "Men always let you down," "Love stinks"). Counselors can help the client replace emotionally charged thinking with rational and concrete thought. The divorce must be reframed not as a symbolic event or an echo of past heartbreaks but as a present-moment life crisis. The client's global interpretations of events ("People can't be trusted") can be challenged with more specific interpretations ("One person broke your trust"). It is useful to ask logical questions at every opportunity. "Do you really think you're going to be penniless and living in the streets?" "Do you really believe that your ex wants to *destroy* you?" "Could it be that the children are being uncooperative for their own reasons and not because your ex is inculcating them against you?" Rational thought is an effective antidote to fear. Support groups can be extremely helpful in allaying fear as well. Sharing in a community of other people who are dealing with the same issues can counter the feelings of disconnection that are integral to fear.

Helping the client increase his present-moment awareness is another effective strategy for counteracting the anxiety that often results from persistent preoccupation with an imagined future. The more clients can stay focused on the present, the less the fear of the unknown can hijack their thinking. Meditation is an excellent practice for developing such awareness. Relaxation, visualization, bodywork, and breathing exercises can also serve this purpose. Clients can be encouraged to read some of the excellent books available on the topic of present-moment awareness, such as those by Ekhart Tolle (1999) and Jon Kabat-Zinn (1990, 2005), which examine the meditative, mindful state in clearly accessible, secular, and demystified terms.

Coming up with *concrete plans* is another way to help clients combat Fear and Anxiety. Early in the divorce process, focusing on *short-term plans* will help the individual make it through the next few hours, days, or weeks. These plans can include simple, concrete considerations such as

- ❖ Where the client will be staying and with whom
- ❖ Professional appointments the client needs to make or keep (lawyer, mediator, financial planner)
- ❖ Social, educational, or recreational activities in which the client might engage in order to feel better (dinner or a movie with a friend, a weekend class at a community college)
- ❖ Support activities (therapy appointment, support group, church event)
- ❖ Self-help activities and "homework assignments" (read a certain book, meditate daily, make a list of personal strengths)
- ❖ Life skill-building activities (open a checking account, research state custody laws online, look for a part-time job)

Later in the divorce process, longer-term plans such as setting up a new family home, starting a new social life, or developing career plans will need to be tailored.

Helplessness

Another major area of vulnerability for clients in the divorce process is the sense of helplessness or powerlessness. This feeling is generally experienced more acutely by a partner who has been the "victim" of a divorce, or who perceives herself that way. If

Partner A initiated the divorce (assuming it was not a joint decision), then he has exerted power or control. Partner B will likely feel helpless or powerless in response to this, at least at the outset. Many clients react to this feeling with anger; some adopt a sense of victimization as part of their postdivorce identity.

A certain measure of helplessness "comes with the territory" of divorce for most clients. As one is suddenly cast in a new role with a new set of demands, one naturally feels unprepared. In a functioning marriage, typically there is a division of labor and responsibility by which each partner specializes in certain tasks. He may fix the cars and she may fix the meals or vice versa. But when the relationship ends, each partner must assume ownership of the full range of adult responsibilities, perhaps for the first time ever. This can include child nurturing, disciplining of the children, bill paying/financial management, housecleaning, grocery shopping, and more. It is rare to feel competent in all of these areas; the divorcing client can become overwhelmed with a sense of helplessness. For women in traditional roles, finances are often the biggest source of helpless feelings; for men, it is often the managing of the children's daily lives. Dealing with new tasks and responsibilities can be an intimidating experience for everyone. For some clients, however, postdivorce feelings of helplessness can become immobilizing.

How to Help

Clients stuck in helplessness often benefit from the encouragement of professionals to feel more empowered on both a *practical* and a *mental/emotional* level.

On a practical level the client may require a boost in his skill levels in some areas. Balancing a checkbook, planning and preparing nutritional meals, and learning to set limits with children are all skills that require learning and practice. If the client is feeling overwhelmed and cannot identify specific areas of helplessness, we might develop a "competency inventory" in which the client makes an honest assessment of the skills that he will need to acquire followed by a plan for developing the needed skills and/or obtaining outside assistance.

The client may benefit from taking a course or two at the local community college or training through a community service agency. Sometimes simply *practicing* a new skill, with a counselor's support and encouragement, is sufficient to learn it. *Homework assignments*— open a checking account in your own name by Tuesday; call a real estate broker by Friday; make a one-week grocery list, etc. — can be quite useful. We might also help the client find a support or social group geared toward a specific skill area such as parenting, investing, or dating. Online there are websites, bulletin boards, and chat rooms dedicated to nearly any skill and interest area imaginable. Many clients feel more comfortable exploring certain issues under the anonymity of the Internet.

Specific interventions to counteract specific areas of weakness can help divorcing clients feel less helpless. These interventions must always be geared toward *coaching* the client in developing new skills, as opposed to doing things *for* the client.

It is equally important that the client learn to *feel* less helpless. Feelings of incompetence can be particularly acute for those who have been in relationships in which they were dependent on their spouse or in which the spouse was invested in making them feel helpless. *Ego building* can help the newly separated feel more competent and ready to face the world. Simple praise and positive reinforcement — pointing out clients' strengths and "catching them doing the right thing" — can go a long way.

Reframing can be a powerful tool. Often when a client is feeling helpless, she is unaware of many of her own innate strengths. By *reframing* personal attributes that the client has dismissed as liabilities we can often help her see them as unrecognized strengths. For example

Initial Statement/Reframed Statement

* ❖ "I'm a pushover."/"I have great empathy for others."
* ❖ "I'm terrible at making decisions."/"I don't like to act impulsively."
* ❖ "I'm bad with math and money."/"I'm a people person."
* ❖ "I don't know how to socialize."/"I don't like small talk, I value meaningful exchanges."

This isn't just "slapping a happy face" on problems; it is a valid way to unearth important qualities in the client that he may be marginalizing.

Assertiveness training may also be useful for those who feel helpless. Standing up for oneself and asking for what one really wants without resorting to blame or attack is an important skill for both women and men. Women, in particular, tend not to speak clearly about what they want when negotiating with their ex-spouses. As a result, they often go along with structures and plans set up for them by their exes or attorneys without exercising their own good judgment about what is best for them or for their family. Men, on the other hand, tend to react angrily when they feel helpless. Sometimes they feel helpless in the face of the legal system or societal pressures. Sometimes they feel helpless in managing the children. Teaching assertiveness skills to men — as an alternative to aggressive or nonassertive behavioral styles — can help them approach their exes in a more productive, less provocative way and become more effective parents. We can refer our clients to the many available books and resources on assertiveness training (e.g., Alberti & Emmons, 2001; Bower & Bower, 1991).

In brief, assertiveness training teaches the speaker to assume full "ownership" of her feelings in order to communicate clearly about her needs. Clients can be taught simple approaches — such as this four-step framework for verbal expression — for resolving problems assertively:

- ❖ State the problem or situation in objective, unemotional terms. ("When the kids come back from visiting you, they tell me they ate a lot of candy and stayed up late every night." Note the neutral, factual language — no blaming.)
- ❖ State how the situation makes you feel. ("I feel frustrated and angry because I work hard to enforce the rules that you and I agreed on. Now the kids seem to view me as the mean parent." Note the "I" language rather than "you" language.)
- ❖ State the observed effects of the problem. ("The kids are tired every Monday morning and have a hard time in

school. They act agitated at bedtime and when it's time to switch houses." Observable facts, rather than interpretations.)

❖ Propose a solution that, if possible, is mutually beneficial. ("I think that if we both enforced the same rules about candy and bedtimes, the kids would be better rested, they'd do better in school, and we'd both have an easier time transitioning them from one house to the other." A win/win proposal.)

Resolving problems in a way that does not include accusations, "should" statements, blame, or negative value judgments is actually quite effective in practice and contributes greatly to feelings of empowerment. Yet it does so without provoking counterforce from the other. Using objective and I-based language is a challenging skill for many clients to learn, but we can practice it with them. If an informal approach is not sufficient — and the client does not exhibit high levels of social anxiety — we can recommend a formal assertiveness training group to help her to develop both verbal and nonverbal skills in self-expression.

Finally, counselors can help the client develop firm *rules and boundaries*, both with the ex-partner and with other people such as the children, extended family, attorneys, and/or other helpers. Sometimes, we must give the client "permission" to start making her own rules — she may be reluctant to do so at first. With our assistance, she can establish boundaries with all of the major players in her postdivorce life. What lines does she want to draw? Where and with whom? Once she is clear on what her boundaries need to be, we then help her create clear, fair, and reasonable rules and support her in articulating those rules to others. It is also important to help her learn to respect the rules and boundaries of others.

How Not *to Help*

We need to work with divorcing clients to help them *develop independence* and a fuller sense of self. We must studiously avoid making choices for them. Rather, we should *present alternatives* to clients and encourage them to make their own choices. While some degree of dependency on the helper is expectable, dependency ought not dominate the relationship. The client needs to move away from looking to us for decision making and crisis intervention and begin looking to us for a discussion of alternatives and a reinforcement of personal strengths. Each time the client takes a step toward greater independence — making a difficult phone call for himself, spending a weekend alone — the helper offers praise and encouragement.

Grief

Grief includes related emotions such as sadness and depression. Grief is, of course, a very natural and appropriate reaction to a life-altering loss, such as divorce. As discussed in chapter 2, the grieving process is a crucial step in readjustment. Here we are not talking so much about the multistaged process of grieving but the acute pain of loss. As mentioned previously, dealing with the loss of a relationship is akin, in some ways, to dealing with the death of a loved one. However, when one ends a long-term relationship through separation or divorce, loss of the relationship itself is only part of the picture.

Loss of role is another source of grief. Traditionally, women have viewed themselves as nurturers. A divorced woman may have a hard time adjusting to the notion of being less than a full-time parent and seeing her ex-husband assume the parenting role some of the time. Men have traditionally viewed themselves as the breadwinners, the competent caretakers. A divorced man can be saddened by the loss of his role as the stable backbone of the family. He may also perceive that his role as provider is underappreciated and unrewarded in the divorce process. Whether actively or more peripherally involved in parenting roles, fathers, like mothers, often feel profoundly sad when time with their children is reduced by the parameters of the divorce.

A client's grief is often also about the *loss of an ideal*. When a marriage ends, the individual not only loses a mate but also loses an entire slate of hopes, dreams, and in many cases comforting illusions. The loss of ideals is often more devastating than the personal loss. The client probably entered the marriage with a vision for life. This vision may have included the white picket fence, the raising of happy children, the birth of grandchildren, and a peaceful, loving retirement. It may also have included unconscious assumptions, such as the idea that personal fulfillment can be attained through marriage.

According to Johnston and Campbell (1988), there are two main reasons that divorcing clients get stuck in Grief. The first is that Grief can awaken the emotions of a prior loss. As we know, strong "negative" feelings that are experienced early in life leave a deep imprint on our emotional patterning. When a later event of the same emotional color (loss, betrayal, abandonment, etc.) occurs, that old pain reawakens and reverberates along with the new pain, creating an emotional reaction of amplified power. For many clients, the power of this type of pain is overwhelming. Grief takes up permanent residence in their psyches.

The other main reason that some clients become stuck in Grief is that loss of the marriage relationship represents a partial *loss of the self.* This is particularly true for clients who have poorly defined ego boundaries due to separation/individuation issues. Their close relationships generally involve a degree of enmeshment. In marriage clients' identity becomes so entwined with that of their partners that they don't know where they stop and their partners begin. This may also be true for the client's relationship with his or her children. The husband, wife, and/or parent relationships define the client and serve as an anchor for his or her sense of integrity. When the relationship with the spouse ends and/or the relationship with children is constricted, it feels as if a part of the self is annihilated. The person no longer knows who he is. The grief that the client feels has as much to do with a loss of *self* as it does with a loss of other. The client no longer feels whole.

How to Help

As clients grieve over the loss of a long-term relationship, they benefit from empathic support. But in addition to helping clients let go of the relationship itself, helpers can assist them to disentangle related sources of grief. We can explore with them the extent to which they are grieving for a lost relationship, lost roles, or lost ideals. Old assumptions must be questioned, roles redefined, and dreams rewritten. This is a sad and difficult process. We can help clients explore which of their ideals may have been sound and which misguided. For example, the notion that another person can "complete me" may need to be challenged over time as may unrealistic notions of the ideal family. The client's emerging belief system will need to incorporate a sense of the divorced self as "okay."

Clients stuck in Grief due to previous traumatic loss benefit from understanding the past pain that their present Grief is reawakening. In addition to focusing on coping skills, we may need to do some skillful questioning to discover earlier instances of loss/betrayal/abandonment. Enabling the client to become consciously aware of past pain and to feel the attendant emotions that may have been repressed will help lower the volume of the present pain and put it in perspective. Providing the client a safe place to mourn past losses affords a level of objective support that the client may not experience elsewhere in her life.

Diving into a new relationship or returning home to live with a parent are common strategies for the dependent client who is dealing with divorce. We can help the client evaluate these choices and coach him in setting healthy boundaries. When helpers model the setting of boundaries in the professional relationship, the client will be encouraged to develop the ability to do so in his other relationships. This is a step toward independent decision making and a fuller sense of individual identity that will enable the client to process his grief and realign his relationships.

Progressing through Grief is an overriding goal for all divorcing clients. To do so, depressed clients may need to get in touch with *anger at the ex-partner*. Grief is an inwardly directed emotion that tends to breed inaction or paralysis. Anger is an outwardly directed emotion that, in proper measure, tends to generate movement that can break the paralysis. However, as we shall discuss later, anger needs to be expressed in healthy, nonhostile ways.

How Not *to Help*

For the client stuck in grief due to identity issues, what helpers *avoid* doing may be as important as positive interventions. Such clients habitually use relationships as a means to bolster their own sense of self and therefore are likely to become dependent on their helpers. They may call us night and day for emergency assistance, rely on us to make decisions for them, and lean on us as indispensable parts of their lives. As helpers, many of us are vulnerable to the siren's song of being needed in this way. It makes us feel useful and important. But, of course, when we foster such dependency in divorcing clients, we are actually stunting their growth, not helping them.

Shame

Yet another emotional "planet" that tends to pull clients into its orbit is shame. Some clients after a divorce not only feel a sense of loss but also a profound sense of wrongness about themselves. Under the banner of shame are related feelings such as guilt, regret, and inadequacy — emotions of negativity directed at the self. The person who is overwhelmed by shame feels that he is somehow *bad* or seriously flawed.

There are many reasons a client might exit a marriage carrying negative feelings about herself. Some of these we might characterize as "normal." For example, a person might have strong moral/religious beliefs about marriage and firmly believe that marriage vows are meant to last a lifetime. Naturally, she is going to feel a degree of personal or moral failure at the dissolution of the marriage. These feelings might even extend, in certain faiths, to feeling sinful in the eyes of God. Or perhaps the individual actually did do a number of regrettable things that helped to cause the breakup. In this case, some degree of remorse is understandable and appropriate. Another common postdivorce feeling is that of inadequacy or low self-esteem — the person feels that she wasn't good enough (attractive enough, smart enough, interesting enough, sexual enough, wealthy enough, etc.) to satisfy the ex-partner.

The client who is stuck in Shame tends to cycle thoughts that reinforce the shame. He may replay painful conversations in his head. These spiral him down into negative self-feelings, which spawn further negative thoughts, which in turn trigger even deeper negative feelings. He may hurl inner insults at himself and entertain thoughts such as "I don't deserve to be happy" on a minute-by-minute basis. The mind returns again and again to these thought patterns like a tongue returning to a painful loose tooth.

Some feelings of shame might be characterized as *neurotic*. These are associated with clients who routinely blame themselves for things that go wrong or who habitually engage in negative self-talk and negative self-conceptualization. Naturally, when a marriage ends, these clients "beat themselves up" more than the average person. There are also feelings of shame that can be considered *characterological*. These are deep-rooted, often unconscious attitudes of shame that give rise to shame-based personalities. We will talk about these briefly under "'Problem' Personalities."

Black-and-white thinking tends to prevail in clients who have shame issues. For those whose shame is neurotic, the black-and-white thinking pertains primarily to their thoughts about themselves. Those with characterological shame have a strong tendency to divide the world into good and bad people, positive and negative experiences, etc. Splitting, polarization, projection, and related psychological devices are commonly employed. Unable to fully accept certain aspects of themselves, these clients often project undesirable characteristics onto the people around them to deal with them as external realities.

How to Help

The simple (some might say simplistic) technique of *thought stopping* can be very effective in interfering with self-hate/self-blame cycles. Thought stopping, a technique originally developed by Wolpe and Lazarus (1966), is based on the principle that thoughts tend to string together like chains, one leading to the next, stirring up the emotions in the process. If the individual can learn to recognize the first in a chain of negative thoughts and immediately call a halt to it, she can stop a spiraling thought/emotion pattern before it can take over.

Thought stopping requires a conscious commitment on the part of the client, and with effort it can become a trustworthy tool. As soon as a familiar negative thought statement starts to arise in the mind, the client simply stops it. A concrete stop signal of some kind can be used. Some people prefer a visual image such as an imagined STOP sign or a red light. Others prefer a mental audio cue, such as the word "Stop," a primal grunt, or a coach's whistle. After a few days of practicing this with very conscious attention — "I'm such a...STOP," "I'll never be a...STOP," "I deserve to be...STOP" — the process starts to become more reflexive. The client can greatly reduce the amount of time spent in negative rumination.

Cognitive restructuring is another method for counteracting negative feelings about the self. Here the client works to identify distorted negative thoughts and replace them with more realistic and productive ones. Beck (Beck, 1976; Beck et al., 1990) defines three levels of cognitive thought. *Automatic thoughts* are fleeting, reflexive thoughts that "play" just below the level of conscious awareness. For a client in shame, these can be thoughts such as, "I'm such an idiot," "Here we go again," or "This is typical." *Assumptions* are projected outcomes that affect a person's actions. They are formed in reaction to early life experiences and are then applied universally in unrelated situations. For example, "If I apply for the job, someone else will only get it," or "If I talk, no one will listen." *Core beliefs* are deep and persistent assumptions that serve as basic rules in a person's life, e.g., the world is a dangerous place, men only want one thing, people always victimize me.

Clients learn to consciously identify these various levels of thought and use logical analysis to evaluate them. More realistic and productive thoughts can then be created to replace the negative ones. Some clients, for example, have persistent beliefs about victimization. For some this is based in the reality of an abusive marriage; for others, however, it is a life script born of being mistreated in childhood. Helping professionals can work with clients to identify when their thinking is maladaptive. An individual who has felt like a victim in one part of his life may extend that thinking across the board, believing that no matter what the situation, he is somehow universally and unfairly singled out for abuse, mistreatment, or bad luck. But, we might ask, what is the mechanism by which such *systematic mistreatment* could possibly occur? Is everyone in the world involved? If so, how often do they meet? (A little humor can help.) How do they communicate with each other? Why are you (client) being singled out? Can a bit of "bad luck" in the past really determine present and future events? How does this occur? By what mechanism? Is it possible instead, we might ask the client, that you are carrying around some negative self-perceptions that function as self-fulfilling prophecies?

Another way to work with clients on a cognitive level is to try, whenever possible, to diffuse black-and-white thinking. Dividing the world into good and bad, true and false, right and wrong, black and white is a logical flaw of the mind. In fact, the world is radically "gray." A glass of water can be called half-full or half-empty or, from a wiser perspective, both at the same time. All human beings possess a rich, complex mixture of characteristics and potentials. These qualities can be seen as positive in one context and negative in another. To categorize someone, even the ex-spouse, as all good or bad, absolutely right or wrong is to engage in a gross form of distortion. It is useful to help clients assess the marriage with an eye toward challenging all-or-nothing beliefs and assumptions. We can then lead them toward constructing a more *realistic interpretation* of their circumstances than they may be currently using as a basis for decision making. When doing so, we may need to combat the influence of friends and extended family members who may be perpetuating the black-and-white interpretations for reasons of their own.

Clients suffering from shame and low self-esteem can also benefit from some of the interventions mentioned above in regards to helplessness — techniques that can enhance their sense of personal effectiveness in the world. However, helpers need to be careful about pushing shame-based clients toward anger. Directing *some* angry attention outward can help snap an intense negative self-focus, but clients with shame-based "problem personalities" (see below) can often become angry in an all-encompassing way. They may have poor impulse control and can easily view the ex-partner as deserving of all the blame and the self as irreproachable.

How Not *to Help*

A major caution is in order here for helping professionals when working with such shame-based individuals. It is all too easy to get drawn into their good vs. bad drama by making rash recommendations or writing ill-advised opinion letters. "This child should never see his father again." "The mother has serious mental health issues and should not be given custody." "The father is a serial abuser who should not be allowed back in the family home." Statements such as these are often made based on the strength of the client's interpretation alone, without the helper ever having met the spouse. This is a serious breech of ethics and sound practice, which we will address further in chapter 10. When a helper becomes caught up in the *rightness* of the client's point of view, it is time to step back, take a fresh look at the case, and perhaps seek professional consultation.

Anger

Anger is one of the most studied yet least understood of emotions, and, when you're working with clients in the divorce process, arguably one of the most important. The contribution anger makes to high-conflict divorce battles is evident in our offices and in the courtroom. Child therapists and researchers have expressed particular concern about the long-term effects on children of angry parent behavior displayed through the process of an acrimonious divorce (Hetherington and Kelly, 2002; Johnston and Roseby,1997; Kelly, J. B., 2000; Wallerstein, Lewis, and Blakeslee, S., 2000).

A number of theoretical formulations have been advanced to define and describe the mechanisms of anger, but a book whose focus is working with divorcing clients is not the place to engage in an academic discussion of the nature of anger. Moreover, if your interventions are focused on helping your client through an emotionally taxing divorce, you're not likely going to have time to address the "deeper" underlying sources of your client's anger, either.

It will be helpful, however, if we can agree on a few basics that will help us to work with angry clients, and with the special intense anger that is often a part of the divorce process:

❖ *Anger is an emotion,* not a form of behavior. Angry feelings may be expressed in many ways — aggressive behavior being one of the most common.

❖ *Anger is universal,* for all practical purposes, and therefore normal, and the expected response to certain life circumstances.

❖ *Anger may be triggered by a wide variety of stimuli* in which the individual feels violated or threatened in some way.

❖ *Anger often occurs as a primary response* to violation, and it also may be a *learned response* which masks fear, sadness or another emotional reaction to vulnerability, threat, or a sense of loss.

❖ *Chronic anger is not healthy,* although brief situational anger responses may help to motivate productive action.

❖ *Appropriate interventions for unhealthy anger* depend upon the unique circumstances of a given client, and may include desensitization to anger triggers, training in effective self-expression, in-depth exploration of the historic emotional foundations of the client's anger, and training in forgiveness.

Anger deserves further attention than we can give to the topic in this chapter. For more in-depth analysis of the topic, I suggest Kassinove & Tafrate, 2002, Potter-Efron (2001), and McKay, Rogers, & McKay (2003).

Anger is intimately connected with both grief *and* shame. Anger is a vital emotion for the client to experience during a healthy divorce process. As we have already seen, it can snap the client out of the grip of grief, helplessness and shame. It can also bring some healthy outer-directed energy to a client who is stuck in an inward spiral.

Still, anger is a tricky emotion to manage, precisely because it is so outer-directed. It tends to seek a personal focus, a recipient for its fiery energy. Since the ex-partner is often viewed as being the cause — either direct or indirect — of the divorce, the anger is frequently focused on the ex. Angry clients may be inclined to hurt, embarrass, attack, insult, scare, demean, strike, undermine or destroy the ex-partner. None of these choices is appropriate or productive. Helpers can guide clients toward *feeling* the emotion of anger in all of its fullness but *harnessing* it in ways that promote health and growth rather than warfare. This is easiest to accomplish with mature and insightful clients and requires more ongoing work with less healthy ones.

Persistent anger can be taken as a sign that something is unresolved or unexpressed in one's life. This might be an action that needs to be taken or an emotion that needs further exploration. As it relates to action, anger can be an effective tool for breaking inertia and motivating a person to take a difficult step. Moving into a new apartment, filing divorce papers, going back to school or taking better control of the family finances might require the galvanizing charge of anger in order for the client to make a move.

As it relates to the emotions, though, stuckness in anger may indicate that the anger is masking, or arising in response to, a fear of vulnerability. Some clients, because of their history or personal makeup, find "weak" or vulnerable emotions unacceptable. An example of this might be the classic macho male who has difficulty owning wounded feelings. When hurt, he automatically shifts into anger, because that emotion is on his approved emotions list. A slightly different situation is one in which the client may be angry because he has been *put in the position* of feeling grief or shame. He becomes angry at the person he perceives to have *caused* this pain and then chooses to focus on the anger rather than the pain. Either way, the anger becomes the dominant focus instead of the wounded feeling.

For some clients, particularly those with deep shame and/or abandonment issues, anger arises in response to a perception that the *core self* has been attacked. These clients feel threatened on a deep level when a loved one leaves them or takes adversarial action. Their anger can be quite extreme and problematic.

How To Help

When a client presents with strong emotions of anger, this can be a Critical Entry Point. We can either respond to the anger at face value or we can use it as an opportunity to do some exploring providing that the client has capacity for insight.

There are three essential ways to help divorcing clients who are stuck in anger or for whom anger is a habitual response. You may help the client

❖ **prevent angry responses** by exploring his or her life history, and the beliefs, attitudes, thoughts, expectations and triggers that may lead to anger.
❖ **explore the emotions** that the anger might be preventing the client from experiencing.
❖ **learn to manage the anger** when it does come up.

Preventing Maladaptive Expressions of Anger

There are many simple techniques clients can learn to use to head off their angry reactions to life. Noticing their **anger triggers** is one that was addressed briefly in the previous chapter. We can work with the client to identify the events that typically trigger angry responses and to recognize the physical and emotional reactions that come up when the trigger occurs. Teaching clients to notice **irrational thoughts** that lead to their anger is another approach (Dryden, 1990; Ellis & Lange, 1994; Ellis & McClaren, 2005; Ellis & Powers, 2000; Kassinove & Tafrate, 2002). The client can then be taught to use thought stopping, relaxation, and/or time-out techniques as soon as he notices the trigger or irrational thought. These techniques include:

❖ Taking several **deep calming breaths**
❖ Repeating a **calming word**, such as "calm"
❖ Taking a **time-out or counting to ten**
❖ Mentally reciting a **short prayer**
❖ Using **coping thoughts**, such these suggested by McKay, Rogers, & McKay (2003):
  ❖ *"I can stay calm and relaxed"*
  ❖ *"Relax and let go."*
  ❖ *"I can deal with this."*
  ❖ *"Just as long as I keep my cool, I'm in control."*
  ❖ *"No one is right; no one is wrong. We just have different needs."*

❖ **Meditation, chanting, prayer and yoga** can all help lessen the client's *overall* anger level and build deep inner resources for coping with anger-inducing situations.

Exploring Anger

Finesse and skill are required to balance an empathic stance with probing questions. When obtaining a subjective history of the marriage and its breakdown, paying attention and asking the right questions is the key. What the client *doesn't say* can be as important as what he does say. Be alert to any past events that the client perceives as offenses or that stir up the anger response. When time allows for an in-depth approach, gently circle in on these areas, probing for deeper feelings. "How did that make you feel?" is a question that may need to be posed often. If the client cannot name an emotion, you can name it for him. "That sounds like it was a betrayal to you. Did it make you feel hurt?" Naming the emotion calls it out of hiding and gives the client permission to feel it. We create the space for the client to safely feel and express emotions that he/she may not be comfortable expressing anywhere else.

For the impulsive client or shame-based individual who feels his very self is under attack, our work can be more challenging. The primary focus generally needs to be on anger management. For those with characterological issues (see "'Problem' Personalities"), getting to the root of the anger will require intensive, long-term therapy *after* the crisis of divorce has been thoroughly resolved.

❖ *"Problem" Personalities*

When working with divorcing clients and families, we all sometimes encounter "problem" personalities. These are clients with extreme anger and blame issues who are typically involved in high-conflict divorces, estimated to be five to ten percent of all divorces. It is up to each of us, as individual helpers, to decide our own threshold for working with such clients. Certain clients will not easily change their behaviors based on behavioral interventions and talk-based therapy. This section will not attempt to thoroughly review psychiatric diagnoses and treatments but will offer some general guidelines for working with problem personalities, particularly in the context of divorce.

Eddy (2005) uses the term "high conflict personalities" and mentions four particular personality types listed in the DSM-IV that he considers to be particularly litigious. These are the Borderline Personality, the Narcissistic Personality, the Antisocial Personality, and the Histrionic Personality. Shapse (2005) has gathered test data using the Millon Clinical Multiaxial Inventory-III on over 100 clients engaged in child custody litigation. The most common cluster of high scores in this population demonstrates significantly high narcissism combined with high scores on the histrionic and/or compulsive scales.

In my experience, the personalities who tend to become embroiled in high conflict divorce often have characteristics common to the above four personality types, with the traits reflected by high peaks on at least two of the three Millon scales. According to Choca, Shanley, and Van Denburg (1992) and Strack (1999), individuals with exceptionally high scores on the narcissism scale tend to be self-centered in their viewpoint. They are often demanding and needy of others' attention and praise. Those who also have histrionic features tend to be emotionally labile and to seek attention in dramatic or seductive ways. Those with compulsive features tend to be rigid in their viewpoints. They may be perfectionistic and moralistic and try to regiment their emotions. They are disinclined to admit their own shortcomings or mistakes.

In general, high-conflict personalities share common characteristics. They often think in black-and-white terms as dictated by their own needs. They frequently project blame onto an external target (usually the spouse, but sometimes the helper) and try to get others on their side. Often they feel victimized. They can all be quite persuasive and/or insistent regarding their viewpoint. Under the stress of divorce or any protracted conflict, they may become extremely hostile. Underneath, they generally lack a cohesive sense of self. The various high-conflict personalities seek to enhance their sense of self in slightly different ways, but they all manifest their "signature" behaviors as means of warding off negative underlying feelings about the self. Thus, they remain focused largely on the "badness" of the other and the righteousness of the self.

Given the underlying fears of these individuals, as characterized by Eddy (i.e., fears of abandonment, being ignored, feeling inferior, or being dominated), it easy to see why the emotional and legal pressures of divorce bring out the worst in them. Of course, the stress of divorce tends to bring out the worst in *most* people, so it can be hard to tell, at first, whether your client has a problem personality or not. Time alone may provide the answer.

Clients with difficult personalities have often been victimized in their lives, sometimes in ways of which they may not be fully aware. It is not always clear to what extent they have been abused in their marital relationship, and this needs to be assessed carefully. Their struggles with their spouses during the break-up period often take on the dynamics of victim/victimizer whether or not there was previous spousal abuse. Frequently both purported victim and alleged victimizer feel mutually abused. It is important to keep this in mind when assessing the dynamics of a breakup. Domestic abuse is discussed further in the next chapter.

Typically, problem personalities engender very strong feelings of countertransference in helpers. Sometimes our feelings are reflections of how the clients themselves feel. Sometimes they are reactions to the ways the clients pull us into their dynamics. Problem clients frequently enlist many helpers who join forces with or against one another in the ensuing divorce drama.

The most common signs that helping professionals are dealing with a problem personality are one or more of the following:

- ❖ A large number of "helpers" are involved.
- ❖ The helper feels disorganized or overwhelmed when working with the client.
- ❖ The helper is inclined to make exceptions to our usual professional standards and practices.

❖ The helper becomes convinced that the client is right and the other spouse is wrong or bad.
❖ The helper feels an imperative to rescue the client from his or her difficulties.
❖ The helper feels as if she or he can never do enough, or do things well enough, for the client.
❖ The helper begins to resent the client.
❖ The client takes up an excess of the helper's time and energy.

How to Help

Helpers should carefully consider the therapeutic goals for working with divorcing clients with problem personalities. Intensive therapy with the goal of long-term personality change may need to be put on hold during the divorce transition when the client's primary needs are to develop coping mechanisms. Our sessions with the client should be scheduled on a regular, but not too frequent, basis. This allows us to help the problem client manage on a practical level, while also preventing him from becoming too dependent on us or becoming a disruptive element in our practice.

Clear *rules and boundaries* are essential. Clear limits on how much help we are willing to offer and how much of our time will be available are organizing for the client. We may need to spell out very specific guidelines such as, "I will not accept night-time phone calls. I will accept up to two phone calls per week, five-minute limit, and one email per week, no more than ten sentences." Then we must stick to the agreement resolutely and literally.

Helpers need to be empathic — but not overly so. We can validate the client as a person, without validating illogical beliefs or getting caught up in the client's battle to be right. It is useful to validate the client's sense of self-esteem and help him focus on healthy ways to enhance his sense of self by reinforcing positive behaviors and highlighting strengths. In other words, we can affirm the person without conceding to his view of the world or affirming his negative behavior (Ury, 1991).

Our work with problem personalities during divorce should retain a *behavioral focus.* How the client *feels* should never be accepted as a justification for his acting one way or another. Our focus should be on whether the action is effective in accomplishing the client's desired goals. Consequences of any behavior are to be emphasized. The client who threatened to have his wife arrested if she picked up the kids, for example, was not looking at the possible consequences of this action — his being seen as a bully, her taking legal action to get back at him, his being less likely to win concessions from her in the future, etc.

Cognitive restructuring, discussed earlier, can be an effective technique when working with problem personalities. DBT, or Dialectical Behavior Therapy (Linehan, 1995), can be another, particularly for emotionally labile clients. DBT was developed as a treatment method for clients with borderline personality disorders who can be overwhelmed by their emotions and are prone to taking impulsive action. Much of the thrust of DBT revolves around learning skills that have been developed in Buddhism, such as present-moment mindfulness, acceptance of one's own feelings, awareness of breathing, radical acceptance of what cannot be changed, and developing the "wise mind" (a level of knowing beyond, but informed by, both the logical mind and the emotions).

How Not *to Help*

When working with problem personalities, it is paramount not to buy into the client's version of reality as "right." Therapeutic work is best focused on coping skills and practical analysis of how to handle situations. Attempting to do psychodynamic or introspective therapies with such clients when they are in crisis runs the risk of fostering inappropriate dependence on the therapist or, in some cases, maintaining clients' tendency to persist in their negative feelings and find justification for antagonistic behaviors. With these clients it is especially important to maintain one's usual professional boundaries. Not only do boundaries provide organization for the client, but they are also protective of the helper's ability to preserve energy and practice within ethical guidelines.

Chapter Five Key Points:

* Normalize feelings of fear.
* Help the client make practical plans.
* Give pragmatic "homework" assignments that build skills and confidence.
* Help the client develop positive self-messages and assertiveness skills.
* Help the client recognize both present and past sources of grief.
* Teach cognitive-behavioral techniques for managing negative thoughts.
* Challenge black-and-white thinking.
* Encourage the client to manage and express anger appropriately.
* Avoid nurturing excessive dependency.
* Avoid engaging clients with problem personalities in intensive "feeling work."
* Maintain professional boundaries.

6 ❖

Domestic Abuse

I t is difficult to discuss divorce without also discussing domestic abuse. Few topics in our counseling practices spark as much polarization of thought. Domestic violence is an area in which black-and-white thinking about who is right and who is wrong tends to obscure subtler shades of gray, often to the detriment of families. A chapter such as this cannot detail how to react to every client in every situation. As an interested practitioner, you'll need to do more reading, thinking, and analyzing of the research data on your own. This chapter is an appetizer, not a main course. Its purpose is to challenge our reflexive thinking and to open our minds to more critical consideration as we deal with divorcing clients.

For the largest part of our cultural history, domestic abuse was minimized or ignored. What happened within a family was generally considered "family business"; a spouse or parent had a right to use physical force at his or her discretion. The outside world did not need to know about it. Over the past several decades our awareness of, and sensitivity to, the issue has grown dramatically. The women's movement has focused attention on male dominance in society, which has been maintained, in part, by male-initiated violence. As a result, the pendulum has swung to the other extreme in many parts of American society, to the point where a "zero tolerance" posture now exists within many sectors of the courts and the helping professions. If one spouse physically strikes the other spouse or a child in any way, then many believe that the incident must be dealt with swiftly and harshly. Mental health practitioners who are mandated reporters feel compelled to call the authorities if there is the possibility that children have experienced or witnessed abuse. Couples are urged to separate and the "abuser" is sometimes removed from the home. But is either of these extreme approaches — ignore or pounce — really helpful to the long-term health of the family? What if the picture really is gray, and not black or white?

Domestic abuse and violence *are* serious issues, very serious ones. We *do* live in a world that has sanctioned male control and dominance over women. Our systems *have* failed to respond adequately. These are troublesome societal issues that must be addressed. But, at the risk of angering some colleagues and readers, the following must also be said: not all abuse is equal, not all accusations of domestic abuse/violence are valid, and not all instances of abuse warrant the same response. If helpers genuinely wish to make the healthiest contribution to the whole family, then we must take the big picture approach advocated elsewhere in this book. We cannot afford facile and reactive thinking when the situation is multidimensional.

❖ *The Importance of the Helper's Response*

When a client comes to your practice reporting a pushing or striking incident, this is a Critical Entry Point. The simplest (and, for some, the most satisfying) response may be to sound the highest alarm — to call for the client to leave the relationship, file a restraining order, seize the children, and retain a lawyer. When we intervene in this way, we feel as if we've protected the family. We've done our part. This is a logical reaction for helping professionals who are well aware of the negative effects of violence on the victim and other family members who witness it. None of us wants to condone domestic abuse. Rather, we want to demonstrate unequivocal opposition.

This discussion, however, calls for a more thoughtful approach. It asks us to exercise reason and nuanced thought as we formulate our responses. The simplest solution may not always be the best. Taking the time to understand the *nature, severity,* and *factuality* of the abuse will give us better tools to help our clients respond. Not all incidents mean the same thing, nor do they represent the same level of danger.

Domestic partners hit or push one another or act in demeaning ways toward one another with greater frequency than we like to admit. The terms "common couple violence" (Johnson, 1995) or "common couple aggression" (Zibbell, 2005) suggest the normative occurrence of some forms of intimate violence. I have been forced to admit, as a practitioner of divorce counseling for several decades, that a certain amount of pushing, slapping, and throwing of household objects does exist within the bounds of many "normal" relationships. This is not to say that practitioners should advocate physical expressions of conflict. Rather, we can acknowledge that aggression does take place among humans and ask ourselves how best to work *with* individuals and families to help lessen the frequency of aggressive acts and minimize their negative impact.

It is shortsighted and injurious to families to advocate the same reaction to every physical exchange. Should children really be taken from a parent on a long-term basis because of a single pushing and shoving incident? The reflexive answer may be yes. The more difficult, soul-searching and multidimensional answer may be no. I will argue for taking the more challenging and complicated route to finding an answer for each particular family: for a *considered*, rather than a *reflexive*, response to our clients' reports of domestic abuse, particularly in divorce cases.

Sometimes domestic abuse *is* a black-and-white issue: we need to get a family out of the house *immediately*. More often the answer is not so clear, particularly when accusations of abuse coincide with the breakdown of a relationship. If a client comes to the office seemingly stunned and upset by physical domestic episode, we need to stop and ask ourselves, "What is really going on here?" Has there been an established pattern of attempted control and dominance by the spouse, or was the incident a one-time occurrence? Often a client can react with shock *precisely because* an abusive incident was so unprecedented. By contrast, it is frequently the habitual and *expected* abuse that typically goes unreported and does the most damage. Not all abuse is the same or has the same impact on the family. Though most of us do not condone *any* form of violence as a means of solving *any* problem, the simple truth is we cannot treat the one-time emotional explosion or the mutual shoving incident the same way we would treat prolonged or repetitive violence. Doing what is truly best for the whole family can be an uncomfortable enterprise that forces us to look beyond what we ourselves might consider personally and politically correct.

❖ *What Is Domestic Abuse?*

Nearly all of us, at one time or another in our adult lives, have resorted to insulting, demeaning, threatening, pushing, jostling, controlling, or manipulating another person. Very few marriages, over the course of their entire history, do not include at least *a few* occurrences that taken out of context could be construed as abusive. As conflict escalates in families to the point that one or both choose to separate, it is not surprising that incidents of abuse increase. Power and control issues are integral to any relationship, particularly long-term ones, and need to be resolved for relationships to continue in a healthy fashion. But when control issues escalate in prolonged and dysfunctional ways, power may be exercised in an abusive fashion.

It often falls upon the helper to distinguish the situation in which some regrettable actions have occurred from that in which dangerous and/or prolonged abuse has existed. As is the case with many complex issues, abuse lies on a continuum rather than an "either/or" scale. We will usually want to explore the nature and severity of the abuse our clients have experienced.

Abuse involves a pattern of intimidating and controlling behavior. The following are some common forms of abuse, all of which are considered in the literature to be forms of *domestic violence* (Dutton & Painter, 1993; O'Leary, 2001; Walker, 1999:

Physical abuse. This includes the full spectrum of hostile physical contact, from pushing, grabbing, and shaking to pinching, biting, and slapping, all the way to striking, choking, beating, and the use of weapons.

Psychological abuse. This includes a range of behaviors or attitudes marked by control, entitlement, exploitation, or a sense of ownership of another person. Such abuse may include isolation of the victim; cutting off a partner from his or her extended family; acts of possessiveness; threats of death or physical harm to self or others; degradation, including humiliation and name-calling; use of rewards or promises in return for desired behaviors; and controlling the distribution and use of money.

Sexual abuse. This includes sexual degradation, ridicule, and objectification; forcing a partner to do acts that are unsafe, unwanted, or uncomfortable; sexual exploitation (forcing someone to look at or participate in pornography, sex with other partners, etc.); rape or assault to the sexual organs; and sexual acts with children.

Stalking. This involves a variety of controlling behaviors including the following: tracking; harassment; excessive "checking in" by phone; use of private detectives; monitoring of Internet usage; sending of unwanted letters, packages, or gifts; and monitoring with hidden cameras.

When a Critical Entry Point occurs and the helper hears of a violent or abusive incident, he walks the tricky path of offering emotional support to the client while trying to assess the true nature of the alleged abuse. The professional first listens empathically and then gently asks questions. The first of these questions revolve around *severity* and *safety*. Is the client safe and does the client *feel* safe in the present? With regard to the incident, was it physically dangerous, did the client *feel* endangered, or were both the case? It is important to recognize that some clients *feel* threatened when the level of danger is small; others minimize their fear although they may be in serious danger.

The second set of questions deals with *context* and *frequency*. Is the incident part of a pervasive pattern of personal control and abuse or does it stem from something else? Is it a one-time incident or a frequent occurrence? There are many abusive incidents in a relationship that do not necessarily fit into an established pattern of injurious abuse. Did the incident occur during a particularly intense argument? Was it a single violent episode that erupted during the heat of the couple's separating?

A third major concern is *intention*. What was the perpetrator's psychological intention in performing the act? Sometimes people behave abusively out of habit and/or lack of skills for coping with their feelings. Abusive behaviors may have been modeled for them in their families, social groups, neighborhoods or cultural groups, or in the mass media. Preventing further abusiveness in such a case might be more a matter of education than deep psychological work. Sometimes a violent incident is a result of poor impulse control or a one-time loss of control due to overwhelming emotional circumstances. In such a case, the *intention* is not to control the partner.

Sometimes pushing and striking by either partner may be mutual and based on poor communication and problem-solving skills. While all abusive behavior has potentially negative consequences, the most damaging abuse tends to flow from a *pervasive intention to control another person*. A basically healthy person *can* suffer a loss of self-control and occasionally resort to violence/abuse. By contrast, when the long-term abuser "loses control" this is actually an attempt to *seize* control of the partner.

A fourth set of questions is about *effect*. Whether the perpetrator intended the abuse or not, has the *effect* on the victim been one of diminishment, intimidation, humiliation, and/or physical harm?

A final set of questions is about the *children*. Have children witnessed the event or been abused themselves and what was their reaction? It is important to point out that the incidence of child abuse is higher in families in which there is domestic violence, and the witnessing of domestic partner abuse puts children at risk (American Psychological Association, 1996; U.S. Department of Justice, Office of Justice Programs, 2003). A full discussion of child abuse is beyond the scope of this volume.

If the children have witnessed parental violence or if they have been abused, most mental health practitioners are required to make a report to the child protective agency in their jurisdiction. Such a report can result in a set of consequences over which the practitioner has little control. It is possible, however, to make the content of such reports reflect a careful analysis of the situation.

Who Is Abusing Whom, and to What Extent?

Before looking at the nature of abuse, it makes sense to address the question, "Who is abusing whom?" There is much disagreement in the field as to the extent of domestic violence/abuse, what constitutes abuse, and the incidence of male-perpetrated versus female-initiated or mutual violence. Most people view domestic abuse as predominantly a male-perpetrated phenomenon. Others cite statistics indicating that women are just as abusive as men. This chapter will not do an exhaustive analysis of the figures, but it will take a quick look. Perhaps when viewed against the "Profiles and Patterns" to be discussed in a moment, the statistics will fall into some kind of intelligent perspective.

Prevalence of Abuse

It is difficult to get an accurate reading as to the extent of domestic violence. There are two main reasons for this: much domestic violence goes unreported and there is disagreement over how to collect and interpret the data. Looking at statistics quoted by The American Bar Association Commission on Domestic Violence, the National Violence against Women Survey (Tjaden & Thoennes, 1998), the National Crime Victimization Survey conducted by the U.S. Department of Justice, Department of Justice Statistics (2003), and statistics reported by Straus and Gelles (1990), a pattern of male-dominated violence seems to emerge:

- ❖ Between 1 million and 4 million instances of domestic violence occur annually.
- ❖ Eighty to ninety-five percent of all reported domestic violence victims are women.
- ❖ One-sixth to one-third of women has experienced domestic violence at some point in their lives.
- ❖ About twenty-eight percent of all annual violence against women is perpetrated by intimates.
- ❖ Roughly five percent of all annual violence against men is perpetrated by intimates.

❖ About half of domestic violence cases go unreported.

❖ About half of the reported cases involve some kind of injury. About fifty percent of the reported injuries are minor. Thus, roughly one-fourth of reported cases involve more serious injuries.

❖ Women are injured six to ten times more often by domestic violence than are men.

While the above statistics point to domestic violence as being primarily a male-on-female phenomenon, this conclusion is too simplistic. Several studies offer data for a different interpretation. Renzetti (1992) found domestic violence in up to fifty-nine percent of lesbian couples. This contrasts with the seventeen percent of gay men who reported physical violence. Renzetti's work and other studies are complicated by the fact that male and female partner aggression may take different forms, with male violence tending to be more injurious but males less likely to perceive/report physical aggression as abusive. It is notable that Strauss and Gelles (1990) reported that severe battering occurred in only two percent of their large community-based sample. In 1993, Strauss additionally reported that equal numbers of violent acts were found to have been committed by both men and women when various forms of couple aggression were factored into the equation. Renzetti (1993) reported another study in which 145 couples seeking therapy were examined: 111 reported some form of marital aggression; slightly more than half of these reported that the aggression was mutual. Out of *this* group, 56.1% reported a low level of victimization for both partners, 26.3% reported that the wife had been more severely victimized than the husband, while 17.5% reported that the husband had suffered more — hardly the monolithic, male-as-sole-abuser model that has dominated societal discourse on this subject.

But some important considerations must be factored in. When we look at the statistics on *injuries and deaths*, we can clearly conclude that the severity, intensity, and harmfulness of violence directed at women, in general, is *much* greater than that directed toward men. When women *are* abusive, their abuse does not generally include routine, systematic attempts at dominance, control, and disempowerment through the use of force. Women's acts of interpersonal violence tend to be more conflict driven (O'Leary, 1993). The classic batterer, whom we will look at below, does indeed seem in the overwhelming majority of cases to be male. However, I must hasten to point out that I have seen "battered men" in my practice as well. They may not suffer the same level of fear and physical endangerment that battered women suffer, but they do show the scars of long-term humiliation, control, and belittling.

What conclusion can we draw from all this? The statistics suggest that both genders behave abusively toward one another, but that a larger percentage of male-dominated domestic violence reaches a more intense and intimidating level. The natural size and strength of men as compared to women, along with a social learning context that condones male aggression, creates a compelling formula by which some, but not all, men are more prone than women to committing physically injurious, control-driven acts of violence. However, the issue is too complex for us to jump to easy conclusions in *any particular case*. Women, too, *can* be abusive. And while most individuals who fit the classic profile of a batterer are males, most males, including those who may have behaved abusively at one time or another, are not persistent batterers.

❖ *Profiles and Patterns of Domestic Violence*

Several theorists have tried to categorize the dominant profiles of violent/abusive behavior that occur in marriages. Two of the most prominent models are presented here. Johnston and Campbell (1993) propose five profiles of domestic violence:

Ongoing and episodic male battering. The classic battering syndrome. The man has a low tolerance for frustration and tends to be possessive, jealous, and dominating. He uses battering as one strategy among many to exert control. Drugs or alcohol sometimes precipitate an actual battering incident.

Female-initiated violence. The woman has explosive outbursts when her needs or ideals are not being met by the spouse. This, too, is often associated with alcohol use. The woman tends to be emotionally labile and prone to throwing objects, scratching, biting, etc. This kind of violence tends to escalate during periods of break-up. Often the male partner is docile or passive-aggressive.

Male-controlling interactive violence. An escalating two-sided dispute leads to verbal abuse and then physical conflict. This kind of violence can be initiated be either partner but is generally dominated by the male. It is not part of an established pattern of control and dominance but tends to be a result of poor learned habits and communication skills.

Separation-engendered and postdivorce trauma. Uncharacteristic violence that occurs around the time of a separation/divorce. The marriage in this case has not been marked by aggression; the incident is a one-time lashing out due to stressful or traumatic events. This type of violence often sparks the victimized spouse to seek help or therapy; the incident is traumatic because it is so unexpected.

Psychotic and paranoid reactions. These can be brought on by an acute phase of mental illness triggered by the divorce or by drug-induced dementia.

Johnson (1995, 2001, 2005) has also proposed categories of domestic violence that have some overlap with Johnston and Campbell's model. His latest conceptualization proposes three primary types of relationship violence which are characterized by different control patterns in the relationship.:

Intimate terrorism. A general, overall pattern of control and domination by one partner, generally, but not exclusively, male. Violence is only one of many tactics used. This abuser is on a campaign to make the spouse feel weak, inferior, isolated, and powerless. He can be dangerous to the ex-partner when the relationship.

Violent resistance. One partner behaves in a violent or threatening manner and then the other reacts with violence, which can sometimes be more intense than the trigger. Violent Resistance is a defensive and protective response and not part of an overall pattern of abuse. *Note: when a victim reacts to a threat or attack with equal or greater force, sometimes the victim can be misidentified as the perpetrator. This mistake sometimes results in a situation whereby women who refuse to submit to violence are diagnosed with pathology.*

Situational couple violence (previously labeled "common couple violence"). Both partners strike out physically at one another, usually as the result of disagreement over some issue. The "violence" is not an attempt on the part of either to psychologically control the other. Typically the involved parties are not abusive outside the home, to each other or anyone else, nor is there sexual or emotional abuse. Johnson has found that situational violence is perpetrated in equal proportions by individuals of both genders.

The Classic Model of Batterer

Perhaps the most publicized view of domestic violence involves a male abuser who inflicts long-term psychological, and often physical, damage. This abuser has identifiable personality traits as summarized by Bancroft (2002).

* The batterer is controlling; he insists on having the last word in arguments and decision making, he may control how the family's money is spent, and he may make rules for the victim about her movements and personal contacts.
* He is manipulative; he misleads people inside and outside of the family about his abusiveness; he twists arguments around to make other people feel at fault.
* He is entitled; he considers himself to have special rights and privileges not applicable to other family members.
* He is disrespectful; he considers his partner less competent, sensitive, and intelligent than he is, often treating her as though she were an inanimate object. He communicates his sense of superiority around the house in various ways.

Bancroft goes on to state that the classic abuser, in fact, often perceives and skillfully portrays himself as the victim. When his wife or children attempt to defend themselves, he regards this as an attack. He stores up grievances and can rattle them off at a moment's notice. By doing so, he can often convince outsiders that the abuse has been provoked or mutual. While some batterers have identifiable, diagnosable psychological problems, the majority do not. They walk among us in all economic and social strata.

❖ *The Cycle of Violence*

According to Lenore Walker (1999), the classic batterer typically exhibits a classic behavior pattern as well. Walker interviewed some 1,500 battered women. With remarkable consistency, they reported that their domestic abuse cycled along a familiar route. What is now commonly referred to as the Cycle of Violence became clarified.

Tension building phase. The relationship is in some sort of equilibrium, then problems start to be experienced and tension starts to build. The abuser becomes more temperamental and begins to blame the victim in some way for the problems(s). The victim, during this period, is often said to "walk on eggshells." She may try to appease or placate the batterer to steer him away from the oncoming abuse.

Explosion. The abuser explodes, attacking the victim either verbally or physically or both. While this incident may appear to be a loss of control on the part of the batterer, it is actually a means of *establishing* control over the victim.

The honeymoon phase. During the honeymoon phase, the abuser is contrite and loving. Having released his tension, he now behaves solicitously toward the spouse. He may buy her flowers and candy. He says that he feels sorry for what he did and may, in fact, genuinely feel that way. He promises that the abuse will never happen again, but at the same time he may attempt to minimize it or explain it away. The victim often collaborates in accepting blame for the incident and downplaying its seriousness. The loving, contrite phase fades after a while and the cycle begins to repeat.

It is important to note that, without solid intervention, the cycle may grow more frequent and more intense over time. The violence gets worse and the honeymoon period grows shorter. Eventually the honeymoon phase may disappear entirely. This is a major warning sign that the victim may now be in serious, ever-present danger.

Walker's cycle has since been revised and refined by others. One model developed by the Mid-Valley Women's Crisis Service (1993) in Salem, Oregon, for example, describes the cycle in six stages rather than three. The first stage is the Abuse itself, followed by Guilt. The abuser then begins to use Rationalization to tell himself that the spouse's behavior somehow caused his own. A phase of "Normal" Behavior comes next, followed by a period of Fantasy and Planning, in which the abuser begins to anticipate how he will next abuse the partner. He then devises the Set-up, manipulating or tricking the victim into doing something that will trigger his next explosion. He might, for example, encourage her to go out with a friend for a drink, without informing her that if she is not home by 11:00, he will interpret this as marital infidelity.

❖ The Victim

There is no single, easily identified profile of an abuse victim. In fact there is considerable resistance in the field to "diagnosing" victims at all, for to do so is seen to imply that some pathology in the recipient helped to invite the abuse. To some, this is just another way to blame the victim. However, the *abuse itself* frequently engenders symptoms, regardless of what psychological traits may have been present beforehand.

In recent years a common way to try to understand women in battering relationships has been Battered Woman Syndrome (Walker, 1984). The concept of Battered Woman Syndrome explains why many women remain in abusive relationships. It is based on the idea of "learned helplessness" noted by Seligman (1975), who studied animals trapped without the possibility of escape from pain. These animals eventually lost their motivation to try to alter or escape their fate. While the "syndrome" has many critics and does not appear in the DSM-IV, it has found its way into the courtroom in criminal proceedings against batterers. A victim of Battered Woman Syndrome is usually described as blaming herself for the abuse, living in great fear for herself and her children, and having an irrational belief that the abuser is omnipotent and omniscient. Women who fit this profile are unlikely to report the abuse because of self-blame and fear of retribution by the mate.

An alternate view of abused women was proposed by Gondolf and Fisher in 1988. In this "Survivor Theory," abused women are seen not as being helpless but as having many strengths that they use to help them survive/escape. They may try to flatter, avoid, or manipulate the abuser to avoid his outbursts. They often *do* turn to family and friends as first-tier supports. Later, as such means prove inadequate, they may turn to police, courts, and social service agencies. Critical Entry Points are often missed. The victims then feel stymied by the weak response of the legal and social services system or the retaliation they receive from the spouse. According to Gondolf and Fisher, it is not really learned helplessness that prevents women from taking action but rather anxiety created by a lack of real-world options, lack of skills in accessing services, and lack of finances.

Most severely battered women present with symptoms of Post-Traumatic Stress Disorder (PTSD). Gondolf and Fisher (1988) state that anywhere from about fifty to seventy-five percent of women presenting with battering issues in clinics and practices nowadays are diagnosed with PTSD. The PSTD diagnosis was originally used to describe symptoms seen in survivors of one-time catastrophic events such as earthquakes, plane crashes, and rape and is now widely used to explain the symptomatology of victims of traumatic domestic violence. If abuse is suspected, checking for PSTD symptoms is a sensible response.

❖ *Assessing the Situation*

Many have found fault with the above models and profiles of abused and abuser, but the models do provide a basic framework. They demonstrate how important it is to recognize which *general* profile or pattern of violence/abuse our clients are really experiencing. Only by understanding the basic dynamics can the helper offer appropriate interventions to the client and family. Before helpers can respond intelligently to a report of abuse, it is important to use the Critical Entry Point as an opportunity to assess the client and her situation. The profiles above can provide a good basic conceptual framework within which to work though, of course, each case will be unique.

Appendix 1 contains a detailed *assessment interview* that can be used when an adult client reports spousal abuse. The interview provides an assessment of the following:

A clear account of what the client recalls as the **first,** **last,** *and* **worst** *incident.* This will provide good parameters for understanding the severity and duration of the abuse.

The power dynamics that have been present throughout the relationship's history. What attracted the partners to one another? Did either attempt to control the other? In what ways?

The level of fear the client is experiencing with respect to the ex-partner. Is the client worried about physical safety? Retribution?

If and how the client may have been restricted by the partner in terms of finances, leisure activities, outside friendships, etc. What were the consequences if the client did not behave as expected or do things just right?

The sequence of events that triggered any given instance(s) of abuse. It is very helpful to have the client give a full narrative reconstruction of at least one specific abusive incident and the events surrounding it. By encouraging detailed memory of events leading up to the abuse, we can better assess the nature of the violent interaction.

Whether there are substance abuse issues in the family. Domestic violence is generally not caused by substance abuse. However, they often co-occur. The use of alcohol or other substances can exacerbate the severity and frequency of abusive behaviors (Fazzone et al, 2001).

Whether your client has ever lashed out. If so, under what circumstances?

Whether the client's account provides evidence of Walker's Cycle of Violence or better fits other prototypes of domestic violence.

Whether the client may be minimizing the incident(s) or playing into the spouse's rationalizations.

In addition, it is useful to ask *how the domestic abuse allegation will likely affect litigation* concerning the divorce. Does one partner stand to gain a great deal by painting the other as abusive?

It is also useful to explore *whether the victim suffered childhood abuse*. What kind of modeling for problem-solving and male-female relations did the client learn as a child? What kind of traumatic experiences does the victim bring into his or her view of the present events?

A central purpose of the assessment interview is to get a fuller, more three-dimensional picture of the incident and its context than the client provides on his own. This means gently asking probing and clarifying questions. Remember, the client's lens is likely to be out of focus during crisis. It is important *not to get drawn automatically into the client's beliefs about the abuse*. The current danger level may be much *higher or lower* than what the client is presenting. We need to assess it realistically. This is no easy task. It can be tricky to sort out the facts while still maintaining the client's trust in our support.

❖ *Children and Domestic Abuse*

Complex considerations arise when children are present in a family in which abuse is charged. Four primary imperatives — what is best for the children, what the children want, what the parents want, and what the legal system may decide — are often at considerable odds with one another. Helping professionals may not have much control over how the court will ultimately decide custody and visitation, but we can try to promote healthy solutions that honor the well-being of all family members.

Studies suggest that both children and adult victims are present in thirty to sixty percent of families in which there is domestic abuse (Bragg, 2003). Thus it is imperative that professionals not only assess the presence and nature of adult interpersonal violence but also the effect of family violence on the children and the possibility of child abuse.

If our professional actions are apt to influence a custody determination, a parenting plan, or a treatment plan for children, it is incumbent upon us to understand the effect of the alleged abuse on the children. We may wish to assess whether any symptoms the children may be presenting are due to experiencing/witnessing actual abuse or simply the vicissitudes of a high-conflict divorce. The following general questions need to be explored: Did the child witness violence? Has the child been abused or is the child in danger of being abused? Does the child have psychological symptoms, and if so, are they consistent with PTSD? Can we rule out another etiology, such as an anxiety disorder? If a child is in danger or there is suspicion of child abuse/neglect, the clinician is generally obligated to file a report with the appropriate authorities.

When interviewing children about domestic violence, it is important to assess the child's level of exposure to family violence, the risk factors for the child being abused, the psychological impact of any violence on the child, and the child's sense of safety and protection within the family. Professionals who question children should have training and experience in working with children and how to communicate with them at a developmentally appropriate level. They need also be cognizant that research indicates that suggestive interviewing can result in the creation of false memories in children (Ceci, Loftus, Leichtman, and Bruck, 1994; Ceci and Bruck, 1995). Sexual abuse evaluations, in particular, should be referred to experts trained in accepted forensic protocols for assessing sexual abuse allegations. Because of the possibility of false accusations in divorce cases, which are discussed later in this chapter, it is crucial that the questioner maintain an objective manner and take care not to influence the child's account of the family dynamics and any reported incidents.

The same general rules for interviewing children that are used in forensic sexual abuse evaluations seem relevant to the questioning of children regarding other kinds of abuse (Carnes, 2002):

- ❖ Build an initial rapport with the child by addressing neutral topics such as school, hobbies, or activities.
- ❖ Word questions appropriately for the child's developmental level.

❖ Give children permission to answer questions in whatever way they want and to say, "I don't know."

❖ Progress slowly to questions that more specifically address the management of conflict in the family.

❖ Use open-ended questions, followed by requests for elaboration.

❖ Be careful not to use leading questions that may guide the child toward describing a specific set of events.

❖ If there is a particular incident that may have happened, indicate that you understand something may have occurred and ask the child to tell you what happened.

❖ Attempt to get the full sequence of events from beginning to end whenever possible, using such prompts as "What happened before (or after) that?"

Appendix 2 provides an original model — incorporating several sources — for interviewing children about domestic violence.

❖ The Dilemma of Domestic Abuse and Child Custody

As we make assessments and propose interventions, we need to keep "dueling considerations" in mind: witnessing or experiencing domestic abuse is harmful to children, but so is deprivation from one or both parents. Our chief calculus must be to weigh these two concerns against one another.

Interpersonal violence in the more severe of the abuse profiles discussed above warrant a strong response. For example, the Ongoing and Episodic Male Batterer and Intimate Terrorist profiles mentioned above are in keeping with Walker's concept of the classic abuser/batterer who causes repeated physical and psychological harm to family members. In these cases, removal of the children from the offending parent and/or supervised visitation are usually warranted. Similarly, supervised and/or limited contact with a parent is warranted if there is evidence of child abuse or neglect. Unless there has been a pattern of ongoing battering, intimate terrorism, abuse related to mental illness, major impulse control issues, and/or ongoing risk of harm to the children,

children do best when they have regular ongoing contact with both parents, with safety controls and treatment interventions in place as necessary (McGill, Deutsch, & Zibbell, 1999). If there are mental health issues with a parent, then custody and contact can be tailored to the parent's level of functioning and response to treatment. If the two parents have been mutually aggressive, but only toward each other, or if the domestic violence is of the one-time, separation-engendered type, then it is generally sufficient to tailor appropriate boundaries between parents and advocate for the children spending time with both.

The latter recommendation can run contrary to current public policy and case law, which has increasingly discouraged granting custody to a perpetrator of *any* act of domestic violence. In 1990, the U.S. Congress passed a resolution stating that, "...credible evidence of physical abuse of a spouse should create a statutory presumption that it is detrimental to the child to be placed in the custody of the abusive spouse...." The National Council of Juvenile and Family Court Judges in 1994 concurred, stating that, "...a determination by the court that domestic or family violence has occurred raises a rebuttable presumption that it is detrimental to the child...to be placed in...custody with the perpetrator...." And so the legal presumption, in a growing number of jurisdictions, is that the child is better off in the primary care of the parent who did not perpetrate abuse.

Sorting Out the Truth — Distorted Beliefs and False Accusations

Professionals need to be especially careful about what to accept as truth when there are children involved. Simply siding with the client and endorsing his accusations without investigation can result in the children being denied access, on a long-term basis, to one of their parents. If, through sheer professional blindness, we serve as a coconspirator in this type of situation or its opposite — accepting a client's *denial* of abuse and allowing the children to remain in an unsafe situation — we have passed a Critical Entry Point and are doing the family a grave injustice.

I cannot emphasize the above point enough. I have seen otherwise competent professionals lose their neutrality and diagnostic prowess far too often when abuse is alleged. It is not uncommon for smart, dedicated, and well-educated helping professionals to accept their clients' stories without question and then to immediately become aggressive advocates of defense strategies. The spouse's therapist (and lawyer) then responds to these strategies in kind. War ensues, all perspective is lost, and the children suffer, often more by the *conflict that ensues* than by the original (alleged) abusive incident(s). Nowhere else in our practice is the need for practiced neutrality greater than when abuse allegations arise.

The story that the divorcing client relates regarding the abuse is not necessarily accurate. Victims and perpetrators often do not recall, or do not report, all aspects of a given incident. The woman who fits the classic profile of a battered woman may be prone to downplaying the violence out of fear, self-blame, and denial. Men who are abused are frequently loath to admit it due to shame. Conversely, the client who is in the anger stage of the divorce process may focus too intense a spotlight on fairly minor events. In this case, relatively innocuous emotional flare-ups are sometimes reported as major forest fires. A mutual shoving incident becomes "that time he tried to push me down the stairs." The same thing can happen when a spouse strikes out physically due to separation-engendered and postdivorce trauma. The shocked victim, in an attempt to make sense of the event, may begin to reinterpret past minor incidents and construct patterns of severe abuse where no *bona fide* pattern may exist.

Some clients who make *false accusations* try to hurt an ex-spouse in order to gain an upper hand in divorce/custody negotiations by accusing the ex of domestic abuse. There is much debate as to the frequency of false allegations. In general, the rate of *purely fabricated* allegations is low. More commonly, a seed of truth is magnified and distorted. Often in cases of the latter type, the accuser actually begins to convince herself of the reality of the abuse. With each subsequent repetition of the stories to sympathetic ears, they become more solidified and "true."

In marriages where there are children, accusations of abuse are often answered with counteraccusations of *parent alienation*. We will discuss parent alienation in more detail in chapter 8. As its name implies, it refers to a situation in which one parent's actions and attitudes cause the disaffection of the children from the other parent. Parent alienation is a controversial term but one that is recognized in many legal and social service systems as both an identifiable family problem and a potential divorce strategy. In fact, it is becoming increasingly common for accusations of abuse to be answered by accusations of parent alienation. Escalating allegations and counterallegations make it hard to identify true cases of either.

Unfortunately, legal precedents do not reflect the complexities of domestic abuse or the possibility of false allegations, reflecting instead a unidimensional abuser-victim model. As a result, allegations of abuse have become part of the win/lose mentality inherent in conflicted divorces. Maccoby and Mnookin (1992), in a large longitudinal study, reported that mutual allegations of abuse are abundant in the roughly nine percent of families that were considered to be "high conflict." Johnston, Soyoung, and Olesen (2005) studied 120 divorced families in which there were multiple allegations of physical/verbal child abuse, neglect, sexual abuse, and domestic partner abuse. The investigators reported at least one allegation of abuse against mothers in fifty-six percent of families and against fathers in seventy-seven percent of families, with mutual allegations in forty-nine percent of families. Allegations included physical abuse, sexual abuse, neglect, and substance abuse. Investigators were able to find some substantiation for *roughly half* of the alleged abuse, with one-quarter involving abuse perpetrated by both parents. They report

> Mothers were more likely to make child sex abuse allegations and drug abuse allegations against fathers than the converse but neither of these types of abuse was substantiated at a higher rate. On the other hand, mothers were also more likely to make allegations of alcohol abuse and domestic violence against fathers than the converse, and both of these kinds of allegations were likely to be substantiated at higher rates than the converse. Note

that the amount of substantiated family abuse of any issue was almost doubled for fathers (fifty-seven percent) compared to mothers (thirty-four percent).... On the other hand, we find that mothers and fathers are equally likely to be responsible for child physical abuse and neglect. (p. 289)

While this research does lend validity to the position that males are more often the perpetrators of physical violence against spouses, it also highlights the serious possibility of false allegations in some high-conflict divorce cases.

It can be extraordinarily difficult for professionals to determine whether allegations are true, false, or partially true. Specialists in interviewing children have developed protocols for interviewing children about suspected sexual abuse (Carnes, 2002). However, such evaluations take time, resources, and highly trained professionals and are often inconclusive. In contrast, the domestic violence and child protective fields have yet to establish well-researched unbiased protocols for assessment of the wide range of domestic violence profiles. As a result, court decisions can sometimes play out in the wrong direction due to the influences of biased or poorly executed evaluations.

Sometimes court decisions result in a child being placed in the custody of a long-term abuser, particularly in cases where an abuser has better legal representation than the spouse or is more coherent in his presentation to the court. On the other hand, an accusation alone — the mere specter of abuse — is often enough to sway a court to err on the side of caution and keep the children away from the accused, at least temporarily. In some cases, mutual "common couple" violence can be successfully portrayed as one sided. Although some courts are beginning to look at the various profiles of abuse when making decisions, policy dictates a lack of sympathy toward even the one-time perpetrator.

So we in the helping professions encounter both fighting fathers and aggrieved mothers — some batterers, some unjustly accused, some engaged in mutual battering or divorce-engendered battering — using both defensive and offensive strategies. While some parents may fight for custody to maintain economic advantage or keep up the dynamics of control, others are forced to fight unfair allegations. In the midst of such controversy, we can forget that most parents want to do what they believe is best for their children. As professionals we need to make the most honest and careful assessment of the family situation possible and to help our clients do the same. That means we need to maintain our neutral perspective so as to avoid becoming caught up in the power games of batterers or the drama games of false accusers.

❖ *Providing a Responsible Response*

It is important to gain as full a picture as possible of the abuse dynamics within the limits of our professional role. If we are unable to assess the dynamics ourselves, a referral to a forensically trained specialist is in order. This is most particularly the case for allegations of sexual abuse. In addition, when we suspect that a child is in danger, professional ethics dictate a referral for evaluation to the appropriate child protective agency.

The goals of our own assessment are to gain as full a picture as possible of what happened regarding the alleged abuse and to assess risk. Only then can we coach the client to respond *realistically and appropriately.* If the abuse seems to be genuine and serious, then our primary focus shifts to the current safety level of family members. What kind of protective measures can the client put in place right now? Will setting boundaries with the spouse be sufficient or is it likely that the boundaries will be violated? In the latter case, the boundaries may need to be given legal teeth in the form of a restraining order or stay-away order. We can help our clients weigh the costs and benefits of seeking such an order, particularly when less formal boundaries are likely to be sufficient. The use of a restraining order as a legal tactic can escalate conflict and lessen the likelihood of reaching a negotiated divorce settlement. On the other hand, a restraining order may be justified when there is good reason to believe that the abusive spouse will not honor the client's stated boundaries without legal enforcement.

It is important to keep in mind that danger to the client can increase when the relationship is ending. In families with a long-term pattern of battering, this can be due to the batterer's feeling that the stakes must be raised to regain control *or* to the intensification of conflict that results from the terminating of a relationship. In cases where no long-term pattern of violence has existed, a divorce action on the part of one partner (i.e., serving the papers) may be the traumatic catalyst that sparks a one-time incident. When trying to ensure safety in such a case, it may be necessary for the client to establish firm boundaries in the short term, which can then be relaxed when the partners have begun to develop independent lives.

If needed, a safety plan or danger management plan should be developed. Safety plans may be appropriate in cases of heated separation as well as prolonged, repeated violence. We can assist the client in making concrete decisions about how to exit the home, whom to call, and where to go should a threatening situation develop. Are there family and friends with whom the client can stay temporarily? What shelters are available and what are their entrance criteria? Are there any nearby motels where the client would not likely be sought out? In potentially dangerous situations, the client should know ahead of time whom to call and where to go. For clients still living with a batterer, it can be useful to hide an "emergency kit" somewhere in the home, with spare car keys, cash, important phone numbers, birth certificate, Social Security card, etc.

❖ ### Treating the Abused Client

As for more comprehensive treatment, it is beyond our present scope to list all the interventions that we might offer when severe recurrent abuse is present. There are many books and resources available for working with abused clients. A very general approach is the following, based in large part on the work of Harway and Hansen (1994, 2004):

Crisis intervention

❖ Assess the marriage for domestic violence using a holistic approach.
❖ Assess the present and future level of danger to the client/family — what are the signs that danger is imminent? Advocate emergency responses if necessary.

❖ Educate the client about domestic violence and validate her experience (based on the profile of domestic violence that has occurred). Identify and point out repetitive cycles, either in the couple's dynamics or in the abuser's patterns. If only one incident occurred, try to frame it in its proper perspective.

❖ Develop and practice a safety or danger-management plan if one is needed.

Short-term counseling

❖ Work on empowerment issues.

❖ Help the client develop independent living skills and attitudes.

❖ Help the client grieve the loss of an idealized relationship and gain a more realistic attitude for the future.

❖ Help the client think through the pros and cons of any legal actions and how to develop an appropriate parenting plan that ensures children's safety and the preservation of a relationship with both parents.

Long-term counseling

❖ Help the client heal the wounds of the troubled relationship and any childhood experiences with abuse that may be feeding the present pain.

❖ Help the client develop trust.

❖ Work from a trauma recovery model to heal resulting psychological problems.

❖ Long-term, intensive work can be done effectively only once the client feels safe, has developed coping skills, and has moved out of crisis mode.

A Caution for Helpers

Maintaining neutrality can be a special challenge when dealing with cases of domestic abuse and violence, especially in high conflict divorce situations. In addition to the typical range of countertransference issues, the therapist/helping professional must contend with several other potentially powerful influences:

Cultural bias. It is often difficult not to project our own cultural preferences on a case. Many of us may believe, for example, that "unfriendly" physical contact of any kind with a child or spouse is always wrong. We will automatically (and understandably) adopt that attitude with clients. But in some communities, routine corporal punishment and/or a certain level of physical exchange among spouses may be considered the norm. If *clients* are comfortable with that, it may not be our place to "reeducate" them or judge them. Of course, injurious violence is unacceptable regardless of cultural concerns, but there is a fair amount of gray area here. A person who is simply following the dictates of his culture may not be a traditional victimizer or victim. It is important to consciously step back from our own assumptions and understand the cultural context of the family.

Desire to be a savior. Rarely will we want to "rescue" a client more than when domestic violence rears it head. But is our desire to be a savior outweighing the overall mental and emotional needs of the client and family? It is wise to take a moment in every case to ask ourselves honestly if the actions we take or the recommendations we make are to help ourselves feel heroic or whether they are truly best for all concerned.

Personal abuse history. Perhaps the helper has her own history of victimization by a parent or mate or has witnessed an alcoholic parent batter the other parent. It is not uncommon for people with histories of abuse to go into the helping professions to "help other victims." This can very easily turn into a subtle "crusade" mentality. If our main purpose for being in the profession is to help victims, we will undoubtedly *find* victims. We must be careful not to allow our own personal agenda and history to color what we're seeing.

As helpers we need to notice our own responses — are we overly impassioned or overly involved with a case? Strong emotions or an inability to "put the case down" tend to indicate that neutrality is slipping away. If this is so, it is all the more important to follow an established protocol for interviewing a family, one that can help us look at the full set of family dynamics. Seeking outside supervision from a neutral party can also be a wise decision for helpers in difficult abuse cases.

Divorce is traumatic under the best of circumstances, but when domestic abuse occurs and/or abuse allegations fly, the emotional temperature is turned up even higher. Reason and moderation are often jettisoned. Family members are vulnerable and the stakes are high. Where there is strong conflict, there is often strong motivation to *win;* sometimes clients vow to say and do "whatever it takes" to achieve victory. Even the most seasoned professionals can fall victim to drama and manipulation. When domestic abuse is on the table, we need to keep our feet planted firmly on the ground and remain sober, reasonable, and honest in our probing. We cannot afford to get swept away by tides of emotion. The family as a whole needs an anchor and is best served by professionals who can play a stabilizing role.

Chapter Six Key Points:

- ❖ Keep an open mind about the various profiles of domestic abuse.
- ❖ Recognize the signs of serious, repeated battering.
- ❖ Take a thorough history of the violence and power dynamics in the relationship.
- ❖ Help clients develop appropriate boundaries and safety plans.
- ❖ Help clients carefully assess their choices of action.
- ❖ Be aware of how your own cultural biases and personal issues may affect your judgment.
- ❖ Be aware of the possibility of false allegations when there are child custody disputes.
- ❖ When interviewing clients about alleged domestic abuse, be careful not to use leading questions based on predetermined assumptions.
- ❖ Keep both parents in contact with their children whenever safe and possible.

7 ❖

Parenting and Divorce

This chapter and the next two deal with the closely intertwined topics of parents and children. It is not possible to talk about one without the other, at least where divorce is concerned. This chapter looks primarily — but not exclusively — at working with parents.

In an ideal world, parents would exhibit their greatest parenting skills during the divorce process, when children have the greatest need. (Of course, in an ideal world, they probably would not be getting divorced at all.) The emotional, logistical, and creative demands placed on them as parents will probably never be greater than they are at this time. The children are feeling confused, unsafe, fretful, traumatized; they need steady wisdom and unwavering reassurance from their parents. Yet, as noted many times, parents are generally in crisis themselves. Their world has just exploded. Either or both of them may be adjusting to extramarital affairs, abandonment, domestic abuse, or legal attacks from a formerly trusted mate. Emotional regression is the norm rather than the exception. Mother and father are often at their all-time lowest reserves in terms of wisdom, perspective, and parental confidence. So very often a sad picture emerges, one in which the children's greatest need for strong parenting coincides with the parents' most depleted ability to provide it.

When we truly appreciate this fact, we realize what an invaluable support we, as counselors, can provide. If we watch carefully for Critical Entry Points, we will find ample opportunities to de-escalate conflict, clarify confusion, and gently bring the parents' attention around to doing what is *best for the children*. Because the parents' mental and emotional states may be skewed at this time, helping professionals may be the only ones who can think objectively and advocate for the family. Countless divorces devolve into warfare simply because no one is there to encourage parents to empathize with the children. Instead, all of the involved parties, including therapists and other helpers, become caught up in the drama and inadvertently lend support to the spiraling dynamics of accusation and strategizing to "win." Getting the parents to focus on the children's needs may not solve the relationship problems that caused the divorce, but it will often serve as a thermostat that can prevent the divorce process from overheating.

Most divorcing parents want to be the best parents they can be. If strongly reminded and encouraged to act in the children's best interests, emotionally healthy parents will typically respond positively, unless they are too distracted by their own pain and anger. Parents are often willing to make difficult adjustments and compromises for the children that they would not make for themselves or the ex-partner. With the encouragement of a helping professional whose focus remains locked unwaveringly on what is best for the children, the parents may discover a reserve of maturity and wisdom that was not initially apparent.

❖ *Parenting Factors That Affect Children's Adjustment*

What are the circumstances that best promote a healthy post-divorce adjustment for children? There is a plethora of literature about children and divorce. Some of the most useful references are Emery (2004), Furstenberg (1991), Hetherington (1999), Hetherington and Kelly (2002), Kelly (2000), Stahl (2000), Wallerstein and Blakeslee (2003), and Wallerstein, Lewis, and Blakeslee (2000), all cited in the bibliography at the end of this volume. In her landmark review of the research on this topic, Joan Kelly identified several key factors that strongly correlate with the successful adjustment of children. An awareness of these factors can help us provide effective parental coaching to our clients.

Ability of parents to resolve conflict. The number one factor correlating with negative adjustment of children is *exposure to conflict*. The more the parents parade their battles in front of the kids, the worse the children fare. Professionals can help parents understand this and modify their behaviors. If we do little else as counselors, we can at least try to influence ex-partners to resolve their conflicts in private and to behave respectfully and peaceably in front of the children. When parents play out their hostilities — subtly or overtly, individually or jointly, verbally or nonverbally — in the presence of the children, there is a high cost. All of the research seems to bear this out.

Mental illness or character disorder of the primary parent. The trauma of divorce is compounded when a child suddenly finds herself in the sole/primary care of an adult who is not capable of coping realistically with the world. But even in cases where there is no diagnosable disorder, a general principle can be applied: the more time the child spends with healthy parents, the better off the child is. If one parent is substantially more integrated than the other, the child will benefit from spending a greater amount of time with that parent.

Parental warmth. During and after divorce, children need a high level of love and reassurance but may not be able to ask for it. They may be too angry and withdrawn. The parent must bridge the emotional gap. Too often, though, the parent remains detached, lost in his own struggle. Parent and child then become emotionally isolated. Simple demonstrativeness — smiles, hugs, praise, laughter — can go a long way toward healing children's wounds of divorce and can have a salving effect on the parent as well.

Competent, authoritative (not authoritarian) parenting. A parent who provides clear expectations and structure without being rigid and dictatorial best aids the child's adjustment to divorce. Baumrind (1991) distinguishes between authoritative and authoritarian parents in this way. "[Authori*tarian* parents] are obedience- and status-oriented, and expect their orders to be obeyed without explanation." They are directive without being responsive. Authori*tative* parents, on the other hand, "... impart clear standards for their children's conduct. They are assertive, but not intrusive and restrictive. Their disciplinary methods are supportive, rather than punitive." Parents who are firm but flexible, confident yet adaptable, have better-adjusted children in the postdivorce arena.

Individual and interpersonal resources of the parent. The more well rounded and well developed the parent is socially and psychologically, the more likely the children are to cope effectively with the changes in the family. Any personal, emotional, and social skills learned by the parent will have direct and indirect effects on the adjustment of the children. This is a strong argument for helpers to encourage parents to work on coping and personal growth rather than to allow regression to become a dominant postdivorce theme.

Involvement with both parents. As difficult as it is for many feuding parents to accept, children need both parents. Even when one parent is clearly the primary caregiver and the other plays a relatively minor role, ongoing contact with *both* parents is strongly correlated with the positive adjustment of children. Unless there are clear arguments to the contrary, such as the high risk of child abuse or neglect, helpers should advocate parenting plans and custody arrangements that include regular, meaningful contact with both parents. Of course we would do well to also keep in mind that one healthy parent is better than two needy and inadequate ones.

❖ Common Issues for Parents in the Divorce Process

If healthier parents make for healthier, better-adjusted children, then anything helping professionals can do to help the parents *become* healthier will improve the family system. Familiarizing ourselves with some of the main issues with which parents grapple during the postdivorce period will help us offer more targeted and effective support.

Parents feel tremendous loss regarding their sense of family

This is equally true for custodial parents, noncustodial parents, and those who share custody. The loss is obvious for a noncustodial parent, often a father who has left the family home. He now comes home to an unfamiliar, empty house or apartment most nights — the absence is palpable. The children and spouse are gone.

But custodial parents suffer deep losses as well. In the majority of cases the custodial parent is the one who was the primary caregiver when the family was intact. This parent will keenly feel the loss of the support functions that the other parent provided. The extra support that the "secondary" parent provided, perhaps by reading the nightly bedtime story or helping enforce discipline, is now missing. Sometimes the presence of the other parent provided a psychological cushion that is now acutely absent. The custodial parent may also experience a sense of emptiness when the children are not at home and are with the other parent.

Often, neither parent understands the degree of loss that the other is feeling. A custodial parent may believe that the ex-partner had not been very involved in the household and thus did not have much to lose. The noncustodial parent may have trouble understanding how the custodial parent could feel loss when he now has the children most of the time. What is difficult for the noncustodial parent to understand in the latter case is that although the custodial parent may now have more *physical* time with the kids, he has probably lost genuine interactive time because days are now filled with functional duties such as feeding, bathing, dressing, transporting, etc.

Whenever we work with parents, we can help them feel less anxious by understanding and normalizing the deep sense of loss they are experiencing. Our empathy can provide a buffer for their anxiety.

Parents feel overwhelmed and incompetent

In the postdivorce environment, both former partners suddenly become single parents. The gaps formerly filled by the partner must now be filled alone. New roles and skills must be quickly assumed. It is frequently the case that both parents feel overwhelmed and less than competent at times. Noncustodial parents may see the children less frequently than before but may find themselves in a position to *do* much more with the children during the time that they do have. Whereas the noncustodial parent may previously have had specialized functions, he now must do everything — cleaning, feeding, clothing, recreational activities. Filling an entire weekend with family structure can be a very daunting task for the uninitiated.

The custodial parent, who may have done the majority of the childcare during the marriage, still probably designated certain areas of lesser competence or appeal — discipline, homework help, fixing things, etc. — to the partner. Now she must assume all of these duties.

Both parents must now deal with the kids in new intervals and in new ways. Helping professionals can understand and normalize the feelings of anxiety that arise as newly separated individuals take on new roles. We can reinforce the notion that new parenting skills take time to master. We can build and reinforce competencies and reframe perceived weaknesses as strengths. Often we can also teach specific skills, such as limit setting, listening, and conflict resolution between children or offer the client innovative parenting solutions based on our readings and our experience with other families.

Sudden changes in lifestyle create anxiety

Since divorced parents typically have the children for longer blocks of time than ever before and go without seeing them for longer blocks as well, they can alternately feel overwhelmed and abandoned as they radically restructure their time. The parent who suddenly has the children more of the time with less support may need to be encouraged to build regular breaks from the children into her weekly schedule. We might encourage her to use the ex-partner as a resource, if at all possible, rather than an enemy. The parent who too often finds herself alone with a glass of wine in an empty nest might be encouraged to look upon the added free time not as a vacuum but as a resource. She may now be able to take courses, join clubs, pursue hobbies, do volunteer work, or take on civic responsibilities that would previously have been impossible. Enriching her life in these ways will make her a stronger and more fulfilled parent during those times when she does have the children. This, in turn, will positively affect the children. Sometimes newly divorced parents may be reluctant to initiate new recreational and social activities out of a sense of guilt. They often feel that enjoyment is a betrayal of the sense of mourning they should be feeling for the "death" of the marriage. Our support and encouragement can be the catalyst for growth.

Parents may lack the coping and communication skills necessary for managing their children and dealing with their ex-spouses

Parents who have not coped well with the separation or who do not know how to manage their feelings do not model adaptive skills for their children. Sometimes the easiest and least intrusive way to teach skills to parents is by offering them skills that *they* can teach their *children*. Parents may be reticent to seek these strategies for themselves but may be eager to find ways to help their children cope. When helpers teach parents techniques for stress reduction, conflict resolution, assertiveness, communication, etc. that they can convey to their children, the adult clients indirectly absorb the skills themselves. For instance, when a parent coaches a child on how to appropriately express her anger or her needs, the parent is likely to also think about how to appropriately express these feelings herself.

Parents become stuck in anger and defensiveness

As noted numerous times, one of the greatest obstacles to a healthy postdivorce adjustment is emotional impasse. Clients become locked in strong emotions of anger, grief, and shame. They also become locked in habitual *postures*, such as attack or defensiveness, or *points of view*, such as "my ex-husband is the bad guy." In any of these cases, bringing attention around to the children can be a helpful catalyst in getting the parents unstuck, at least partially or temporarily. Whereas a parent might not be able to surrender her hardened posture for herself or her ex, she may be able to do so for the children. Is it really healthy for *the child* to continually hear his father referred to as callous and uncaring? To hear his mother called a selfish cheater? Clearly the answer is no. And so, we must encourage parents to develop vital awareness of the needs of the children — not just a passing consideration, but a genuine willingness to put themselves in their kids' shoes. Empathy for their children is often the only route around the parents' own roadblocks.

Parents can become enmeshed with their children

A common problem in the postdivorce landscape is an inability to distinguish between the needs and emotions of the self and those of the child. The parent, feeling insecure and traumatized, projects her own feelings onto the children. It is not uncommon to see divorced parents, especially mothers who have been the primary caretaker, unwilling to give up breastfeeding or unable to let their child walk unaccompanied into a classroom because of their perception of the child's loneliness or anxiety. Such a client must be encouraged to look at her own boundaries and sense of identity. This can be frightening, of course. Often, we can reach such clients by coaching them in helping the children manage *their* "loneliness" and separation anxiety. As we ask the enmeshed client to eliminate "check in" phone calls to the ex's house when the kids are there, we simultaneously praise her for doing a good job helping the children manage their nervousness about being away from home. Over time, with our help the client can learn to help the child (and herself) recognize that both of them can handle being apart when the child spends time with the other parent.

Holidays and special occasions tend to escalate conflict and anxiety

Holidays, such as Christmas, or special occasions, such as weddings and funerals, frequently stir up conflict and strong emotions in separated parents. Often each ex-partner has deep emotional commitments to celebrating holidays in a particular way and may be very resistant to changing treasured routines. Parents may be willing to do battle over this issue.

Helpers can assist clients to anticipate special occasions and holidays well in advance. Pointing out that the ex-partner is likely to have her own agenda for the event can eliminate the element of surprise (which triggers defensiveness) and enable the client to put some early thought into how to manage the special occasion. Helpers can strategize with their clients as to how to negotiate a structure that works for the children so that the kids do not get caught between the competing demands of the parents. Helping professionals can also help clients think about how to create new rituals for celebrating holidays, whether alone or with the children.

It can be useful to talk with insightful clients about separating their own feelings about celebrating Christmas or a child's birthday from those of the children. For parents who are enmeshed with their children, learning how to help their kids adapt to a holiday or special occasion can be a catalyst for their own coping.

❖ *Parenting Plans*

At some point, if the ex-partners have children they will need to develop a formal parenting plan. This is an agreement, on paper, that spells out how parenting duties will be handled during the postdivorce period. The heart of the parenting plan is the residency schedule — where the children will stay at what times and with whom. Often clients will want to discuss these issues with counselors or other helping professionals. While we cannot provide legal advice, it is useful for us to be aware of some of the parameters of an effective parenting plan and some of the dilemmas inherent in custody disputes.

An effective parenting plan should contain a regular schedule for the children to be with each parent; provisions for holidays, vacations, and special occasions; mechanisms for communication between parents and children; and ways to facilitate communication and conflict resolution between the parents. Well thought-out plans between cooperative parties may also contain a statement of parenting philosophy. This is an overall agreement about how the two ex-partners wish to conduct themselves as parents and the principles of childrearing they wish to embrace. If the client seeks our advice about developing a plan, this can be a Critical Entry Point. The negotiation of a parenting plan is an excellent opportunity for the two parties to formally clarify their parenting ideals and communication expectations. The plan can serve as a solid philosophical rudder when seas get rough.

As with anything else in the divorce process, the parenting plan should be firm but flexible. It should be firm, in that both parents stick to it reliably, but flexible, in that it is open to revision and review at regular intervals. Parents who communicate well with one another can tolerate more flexibility in their parenting plans than parents who are in conflict. In the latter case, eliminating ambiguity up front will help reduce conflict and provide the family with a clear roadmap. However, even when there is a need for a very specific plan, parents sometimes make the mistake of allowing the plan to be written in stone. As the children get older and/or family circumstances change over time, the original plan may no longer be optimal.

Research suggests that consistency and regularity of contact for children with their parents assists in their development (Pruett, Ebling, and Insabella, 2004). The best parenting plans provide for regularity but also include provisions for change as children's developmental needs change. With younger children, for example, more frequent stays with each parent for shorter durations are developmentally appropriate. The consolidation of attachment with parents is a primary need of the child at this stage. As the child grows older, longer stays and correspondingly longer separations will probably make more sense.

Ideally a *review process* should be built into the parenting plan with both parents agreeing to meet, for example, every two years either alone or with a third party to refine and readjust the plan. For parents who get along well, the parenting plan can be reviewed as needed. Helpers can refer parents to any of several books available for developing parenting plans and facilitating children's postdivorce adjustment. Those by Ricci (1997), Wallerstein and Blakeslee (2003), Long and Forehand (2002), and Emery (2004) listed in the bibliography, and the website of the Association of Family and Conciliation Courts (www.afcc.org) are good resources. Appendix 3 also provides some guidelines for creating developmentally appropriate parenting plans.

Keep in mind that there is no magic formula for the optimal plan. There is no solid research that one plan is better than another as long as the plan fosters strong parent-child relationships. The plan ought not be an instrument by which one parent exacts revenge or punishment on the other. Unless there is strong reason for deciding otherwise (such as abuse or mental illness), the plan should allow for the children to spend substantial time with both parents according to a timetable that is practically feasible and that makes sense in light of the children's needs. Some prominent divorce researchers point to the benefit of both mothers and fathers' postdivorce involvement in children's lives from an early age. (Kelly and Lamb, 2000; Warshak, 2000; Lamb & Kelly, 2001; Pruett & Pruett, 1998). Contrary to common assumptions, recent research also suggests that young children can tolerate overnights with multiple caregivers, and a schedule which includes such overnights may benefit children's social development (Pruett, Ebling, and Insabella, 2004).

It is useful to remind parents that transitions from one home to another have the potential of reactivating the feelings associated with the divorce and can be disorganizing. Two opposing concerns must be balanced in a parenting plan: (1) maximizing contact with both parents vs. (2) minimizing disruption to the children. Switching homes too *infrequently* can be painful and disruptive because children may miss one parent if they lose touch with him or her for too long a period. Switching homes too *frequently*, on the other hand, can be disruptive because the child never has a chance to really adjust to either home. There is no sense of stability.

Good parenting plans are based primarily on the interests of the children. Of course, practicality demands that the needs of the parents be considered too, but the needs of the children should be placed first rather than a distant second. Four basic levels of need should be considered:

- ❖ Developmental needs. As already noted, the needs of a two-year-old are different from those of a nine-year-old. The plan should address growth-based needs and adapt to them.
- ❖ Special needs. If any of the children have special learning requirements or psychological needs or are physically disabled, then these special needs must be taken into account.
- ❖ Practical needs. If a child is in Little League or ballet lessons, for example, and this activity is important to the child (and not being used as a time-control lever by a parent), then it should be accommodated in the planning whenever possible.

❖ Temperamental needs. The personalities of the children should be considered as well. If a child has a very anxious time with transitions, for example, then parents might seek to minimize or ameliorate these for that child by adjusting the number of transitions and/or the time and location of pickups and drop offs.

Sometimes siblings differ greatly from one another in age and need. In some cases, children's personalities and interests are so divergent that it is virtually impossible to schedule activities for them to do together. In such cases it may be necessary to create *individualized plans* or plan components for each child. Building in individual time with each of the children may be desirable even if the children function well as a group.

The following additional considerations underlie a sound parenting plan in high-conflict families:

❖ It is designed to minimize children's exposure to conflict. Transitions can be planned to avoid confrontation by having children returned directly to school rather than to the other parent's home and/or by building in clarity about the methods of exchange.
❖ It is based on the *practical* availability of each parent, not on forced or idealized schedules.
❖ It is based, ideally, on the mental health of the parents. Bluntly put, unhealthy parents should spend less time with the children. This is an ideal that is not always realizable.

The parenting schedule is very likely not as important as the *quality* of contact that the child maintains with both parents. Squabbling ex-parents often become overly focused on the *amount* of time they spend with the children. They go to battle over days, hours, and in some cases, minutes. Research continually confirms, however, that it is the *substance* of the time not the *quantity* of time spent with each parent that matters, so long as significant parental involvement with two healthy parents is maintained. We can help parents understand this and to try to defuse the "time wars." The parent who sees the children every other weekend, plus one evening in between, may feel justifiably cheated but can be reminded that he plays just as important a role in the child's development as the custodial parent. If this parent's visits with the children are characterized by genuine presence and authentic interaction (not just working on the computer while the child plays Nintendo), we can assure the parent that he is playing a vital part in raising the child.

If parents cannot agree on a parenting plan, they may need to look to the court to determine custody and a visitation schedule. In contested custody cases, the court often appoints a child custody evaluator, also known in some locations as a guardian *ad litem*, to investigate the family and provide information to the court. In many states, the child custody evaluator makes formal recommendations to the court. Such an evaluation may be conducted by court personnel, but frequently it is funded privately by the family. This can be an anxiety-provoking and expensive procedure for families. We can help clients learn about the procedures and costs of a custody evaluation in their jurisdiction and evaluate for themselves whether fighting a custody battle is worth the financial and emotional toll.

❖ *Coparenting: Cooperative vs. Parallel Styles*

Family therapist and prominent divorce specialist Constance Ahrons (1994) has coined several colorful alliterative terms to describe the continuum of relationships into which divorced parents fall: perfect pals, cooperative colleagues, angry associates, fiery foes, and dissolved duos. But no matter what type of post-divorce relationship the ex-partners establish, they will need to find a way to effectively and peacefully coparent the children during and after the divorce process.

A productive coparenting relationship often occurs on a continuum from Cooperative Parenting to Parallel Parenting. Cooperative Parenting, often touted as the ideal, embodies the following characteristics:

❖ The parents communicate often and openly about the children. They work together as genuine partners, at least where the children are concerned.

❖ The parents do their best to enforce consistent rules and expectations across both households.

❖ The parents make all major decisions and resolve all major issues about the child together.

❖ Schedules and rules remain flexible and subject to change based on the needs of all parties.

❖ Smooth transitions between households are facilitated.

❖ A child-centered parenting philosophy is adopted.

Cooperative Parenting is comforting and effective with the children and, when handled adroitly, produces the lowest levels of stress for all involved. If the parents fit into either of Ahrons's first two categories — perfect pals or cooperative colleagues — then this style certainly seems indicated. However many, if not most, parents fail to remain on good terms. Cooperative parenting is an ideal that works only when both parents genuinely *want and are able* to work together, without hidden agendas and without conflict.

Furstenberg and Cherlin (1991) first coined the term *parallel parenting* to describe another adaptive style of postdivorce parenting, and this style of coparenting has gained wide acceptance as a concept to be taught in classes for divorcing parents (Fuhrman & McGill, 1995). In parallel parenting, both parents "maintain separate and segregated relationships with their children and have a tacit agreement not to interfere in each other's lives" (Furstenberg and Cherlin, 40). Like parallel play between children, parallel parenting allows both parents to conduct their parenting duties "side by side," without much acknowledgement of, or interaction with, one another. Some characteristics of parallel parenting are

❖ Parents do not communicate openly and regularly but only around emergencies and deviations from the parenting plan.

❖ Parents often have businesslike communication. They may prefer not to talk in person or by phone but use "cooler" methods of communication such as email, third parties, or a shared parenting log.

* ❖ The parenting plan is followed closely and without much flexibility.
* ❖ Each household maintains its own rules, structures, and expectations independent of the other.
* ❖ Each parent accepts and endorses the other's parental authority without necessarily agreeing with the other's approach.
* ❖ Transitions from one household to the other involve little or no contact between the parents.

At first glance, parallel parenting might seem cold and undesirable, but it makes good sense for conflicted families when we consider the idea that *minimizing parental conflict* is an overriding goal. Cooperation requires good communication skills and the ability to compromise. It is often the lack of these very qualities that has led to the divorce in the first place. Ongoing "communication" between two people who harbor major resentments and contentions usually results in conflict and confrontations. It is often preferable to simply acknowledge that both parents have different styles and that both will parent as they see fit.

Children can, in fact, adapt to this type of situation much more easily than one in which there is constant conflict as the ex-partners ineptly strive to "cooperate" and enforce consistent rules. It is not so different from a school setting in which each teacher's classroom has its own culture, climate, and rules. Children learn very quickly that certain behaviors may be tolerated in one classroom but not in another. They are able to adjust to different sets of expectations without any known adverse effects.

A strong example of the power of parallel parenting versus flawed cooperative parenting occurred in an actual case where the child had a stubborn problem with incontinence. The divorced parents had tried many techniques and had eventually consulted medical and psychological experts at a well-respected hospital clinic. The specialists gave the parents a plan and technique to use, but the two parents, locked in conflict as they habitually were, could not agree on precisely how to implement the plan. Both parents were invested in the child's treatment and had defensible points of view. The struggle went on for months without any improvement in the child's condition. (In fact, one could argue that the child's persistent encopresis had the secondary gain for both child and parents of keeping the parents in communication with one another, albeit in conflict.) Finally, after an emergency conference call with all parties and some coaching of the involved professional staff, each parent was given permission to work with the child according to his or her own schedule. Shortly thereafter, the child's medical problem "miraculously" cleared up.

The majority of parents find themselves operating somewhere on a continuum between cooperative and parallel parenting. The main point to remember is that positive parental *involvement* is a strong predictor of healthy adjustment while parental *conflict* is a strong predictor of the opposite. Helpers can advocate for whichever coparenting arrangement promotes the most positive parental involvement with the least amount of conflict, even though the arrangement may not seem ideal in many ways.

Of course for parallel parenting to work, both parents must be capable of sound independent parenting and largely free of mental health, abuse, and addiction issues. Basic guidelines we might coach the parallel parents to follow are

- ❖ Relinquish all attempts to control or interfere with the ex-partner.
- ❖ Behave in a courteous, businesslike manner toward one another. Neither hostility nor inappropriate gestures of intimacy are advisable.
- ❖ Do not plan activities for the child to occur on the other parent's watch. Always consult the other parent first.
- ❖ Use "cool" communication methods that do not promote conflict, such as email or a notebook that travels in the child's backpack for the provision of concrete information such as what the child ate, what medicines were given, or notification of a school event.

❖ If you need to talk to one another, do so out of earshot of the child.

❖ Consider using a third party to assist with communications if the conflict level is high.

❖ When the child has a problem with the other parent, encourage the child to speak to that person directly with assistance of an outside party if necessary.

❖ Be dependable in following the schedule.

❖ Do not pressure the child for information about the other parent.

❖ Do not use the child as a go-between or as a means of communicating with the other parent.

❖ Do not speak negatively to the child about the other parent. Encourage a fundamental attitude of respect for the other parent.

❖ *Repartnering*

Sooner or later, one or both parents will probably find new partners. It is often useful for the parent to engage in professional counseling to assess her choice of a new partner as well as to discuss whether and how to bring a new love interest into the child's life.

The introduction of a new adult can disrupt the equilibrium of the family system. Parents often need guidance to help the children adjust. The possibility of absorbing a new parental figure into their lives will often rekindle children's feelings of loss of the original family constellation. Feelings of jealousy are common as the parent's time and affections are now split with a new person. Introducing a new partner may also stir up conflict between the two parents, even when such does not seem justified or rational. This may be due to residual romantic bonds with the ex or fears of having one's parental position usurped by a new "father" or "mother."

Determining what role the new partner will play in the family is an extremely delicate matter that requires time, discussion, emotional consensus, and gentle experimentation. One of the biggest mistakes parents make is moving too fast. Sometimes the parent, riding the "high" of a new relationship, rushes recklessly into sharing the experience with the children. In other cases, the parent simply decides that it is his right to act autonomously on the matter of relationships and demands that the children adjust. Both approaches run the risk of doing damage to the parent-child relationship. We can help parents avoid these mistakes by focusing clearly on the children's needs and feelings.

On the other hand, some parents are held hostage by their children's negative attitudes toward new partners and find themselves *unable* to form new relationships. Or they may use concern for the children as a handy excuse to avoid taking a new romantic risk. Counselors often need to help clients find the balance between moving too fast and not moving at all.

Some basic "rules" of repartnering that helping professionals can impart to clients are

Move slowly. Do not introduce dates and casual romances to the children. Wait until a relationship seems likely to become a long-term, exclusive arrangement. Waiting six months or more is a good general rule of thumb, though this may vary. If in doubt, err on the side of caution.

Minimize loss for the children. Parents who play "musical partners" and bring many new adults into their children's lives run the risk of creating repeated new losses for children who are already struggling with loss. Children can then become emotionally calloused or withdrawn. When parents spend more time with the new partner(s) than with the children, children may feel abandoned or jealous. It can be difficult for parents who are filling their own emptiness to step back from their new relationship in order to give their children individual time and attention.

Set early and firm boundaries with everyone. This includes the new partner, the ex-partner, and the children. A new partner may begin to make unreasonable time/attention demands and ask for unwelcome changes in family customs. Ex-partners can become intrusive and "in the interest of the children" try to dictate rules about the new partnership. The children themselves will often attempt to manipulate the parent's new relationship unfairly. The individual must make firm decisions about how much influence she will allow each relationship to have on the others and then clearly enforce those boundaries with everyone concerned.

Choose a mature, generous, and resilient partner for a long-term relationship. If clients are amenable, we can help them evaluate prospective new relationships. A new partner who lacks flexibility and has unrealistic expectations about having his own needs fulfilled through parenting the partner's children will have difficulty. The prospective stepparent is likely to be subjected to rejection, suspicion, manipulation, testing, and even outright hostility from various members of the family system during the repartnering process.

Set realistic expectations. Do not expect to have an instant family without conflict. Realize that you will likely be caught in the middle between your children's desire for your attention and that of your partner. Do not expect children to quickly bond with your new partner. This will take time. Understand the there will be an extended adjustment period as new family rules become established.

Become educated about the dynamics of stepfamilies. The Stepfamily Association of America (www.saafamilies.org) has excellent informational resources and listings of support groups. Other excellent sources about stepfamilies include Visher and Visher (1996), Papernow (1993), and Einstein and Albert (2005).

❖ A Caution for Helpers

A parent who is involved in a high-conflict divorce may attempt to persuade you that the other parent is incompetent or inadequate. It is all-too-easy to buy into your client's view and lose your neutrality. The helping professional who assists one parent is best advised not to assume that the client's assessment of the other parent is accurate. Focus instead on your client's ability to parent the child(ren), and do what you can to keep the child(ren) out of the middle of parental conflict. The helping professional who maintains neutrality regarding the relative competence of the two parents provides a model for the client-parent to do the same with the children, and avoids fueling inter-parental conflict and blame.

Chapter Seven Key Points

- ❖ Stand up for what is best for the children.
- ❖ Promote involvement of children with both parents.
- ❖ Help parents keep children out of parental conflict.
- ❖ Normalize parents' feelings of loss, anxiety, and disempowerment.
- ❖ Stress quality of parenting time vs. quantity.
- ❖ Educate parents about parallel parenting.
- ❖ Advocate slow introduction of new partners to children.
- ❖ Support parents in setting limits.
- ❖ Encourage parents to be flexible regarding the parenting schedule as children get older.

Parental Alienation

An important Critical Entry Point occurs when a helper becomes aware of a situation in which a child of a high-conflict divorce spends progressively less time with one parent and/or voices strong objection to being with that parent. The helper's response can be crucial in the maintenance of the parent-child relationship. To determine an appropriate response, it is important for the professional to diagnose fully the reasons for the parental rejection. As with other aspects of the divorce, it is crucial to look at the big picture.

In such cases, we may or may not be seeing a dynamic that has come to be known as "parental alienation" (Clawar & Rivlin, 1991; Darnell, 1998; Gardner, 1989, 1999, 2002; Rand, 1997; Warshak, 2001a, 2001b). Parental alienation occurs when a child becomes allied with one parent and disparages or rejects the other. In extreme cases, the child may refuse to see the rejected parent. We have discussed the complexities of domestic violence allegations in divorce; the dynamics of parental rejection are equally controversial and complex. Cases of parental rejection often involve allegations of physical or sexual abuse of the child, which the target parent counters with claims of parental alienation instigated by the other parent. Each case warrants good diagnosis and appropriate early intervention.

Research suggests that some aspects of alienation often arise during and after the dissolution of families where there is a legal dispute over custody. Clawar and Rivlin (1991) found that fully eighty percent of high-conflict divorcing parents practice some form of parent-estranging behaviors. Janet Johnston (1993) found that forty-three percent of children in her sample of families with disputed custody issues were in strong alliances with one parent and twenty-nine percent in mild alliances. Most often, children who fully reject a parent are preadolescent or adolescent, but younger children may display many rejecting behaviors toward a parent. Generally, but not always, children are in an alliance with a custodial parent and target the noncustodial one.

A common cluster of symptoms in such families prompted Gardner to coin the term "parental alienation syndrome" or PAS. Depending on the severity of the problem, a child who allegedly suffers from PAS may exhibit all or some of the following behaviors, as described by Rand (1997):

- The child is aligned with the alienating parent in a campaign of denigration against the target parent, with the child making active contributions.
- Rationalizations for deprecating the target parent are often weak, frivolous, or absurd.
- Animosity toward the rejected parent lacks the ambivalence normal to human relationships.
- The child asserts that the decision to reject the target parent is his or her own.
- The child reflexively supports the parent with whom he or she is aligned.
- The child expresses guiltless disregard for the feelings of the target or hated parent.
- Borrowed scenarios are present, i.e., the child's statements reflect themes and terminology of the alienating parent.
- Animosity is spread to the extended family and others associated with the hated parent.

Gardner's notion of a "syndrome" sparked controversy in the psychological community because the term implies a discrete set of symptoms with a consistent constellation of causes. Gardner placed the blame for PAS squarely on the shoulders of an alienating custodial parent. In contrast to this one-dimensional approach, Kelly and Johnston (2001) have proposed that not all children of divorce who reject a parent do so because they are influenced by the other parent. Rather, the rejection is likely to have multiple causes. These authors suggest that the child's post-divorce affinities with the parent(s) lie on a continuum, as described below. These five categories can also be viewed as the stages through which a child might pass as she grows progressively estranged from one parent. They are

- ❖ Positive relationships with both parents
- ❖ Affinity with one parent
- ❖ Allied child — child has formed an alliance with one parent
- ❖ Estranged child — child has become distant from one parent, with corresponding negative attitudes
- ❖ Alienated child — relationship with one parent has broken down completely

Garber (2004, 2005) views alienation from the perspective of developmental attachment theory and uses terminology somewhat differently from Kelly and Johnston. He employs Bowlby's (1969) notion that the child's "internal working model" of the parents governs the nature of his or her attachments to each of them. The quality of children's internal models can change over time in response to their experiences. Garber believes that "aligning" and "alienating" messages occur in most families to some degree or another. Aligning messages *enable* security of attachment, whereas alienating communications *inhibit* relational security. "Coparental alienation" is the term Garber uses for when a parent sends alienating messages to a child about the other parent. Children sometimes adjust their internal working model about one parent based on the messages they receive from the other. The coparental message may be accurate or inaccurate and the parent described may be sensitive or insensitive to the child's needs. Children become *alienated*, in Garber's terminology, when they accommodate their internal schema based on inaccurate alienating messages from one parent. If an alienating message about an insensitive parent is *accurate*, however, the child might form an appropriate *estrangement* from that parent. Garber uses the term "polarized children" to describe children who have adopted extreme attitudes and emotions toward one of their parents.

This author agrees that the reasons for parental rejection are often multiple and complex. While the rejection of one parent may sometimes result from the deliberate machinations of the other, frequently the problem is multi-causal. As with other aspects of divorce, it is helpful to use Janet Johnston's three-tiered model described in chapter 2. We need to look at the intrapsychic dynamics of the individual, the interactive dynamics of the family, and the influences of the wider social sphere to fully understand all of the contributing factors to parental alienation in any given case.

❖ Individual/Intrapsychic Dynamics

No matter what the helper's role, it is useful for him to obtain as clear a picture as possible of the following issues regarding each family member:

The allied parent

Is there evidence of long-term psychopathology? In particular, is there evidence that this parent fits the profile of one of the problem personalities listed in chapter 5? How is this parent adjusting to the divorce? If there is anxiety, is it apparent only with respect to the other parent, or is it more generalized? What is the parent's belief system about the other parent and how has this changed over time? What is the parent's relational history with her own family of origin? Does the parent have an abuse history? Does the parent have the capacity for empathy with the child?

Allied parents may be angry at the other parent and retaliate by limiting access to the child. Others are genuinely anxious about the child seeing the other parent due to their experience of the other parent as abusive or neglectful. Sometimes their concerns are appropriate, but sometimes they are overblown. Anxious parents may fear letting go of their children because of their own sense of vulnerability. Sometimes the parent has a history of being victimized earlier in life and carries this sense of victimization to the present. In some cases, the allied parent is not able to tolerate and appropriately respond to the child's full range of feelings because any anger the child might express toward the allied parent or positive feelings toward the other parent can feel like a personal betrayal.

The alienated parent

Again, is there evidence of long-term psychopathology? How is *this* parent adjusting to the divorce? Has this parent historically been involved with the child? Can the parent empathize with the child and understand the stress that the child experiences? What is this parent's view of the other parent and of the child? How well does this parent control his impulses?

There is no evidence clearly demonstrating the relationship between psychological disorder and parent alienation. Some rejected parents have indeed been good parents but events related to the divorce have triggered the child's anger, which in turn may have been reinforced by the other parent. Some rejected parents, however, have contributed in some way to the child's disfavor of them. Some noncustodial parents have been relatively absent in the home and have little experience parenting the child. These parents need to develop a more solid relationship over time. Some alienated parents have difficulty relating to the child due to differences in temperament or their own poor social skills. Some have indeed been emotionally neglectful and/or abusive, but the degree to which this has occurred needs to be assessed. In some cases, the alienated parent fits the profile of the narcissistic problem personality mentioned in chapter 5 and thus has been unable to respond empathically to the child's needs. However, even abuse or lack of empathy does not mean that there is no value in the parent-child relationship provided the contact can be structured in ways that feel safe to the child.

The child

What is the child's developmental history? What is his relationship history with each parent? How has his internal working model of the parent changed over time? Does the child display anxiety, and is this anxiety focused on the target parent or does it apply in other aspects of his life? If there are questions of abuse, does the child have symptoms of post-traumatic stress disorder? Can the child express a full range of emotions? Does the child mirror the allied parent's words when describing the alienated parent? Does the child's explanation of events make sense or are there holes and contradictions? Are his reactions appropriate to the stated "crimes" of the alienated parent? Does the child have flip-flopping views of the parent(s)?

Children who reject a parent are often highly anxious. Sometimes this is appropriate to the situation because the child has experienced or witnessed one or more traumatic events. However, in many cases the level of anxiety is greater than one would expect given the events that transpired. Often, it is not clear which is the case.

Once a polarized child develops a strongly held negative internal working model of a parent, the child may adapt or distort information from or about that parent to fit the belief system. In a recent case, for example, the father and mother had a disagreement over whose role it was to pay for certain extracurricular activities for the son. The father asked the mother to consider whether she might perhaps pay a portion of the bill. When the child reported the story, it became, "My Dad refuses to pay for hockey, so I can't play." A mild disagreement had been filtered through the child's negative internal working model of the father.

Even though polarized children often play the rejecting role themselves, it is common for them to assimilate a view of the parent as not caring about them. The child both mirrors the perceived rejection and filters input from the parent in a way that reinforces the perception of not being cared about. It is not surprising that children in this relational dilemma often have deep-seated feelings that they are not worthy of their parents' affection.

Some children flip-flop in their view of a parent depending on whom they are with. Garber (2004) refers to such children as "chameleons." Chameleon children may appear to be allied with whichever parent they are with at a particular time. They will provide negative reports about the other parent to the current parent and may indeed believe them to be true at the time. After they transition to the rejected parent's home, their behaviors and their internal working models shift. Such children have difficulty holding divergent internal models of their parents at one time. When chameleon children move from home to home, their transitions can be full of pain and conflict. In one extreme case, for example, two girls were told by their father that their mother, with whom they resided, was extremely emotionally disturbed. When they came home to mother's house, they would refuse to take off their coats and would scrutinize their mother's every move until they were certain that she was safe to be with. It generally took two full days for the girls to be able to trust her. By their third day home, they were happily ensconced with their mother, trusted her, and believed that their father was "mean" to her.

❖ *Family Dynamics*

The interactions between family members hold important clues as to why a parent is being rejected. It is useful to explore the current and past dynamics of the various "interactive subsystems" of a family.

The couple

What were the dynamics of the couple prior to divorce? How did the couple break up? What have been the divorce dynamics? What are the current legal issues between them?

We have already discussed many of the issues related to high-conflict couples in previous chapters. Of particular relevance here is the question of domestic violence. It is important to do a thorough evaluation of the alleged abuse and its severity. It is also important to assess the current level of conflict and how it manifests in the legal struggle between the couple. In the case of the boy who believed his father did not care about him because he would not pay for hockey, the parents had been embroiled in litigation for over a year and a half about money. In addition to litigation in family court, the mother was suing the father in civil court for $500,000.

The sibling subsystem

Do all the children in the family feel/act the same way toward the affected parent? Have they bonded together? Is one child allowed to have her own opinion about the parent or is there an unwritten rule that they must view things the same way?

In polarized families, siblings sometimes, but not always, present a unified front against the rejected parent. Sometimes it feels safer for a child to join with the others in opinion and action. On the other hand, children may vary strongly in their history and affections regarding the alienated parent. Child A, for example, may have always allied with one parent, while Child B may have allied with the other. The current alienation dynamic is a heightening of this polarization. In such cases the children may develop conflicts with *one another* that mirror the conflict between the parents.

The allied parent-child subsystem

What has been the relationship over time? How has it changed? What is the nature of their attachment? Does the child have difficulty separating from the parent? Does this parent say negative things about the other parent to the child? Does this parent use the child as a confidant? Does the child mirror the parent's words? Is the parent emotionally or physically abusive to the child?

Allied parents and children tend to have close relationships, but sometimes children fear the consequences if they individuate from the allied parent. In some cases, the child feels protective of the parent perceived as having been wronged in the marriage. In other cases, the parent has been the child's protector from an abusive parent. Some children have an insecure attachment to the allied parent, who is most often the primary caretaker, and may fear abandonment by that parent. In some cases, the child has become a companion to the allied parent who is having trouble feeling whole on her own.

The rejected parent-child subsystem

How has *this* relationship changed over time? Does the interaction between parent and child change over time when the child is alone with that parent? Does the parent make comments to the child about the other parent? Can the parent empathize with the child or does she impose her own point of view? Is there credible evidence of physical or emotional abuse to the child?

It is useful to get a full history of the child's relationship with the rejected parent from the point of view of the child, each parent, and others who may know the family. The current relationship may be an extreme of what existed before, or it may be a new dynamic. When the relationship has changed dramatically, it pays to explore the events surrounding the change. Children who have had a positive history with a parent are more likely to regain it than children whose previous relationship has been minimal or conflicted.

The parent-parent-child subsystem

In what ways does the child play into the parental conflict? Has the child historically been the focus of parental conflict? What happens before, during, and after the child transitions from one parent to the other?

In some families, one or more of the children have been the focal point of parental conflict. Sometimes this is the child for whom there have been the greatest expectations. In other families it is a child with special needs or the child with the most difficult temperament. In many families where the parental relationship has been strained, one or more children have been triangulated into the family system as one parent's ally against the other. As a high-conflict divorce progresses, the child's polarization becomes more solidified.

We will want to find out how the parents interact at the time of transition. In one case, the parents exchanged the child at a local restaurant because the mother was afraid of a confrontation with the father. The two had agreed not to talk with one another during the transition. The mother did not make eye contact or say hello to the father. Despite the mother's *words* of encouragement about the child going with the father, her body language relayed resentment and fear. The child clung to the mother and frequently would not go with the father.

❖ External Influences

We can also examine the interplay between any of the *related* parties and family members. A variety of outside influences provide and receive feedback to/from members of the nuclear family. Such influences include the extended family, the legal system, friends, and such helpers as the child's school counselor, therapists, custody evaluators, etc. As these external forces become involved, they often reinforce the thinking of the parent and/or children with whom they personally have relationships. It is not unusual for one parent and his "team" of allied family members friends and professionals to cast the other parent as an abuser, while the other parent's "team" counters with accusations of parent alienation. Each side can present a convincing argument when seen in isolation.

Extended family

What is each parent's relationship with extended family? What kinds of attachments has the parent had to his or her family members? Were family members actively involved with the couple and/or a source of conflict in the marriage? What is the attitude of one parent's family about the other? Has the parent come to rely more on family since the separation? What do family members believe and say about the ex-spouse? How involved are they with the polarized children?

Extended family can become embroiled in the conflict as a couple comes apart. Sometimes family members are already a major influence in the family and may be a source of conflict. When couples break up, the parties often turn to these family members for emotional or financial support. Old family alliances can deepen and new ones form. Family members may become involved in the couple's dispute over money as grandparents try to protect grandchildren by helping to secure assets. Divorce can wound a family's sense of pride — i.e., something is "wrong" or shameful in the event and the family must prove the other side is blameworthy to save face.

The family's cultural or religious ties can further heighten the hostility between the ex-spouses and the need for one parent to bring the child into his family "fold." When the couple bond is broken, a parent may realign with the family values and beliefs as he turns toward family members for support. The following case of an Indian immigrant family is an example of how extended family can greatly contribute to polarization.

The couple met in graduate school in the United States and married in a small civil ceremony. After graduation, both worked as engineers. The wife's family had never approved of the husband because his family was of a different caste in India. The wife's family had been of an intellectual class, but were not wealthy. The husband's father, however, had become a successful businessman and had considerable assets. He never liked the mother's family because he believed they wanted his family's money but did not approve of his son's background. The couple eventually had two girls.

After the maternal grandfather's death, the maternal grandmother moved to the United States and lived in an in-law apartment in the family home. The grandmother often babysat the children while the parents worked. She and the husband did not get along. Arguments often took place regarding the wife's relationship with her mother. The children often heard their parents screaming and finally witnessed a pushing and shoving incident in which their father left the house in a rage. The children's mother filed a restraining order. A high-conflict divorce ensued, with much wrangling over child support and ownership of the house. From this point forward, the children's negative belief system about their father was heavily reinforced by their mother and grandmother. The family's cultural prejudice against the husband's family's caste contributed a great deal of fuel to the growing alienation of the father.

Culture

The cultural influences in this and many such cases should not be overlooked. The girls in the case just described actually made racial slurs against their own father, referencing his darker skin. These cultural biases were ingrained in the beliefs of the family and were reinforced by the maternal grandmother and extended family. While the mother claimed to repudiate the cultural biases, her children expressed them openly in their statements about the father.

As with any therapeutic relationship, helpers dealing with alienation cases would do well to remain sensitive to potential cultural influences (McGoldrick, Gordano, & Garcia-Preto, 2005). While not always as obvious as in the case discussed here, cultural issues are nonetheless frequent contributors to family discord and must be thoroughly considered in evaluation of possible helping interventions.

❖ How to Help

The most important point for helpers to remember is that our interventions at Critical Entry Points can be important in the *prevention of* parent alienation. Helpers should take care not to unwittingly feed family polarization. Rather, we need to maintain a neutral stance with regard to the parental conflict and take the time to fully diagnose the family dynamics. When we spot the warning signs of parent alienation we need to look for ways to empathize with our client while avoiding contributing to the estrangement by accepting a unilateral view of events. As with all issues that arise in high-conflict divorce, we need to assess the history and dynamics of the family system, with attention in this case to the parent-child subsystems as well as the couple.

Parental alienation is far easier to forestall than it is to reverse once it has become full blown. There is a good deal of controversy over how to work with families in which there appears to be pathological alienation. Once it occurs, it often takes a team approach along with court intervention to remediate the situation. In such circumstances, perhaps even more than in others, the maintenance of neutrality and a family systems perspective to treatment are paramount. It is especially important for the helping professional to be clear about her role and to maintain contact with all helpers involved with the case (given, of course, the required client permission to discuss the case with other professionals who may be involved).

Interventions

Among the red flags that can signal family polarization are a series of blocked visits or a highly contested visitation episode.

Frequent *missed* visits or questionable events/excuses that result in limiting one parent's time with the children are also warning signs. When we decide there is cause for concern, it is paramount to get both parents' points of view so that we can keep a balanced perspective. Keeping the child involved with the estranged parent, regardless of how the child may protest, also prevents alienation. If there are concerns about safety, supervised visits can be implemented as a way to keep the child in contact with the feared parent.

Dealing with the allied parent

Allied parents can present difficult challenges for helping professionals. When dealing with the allied parent, it can be helpful to educate him about the dangers of alienation and focus on the welfare of the child. Professionals can point out that children fare much more poorly in school and in general when they lose a relationship with one parent or get drawn into black-and-white, good vs. bad thinking about a parent. We can help isolate the parent's concerns about the ex from those of the child.

Often, allied parents need extra encouragement and support to set rules regarding expectations that the child see the other parent. This is particularly difficult for the parent who believes that the child has little to gain from seeing the other parent. It is incumbent upon counselors to help the allied parent to consider the potential value of letting go and allowing the child to form her own relationship with the other parent.

In some cases, the allied parent may feel threatened by the child's forming a relationship with the estranged parent. In such cases, the helper must support the parent in managing his own anxiety and/or loneliness. Sometimes it is not possible to address this directly. Rather, counselors can provide parents with tools to help children manage their anxiety. In so doing, helpers are also indirectly providing tools for the parent as well. Anxious parents can be reminded about the strategies listed in chapter 8 for helping children with transitions. They can also be taught relaxation techniques and cognitive-behavioral strategies such as those mentioned in chapter 5, which they, in turn, can reinforce with their children.

Some allied parents have poor or selective limit-setting skills. They may routinely tell kids that they need to go to school but not that they need to see the other parent. Such parents may claim to feel sorry for the child because of the pain that has been caused by the bad marriage or the traumatic divorce. Others do not want to become the "bad guy" by pushing children too hard. In both cases, counselors can work with parents to tolerate the temporary negative feelings that children may express when the parent sets clear limits. With adolescents, the situation is complicated by their developmental needs. It is a balancing act to allow them some control over their schedule while still insisting that the relationship with the other parent is a must-do. In some of these cases, the helper can help the parent or parents negotiate a schedule that is better matched to the maturing child's schedule and relational needs.

Helping children recall positive memories is a beneficial practice we can encourage parents to try. In some cases, parents will deny that there ever *were* positive experiences. Whenever possible, however, parents can be encouraged to share with their children pictures or videos that convey positive images of their family relationships. A parent may not do this for him or herself, but can often be encouraged to do so for the child's sake. The counselor can support this effort by offering to look through old pictures with the client first, helping to identify positive themes. Looking at the past, of course, can also bring up tremendous sadness for the parent, along with a fear of making the child similarly sad. Counselors can support parents when such feelings arise and help them anticipate and accept sad feelings that may come up in their children.

In one recent case, a mother was convinced that the child was traumatized by the father who had yelled a great deal when the child was young and had pinned the mother to the wall in a volatile fight in front of the child shortly before the marriage ended. Mother wanted to believe that the child had PTSD. The child had not seen the father in three years, due to the mother's belief that the father was abusive and that the child is afraid of him. In therapy, however, the child, now 9, told the counselor that seeing her father made her very sad because he could not be the father she wanted. Sadness is quite different from fear. The mother needed to hear about the child's sadness and then cope with her own in order to make forward progress in reestablishing the child's relationship with her father.

Assisting the estranged parent

The parent who does not see her child over extended periods of time can become extremely angry and feel a strong sense of injustice, particularly if she feels wrongly accused of abuse or bad parenting. For such parents, an open-minded helping professional may be the first person in the divorce process who has seemed sympathetic. While it may not feel like "enough" to the counseling professional, it is often profoundly helpful for a rejected parent simply to be heard and validated. Within a context of acceptance, some rejected parents are remarkably able to identify the child's anxiety and pain. When a parent can empathize with the child's plight, she is better able to react to the child's rejection with patience and calm. Parents who cannot do this often run the risk of digging themselves into a deeper hole of rejection as the child sees the parent's angry insistence on "the truth" as proof of the parent's concern only for herself.

The helper can also try to foster clear ways for parents and children to communicate when they do not see one another. Emails, phone calls, greeting cards, etc. can be less intrusive ways for parents to keep in touch with a child who wants to limit direct contact. For parents who have been rejected, maintaining contact in such ways can forestall the child's internalizing a belief that the parent does not care and leave the door open for future contact.

Some children seem able to tolerate intermittent contact with a disliked parent. The reasons for this may vary. Some children simply do not feel they have common interests with the less involved parent. Others, particularly adolescents, have a developmentally appropriate need to be more involved with peers rather than "forced" to spend time with a parent. In cases of extreme alienation, a child may feel that he can see the disliked parent only intermittently without breaching his loyalty to the aligned parent. We can help rejected parents understand these issues so that they can let go of a rigid schedule and give the child more leeway. For example, shorter visits such as "four hours every other Sunday with some dinners in between" might be more workable and developmentally appropriate than extended weekend visits. (Keep in mind that a formal parenting agreement or court decree may govern visitation schedules. Changes in schedule may require a modification approved by the court.)

For estranged parents who are in touch with their children and who are able to maintain good impulse control, it is sometimes helpful for them to learn to skillfully challenge their children's distorted views of reality. This is a process that comes from repeated exposure to behaviors and experiences that differ from the child's anticipated beliefs about the parent. Warshak (2001b) offers useful suggestions for parents who are in a position to counteract their children's negative beliefs.

Helping alienated children

Therapists and counselors working with children who refuse visitation must be particularly sensitized to the need of children to experience support for their full range of feelings. It can be tricky to provide empathy without agreeing with the child's distortions. Gentle questioning and challenging of the child's viewpoints can be gingerly introduced once an alliance is established with the child.

If a child is anxious about seeing a parent, it can be useful to teach the child techniques for managing anxiety, including deep breathing and turning off negative thoughts. Sometimes children are anxious because they are focused on one or more bad memories. In such cases, a therapist can help the child consider whether there are also positive memories. If seeing a parent brings up *sadness*, the therapist can support the child through the grief process. In some cases, the estranged parent may indeed fall short of the child's wishes and expectations. The counselor needs to help the child develop realistic expectations about what is possible, rather than focusing only on what is missing.

It can be crucial for a child to process a visit with an estranged parent very shortly after the visit. If a visitation supervisor or family therapist has been involved, she can review the visit with the child or convey the details of the visit with the child's therapist to review it in turn with the child. It is not uncommon for children to have forgotten things that happened in the visit that differ from their selective memory of the visit being "bad" or "scary." It can be particularly effective for the helper to review all aspects of a visit first with a child and then again with the child and the allied parent.

Parameters of Treatment for Extremely Polarized Families

If alienation or estrangement has already occurred, it is likely that the child's negative views and/or fears about the rejected parent will continue to mount and multiply unless treatment occurs. Treatment of entrenched cases is extremely difficult. The following advice is offered for those who attempt treatment based in part on the works of Ward (2005) and Warshak (2001b, 2003):

- ❖ Treatment contracts and visitation schedules may need to be ordered by the court and monitored for compliance by a court officer or a parenting coordinator (see chapter 9).
- ❖ Court-ordered sanctions may be necessary for allied parents who encourage extreme cases of alienation.
- ❖ If children are amenable and parents are cooperative, children can benefit from having their own neutral therapist who maintains confidentiality and who gets information about the child from both parents.
- ❖ Therapeutic family intervention will also be necessary and should be undertaken by a therapist other than the one seeing the child. When working with the family, the family counselor should see family members in varied groupings — child with Parent A, child with Parent B, child alone, parents alone without child — from time to time.

    Goals of treatment for both family and child therapy will include remedying distortions in thinking, helping the child individuate from the allied parent and helping the child feel safe with the alienated parent.

❖ The helper can coach the allied parent on how to allow the child to separate and comfortably encourage contact with parent B.

❖ The helper can coach the rejected parent to be patient and empathic and to reach out to the child consistently, in appropriate ways, despite possible rejection by the child.

❖ The helper may wish to involve extended family if they are strong influences on the parents or the children.

❖ Interventions may fail for a variety of reasons. If this occurs, the helper can assist the rejected parent to cope with the loss of the relationship. If possible, the rejected parent should be encouraged to let the child know she still cares by sending periodic letters, emails, or phone messages that do not demand a response.

Chapter Eight-A Key Points

❖ Maintain a big picture perspective when working with polarized families.

❖ Watch for signs of parental alienation and intervene early.

❖ Facilitate continued safe contact with children and estranged parents.

❖ Support allied parents in setting limits with their children.

❖ Encourage and support healthy coping strategies for dealing with separations between allied parents and their children.

❖ Provide support and coaching for estranged parents.

❖ Help children to recall a broad range of memories.

❖ Slowly and gently challenge children's distorted thinking.

9 ❖

Children and Divorce

Children do not generally cause their parents' marital crises. They have no control over their parents' maturity levels, psychological make-ups, behaviors, or decisions about the breakup of the family. Yet divorce fractures children's lives as much as, or more than, it does their parents'. We can regularly remind parents about the magnitude of trauma that divorce represents to kids so that they can respond to their children's needs during and after the separation. Divorce will always leave emotional scars, but it does not have to permanently destroy lives.

When children are faced with divorce, they progress through most of the same stages of emotional adjustment that adults do — anger, denial, sadness, etc. But children generally lack the linguistic tools and cognitive skills to process the experience in adult terms. When parents are mystified by a child's withdrawal or acting-out behaviors, they need to be reminded that the child is simply reacting to an extremely confusing and painful situation with the only tools she possesses at her developmental level.

It is important to help parents understand that it is normal for a child, as it would be for an adult, to have adjustment difficulties during a divorce. Often parents leap to blaming the ex-partner for problem behaviors in the child or assume that something is psychologically amiss, when the child is merely moving in her own way through the grief process. The child's expressions of strong emotions are actually quite healthy, as long as the child is not injurious to herself or others or unable to function. It is only when symptoms are extreme or prolonged that the situation warrants extended intervention by a mental health professional. In most cases, professional intervention with children, if desired at all, need only be short term or intermittent with the goals of resolving the grief process and developing skills for coping with stresses inherent in the reorganization of the family.

❖ *Telling the Children*

One of the very first questions parents may ask helping professionals is, "How should we tell the kids that we're getting divorced?" While no two cases are exactly alike, there are some general guidelines that professionals can share with parents:

Tell the children **before** *the family comes apart.* If possible, parents will want to tell the children of the impending divorce while the family is still intact. Letting the children digest the upcoming divorce "in bites," rather than all at once, can help prevent extreme reactions. The actual separation, when it occurs, will still be difficult but will be less so if it has been preceded by a period of anticipation, discussion, and preparation.

Tell the children at a time when the parents can be emotionally available. Parents should plan to be with the children, or at least available to them, for a substantial period of time after breaking the news. Telling children twenty minutes before departing for work or before the kids leave for school or camp is inadvisable. Children need plenty of time to cry, get angry, ask questions, and to be comforted and reassured. They will not be able to swallow the news in five or ten minutes and may need to engage in several rounds of questioning and emotional reactions.

Talk to the children together when possible. Both parents should be present for such an important discussion. If possible, they should temporarily put their conflicts aside in order to give the children some semblance of a united front and a coherent explanation of the separation. If the parents are not capable of talking to the children together, they should take turns. In this way the children will be given a balanced perspective, without one parent's point of view dominating the presentation.

Tell the children that the marriage was based on love, if indeed it was. It is important for the children to know that the marriage that gave them emotional sustenance for years was not a sham but was based on love. If the parents cannot claim any love of one another, even in the past, then they should at least make it clear that both of them love the children unequivocally.

Know which questions you will not answer. If the partners are cooperating with one another, they should talk privately before approaching the children. They should decide together, ahead of time, which tough questions they will answer — and how — and which ones they will not.

Be honest, but tell children only what they need to know. There are some details that children do not need to know. Some information will only be confusing and destructive to their relationship with one or both parents. Maintain healthy parental boundaries when talking to the children. If there has been an extramarital affair, the children probably do not need to know. However some children, particularly older children, may ask pointed questions about it. In some cases, the "wronged" parent insists that "the truth" be told. When children must be told about infidelity or other sensitive matters, discussions should be kept in broad terms and presented in a way that preserves respect for the "offending" parent.

Tell the children about the breakdown in terms they can understand. This is not always easy, particularly with young children who have little understanding of the complexities of adult relationships. Parents can help the child to understand that there are different ways of loving people and that sometimes these ways change. There are numerous children's books that can be useful aids in explaining divorce to children such as those by MacGregor (2001, 2005). Referring to familiar situations in children's lives — characters in books and TV shows, friends and neighbors, pets — that are emotionally analogous to the breakdown can aid the child's understanding.

Assure children that they are not to blame for the divorce. Young children who do not yet understand cause and effect may react to the news of divorce with self-blame. Older children who have been the focus of arguments between their parents may also internalize blame. Since children may not always express these beliefs openly, a parent may want to anticipate that the child will feel this way and clearly explain that the divorce is not his fault. This may need to be done repeatedly.

Anticipate the logistics beforehand. Before speaking to the children, parents should try to work out the major practical and logistical issues. When the children hear of the separation, they are likely to have a great many questions concerning how the divorce will affect them. Will they have to move? Will they still see both parents? Will they have to change schools? Insufficient or ambiguous answers to such questions can add to children's stress and anxiety.

Tell children that they will be given care and attention. Fear of loss is the dominating emotion for children when they hear about a divorce. Parents need to demonstrate that the children's needs are being honored as the family reorganizes. Parents need to recognize the immediacy of their children's basic concerns, such as "Who will read me my bedtime story?"

Give children permission to have a loving, satisfying relationship with both parents. It is important to set the tone, from the outset, that each parent fully expects and permits the child to maintain a bonded relationship with the other parent. It is in the child's interest to be free to continue loving both parents without any fear of betraying or weakening the relationship with either one.

Let the children know that the decision is final and nonnegotiable, if this is the case. It is important to empathize with the children's feelings, but it is also important to let them know that the decision to divorce is a final adult decision. No amount of "good" or "bad" behavior on the part of the children will result in the parents getting back together again. Leaving children with the hope of parental reconciliation, when such is unlikely, is usually a mistake. It retards the child's ultimate adjustment in the same way that saying a deceased parent has "gone away for a while" does.

❖ *Children React — Some Common General Issues*

There is no way around the fact that the dissolution of the family will be a painful experience for the children. Healing will happen in fits and starts, over time. Strong emotions and acting-out behaviors are to be expected. In fact, the child who appears to react calmly and indifferently to divorce may be a greater cause for concern than one who displays her feelings openly. As a general rule, divorcing parents can expect children's adjustment to take several months to a year. In high-conflict divorces with prolonged litigation or in cases where the parents themselves are unable to adjust, children's adjustment problems will likely be more chronic.

The nature of a child's reactions depends upon his disposition and age. Regression is quite common, as is anger and aggression. Anxiety, particularly separation anxiety, may occur, especially in families in which the child is enmeshed with the emotional needs of a primary parent. Depression or feelings of sadness in older children are normal too. As children adjust, their feelings and concerns may change on a daily or weekly basis.

Children may have different reactions with different parents. Sometimes they parrot their parents' concerns about one another. They may tell one parent one thing and the other parent another, based on what they think the parents want to hear or are able to hear. In some cases the child may have reunification fantasies and may, consciously or unconsciously, exhibit certain behaviors to try to bring the parents back together. One common example of this is a child who suddenly has difficulty in school. Knowing that both parents are invested in her education, she secretly hopes that her school struggles will force the parents to come together to help solve them.

Preteens and adolescents can play one parent against the other. This is most successful in families in which the parents do not communicate well. "But Dad said I could," may be a common refrain. It is easy for parents to assume that the other parent did indeed give permission for the child to have her ears pierced or to stay out late when this may not be the case. Thus it is crucial that the parents maintain some mechanism of communication, whether by telephone or email or through a third party.

It is important to help parents understand that any or all of the above reactions fall within the range of normal behaviors and do not necessarily require outside intervention. The breadth and depth of the child's problems will tend to be a function of (1) the level of conflict between the parents, (2) the healthiness of the child's relationship with the parents, and (3) the individual strengths and resources of the child.

❖ *Children and High-Conflict Divorce*

Children in any divorce will have adjustment problems, but children in high-conflict divorces are likely to have symptoms of a more serious and enduring nature. These problems will manifest on the emotional, social, and behavioral levels. Children caught in the middle of an extended parental struggle tend to be hypervigilant, to be prone to aggression and depression, and to have a black-and-white world view (Johnston & Roseby, 1997). In other words, they demonstrate traits similar to those of their character-disordered parents as discussed earlier in chapter 5. Considering the situation in which these children find themselves, it is unlikely that they would *not* have serious adjustment problems. Their parents pull them in opposite directions, often forcing them to reconcile two very different versions of reality. Thus, the children are unable to mature normally on a cognitive and emotional level.

> *Consider the case of teenage Sally, whose custodial mother routinely tried to set rules, which Sally routinely broke. The father, rather than communicate with his ex-wife, undermined mom's rules and blamed all of his daughter's problems on his ex. With this added fuel for her anger at mom, Sally began to act out more dangerously, cutting herself, stealing, and drinking. Sally was finally hospitalized and diagnosed with borderline personality disorder. Upon release from the hospital, she told mom she was sorry and wanted to go away with her for an upcoming holiday. But . . . she told dad the same thing. The parents argued, Sally cut herself again, and no one went anywhere for the holiday. On and on the battle went, both externally — between the parents — and inside Sally.*

Children like Sally, who are stuck in the middle, become symptomatic when they are forced to synthesize their parents' opposed realities. *The children* become the fulcrum on which the parents' battle seesaws. When warring parents maintain rigid postures and refuse to engage or compromise with each other, the child is forced into the impossible position of living in two worlds. Typically, each parent blames the other for the "problems" that the child is having, rather than seeing these as normal reactions to an abnormal and complex situation. Mutual accusations escalate and perpetuate the child's maladaptive behaviors. The manifestation of serious problems in a child can often represent a Critical Entry Point for helpers. It is a challenge for professionals who work with high-conflict parents to help them accept responsibility for the ways in which they themselves *create* their children's adjustment problems. In cases where parents are unable to change their behaviors, providing a safe harbor for the child outside of the family may be the most helpful intervention.

Johnston and Roseby emphasize that damage to children's self-image often occurs in high-conflict divorce. Since children's self-images result in part from their identification with their parents, when one parent rejects or insults the other parent, children often internalize this negative portrayal. Children can feel as if a part of themselves is being negated or rejected. If we can help divorcing parents to understand this dynamic, we can prompt a critical shift in the way they choose to play out their conflicts.

❖ *Divorce and Developmental Stages*

It is important for helping professionals and the parents with whom they work to recognize that children's needs and tolerances change as they age. Postdivorce arrangements need to adjust to these changes. A brief look at the specific needs of children in the major age groups from infancy to early adulthood and how parents can address these needs is contained in appendix 3.

In general, as children grow older

- ❖ They become better able to understand the family dynamics.
- ❖ They are more adept at expressing their concerns and needs.
- ❖ They can better adjust to different parenting styles.

❖ They do not require as much routine and consistency.
❖ They have stronger peer relationships, which become increasingly more central in their lives.
❖ They can go for longer periods without seeing each parent.
❖ They have more demanding and complex schedules.
❖ They generally prefer, and do better with, fewer transitions between households.

❖ *Transitions between Homes*

Transitioning from one parent's home to the other can evoke strong feelings for all members of the divorcing family. Transitions often spark regression and anxiety in the children and conflict between the adults. It is normal for children to have some negative reaction to the strain of switching gears from one home to another. For many children, particularly in newly separated families, the emotional charge of the original separation may be reactivated each time the children switch parents and homes. In conflicted families there is the additional stress of the cognitive shift in belief systems that occurs with each transition. It may take hours or days for that readjustment to occur. The child who is in frequent transition between opposing household cultures may never feel completely settled.

Children fare much better when parents take the time to *positively prepare* them for transitions. Preparations may begin hours before the physical transition itself. The child can be prompted to start thinking about the move, finishing activities, packing, tying up loose ends. Soothing the child and talking to her about the transition is important, as is a supportive, encouraging attitude. "You're going to have a great time at your Dad's." If parents themselves feel anxious, resentful, angry, resistant, or ambivalent about the transition, they often will not do positive preparation work with the children or will not do it convincingly or sufficiently. Helping professionals can aid parents to overcome their own emotional predispositions and recognize the needs of the transitioning child.

When children have difficulty with transition, it is generally useful for the parents to build routine and structure around the transition. In cases where there is a high level of parental conflict, children may worry that their parents will fight or break down emotionally when they see one another. Pickups or drop-offs in neutral locations or rules about each parent remaining outside of the other's home can help ease anxiety. One family, for example, always handles transitions at a local fast food restaurant that has a play area that the children enjoy.

Helping professionals can reinforce the following points for parents:

❖ The parent who *presently* has the children should manage the transition and encourage the child to have a good time with the other parent.

❖ Parents should do frequent time countdowns with the children as the transition approaches. "In two hours you're going to your father's." "Better save your videogame; you're going to your mom's in fifteen minutes," etc.

❖ For young children, it is helpful if parents can maintain the basic routines and schedules of eating, napping, and bedtimes between homes.

❖ It is advisable to set up a comfortable personal space and a good assortment of personal items in both homes.

❖ It is important to set up good personal boundaries and a sense of private space in each home for each child. As children enter adolescence, issues of modesty must be addressed.

❖ Parents may need to allow children adjustment time when they transition to the new home.

❖ Parents should take care not to grill the children about life in the other home or express judgment about the other parent's parenting skills, e.g., "Did your father feed you today?" "When was the last time your mother washed your clothes?"

Counseling professionals can help parents understand that transitioning may be difficult under the best of circumstances. If a child is difficult to discipline, moody, or agitated when he arrives from the other home, this does not necessarily mean that the other parent is doing a bad job. It may be just part of that child's readjustment. If the child is having trouble sleeping or paying attention in school after a transition, this may simply mean that she needs a longer adjustment time. Parents might consider altering the schedule so that the transitions occur earlier in the day or on different days. For some children, it is easier to return directly *to school* after a weekend visit than to come home on Sunday night, reintegrate into a new space, and then go off to school the next morning.

❖ *Counseling Children*

Parents often assume that children need counseling when their parents divorce. This may or may not be the case. Often, the most effective way to smooth children's adjustment is to work with their parents. Since the parents' mental and emotional health is a key factor in children's postdivorce adjustment, improving the adults' skills and enhancing their adjustment is vital for the well-being of the children in the long term. However, when the parents are too caught up in their own personal or interactive struggles to provide an environment in which the kids may express themselves honestly, professional counseling can provide children a neutral and safe place to explore their feelings with a positive adult role model.

When working with children, it is good policy to verify the custodial status of the parents. If a parent states that he has full or joint custody of the children, the professional can ask to see the paperwork, "as a matter of policy." Sometimes parents do not fully know or understand their custody arrangement; others falsify or embellish their custody status as a way of trying to exert control. On a practical level, mental health professionals need to be aware of state laws regarding seeing children in counseling. Some states require signed consent from both parents if both are the legal custodians; others require only one parent's agreement. Even in the latter case, either parent can *rescind* the consent for treatment and may do so if she feels that the helping professional is taking sides. Thus logic dictates that if there is joint legal custody, it is important to have permission to treat the child from both parents.

It is highly advisable from the beginning to establish and maintain contact *with both parents*, even if they do not both have legal custody. It is not possible to help children have a balanced view of their life situation when the helper has imbalanced information, nor is it possible to help children function well in both households if talking occurs only with the head of one. Also, if communication with both parents is not established early, the excluded parent may adopt a hostile attitude toward the counselor and seek to undermine the counseling process. Conversely, reaching out to both parents conveys, both to the child and to the parents, a strong intention to proceed fairly and openly without taking sides. In cases where one parent does not want a counselor to contact the other, it is important to explore the reasons. Such resistance can often indicate that the parent is hoping to triangulate the helping professional into the conflict as an ally or a witness in legal proceedings. It is therefore useful to explain to the parent who brings a child to therapy that it is a matter of policy to speak to both parents. Most parents accept this if they understand that the other parent might seek to block therapy if he is left "out of the loop." The parent who seeks therapy for a child is unlikely to argue with the logic that it is in the child's best interest for the counselor to understand problems the child may be having in both homes.

Mental health professionals and other helpers need to be clear with all parties about the rules of confidentiality. In most cases this means that they will not discuss the child's case in detail with the parents, but will give them only a general "status report," unless the child is in danger. It is important to explain to parents the therapeutic importance of confidentiality at the beginning of the counseling relationship and to get their buy-in. While parents may have the legal right to request their child's records, it is useful to have them sign an agreement stipulating that the child retains confidentiality within the therapeutic setting.

An example of wording that can be contained in the initial therapeutic contract is the following:

> The law allows parents to examine the treatment records of their children who are under 18 years of age, unless I believe this review would be harmful to the patient and his or her treatment. Because privacy in psychotherapy is often crucial to successful progress, particularly with teenagers, it is my policy to provide parents with general information about the progress of the child's treatment and his or her attendance at scheduled sessions. Upon request, I will also provide parents with a summary of their child's treatment. I will otherwise maintain the child's confidentiality except in circumstances when I feel that the child is in danger or is a danger to someone else. In such case, I will notify the parents of my concern. Before giving parents any information, I will discuss the matter with the child and do my best to handle any objections he or she may have.

As professionals embark on therapeutic work with a child, the following concerns may be fruitfully kept in mind:

Safety. It is important to explore, with the child, ways to help her feel safe within the counseling setting. Many children have a difficult time believing that they have unfettered permission to speak about their parents without fear of reprisals. The child's feelings of emotional and physical safety in both of their homes and in the world at large may also be explored. This is particularly true for children who have been abused or have witnessed violence between their parents. A major goal of treatment is the child's development of an inner sense of security.

Assertiveness. Helping the child to express her needs with others, especially with her parents, can be a therapeutic goal. The child needs to find comfortable and effective ways to ask the parents to keep her out of the middle or to stop fighting in front of her.

Verbal expressiveness. Part of therapy work with a child involves expanding the child's emotional vocabulary, helping her learn new and better ways of verbally expressing what she is feeling.

Control/Mastery. Kids of divorce often feel quite out of control. Counselors can find ways to give children a sense of control over numerous aspects of their lives. Building practical competencies and helping children develop control over their emotions are important goals. The use of storytelling and play are good ways to reinforce young children's sense of control and competence.

Coping. Therapists must often teach young clients practical techniques for relaxation, self-soothing, managing fear and anxiety, and coping with new situations. Children benefit greatly from having clearly identified strategies for dealing with uncomfortable situations, such as feeling scared at mom's new home or being unable to sleep when they go to their dad's.

"Gray" thinking. As noted already, children of divorce can easily be drawn into black/white, good/bad thinking that can alienate them from one parent or the other. While concrete thinking may be developmentally appropriate for younger children, therapists can work with kids as they mature to help them see the gray areas in their family lives and gain a broader perspective about the strengths and weaknesses of each of their parents.

How not *to help*

A caution is in order for helpers who work with children of high-conflict divorce, especially when there are allegations of abuse or poor parenting. It is often tempting to ask children questions to ascertain the "facts" about what the child has experienced. That is not the job of the counselor when working with the child. Rather, the overall goal of therapy with children is to *help children cope* appropriately with the divorce transition and with the issues they face in their lives.

Some therapists seek to uncover memories of unpleasant incidents or alleged abuse at the expense of addressing children's immediate concerns about managing their anxiety. While there is a place for therapeutic detective work, it should be secondary to helping the child feel better and safer in the present moment.

> *Mary, a child who allegedly revealed an incident of sexual abuse to her mother during the course of a custody dispute, was questioned by a sexual abuse evaluator and then relentlessly by her therapist who sought to uncover the details of the abuse to help Mary "manage her feelings." Mary, who became avoidant of her father, never made a disclosure. Over time, she became*

avoidant of therapy and other helpers such as her school counselor. For the remainder of her childhood and adolescence, she resisted getting help with her increasing symptoms of anxiety and depression.

Children can become resistant to treatment if a therapist persists in too much digging and questioning. When the therapist focuses instead on helping the child feel safe and comfortable, details from the past can and will bubble up at their own pace and then can be addressed.

❖ *Tips for Effective Intervention*

The following are some general guiding principles for working with children of divorce:

- ❖ Communicate with the child at his or her own level.
- ❖ Listen empathically.
- ❖ Be nondirective and let the child take the lead, at least some of the time. Grilling the child with questions is counterproductive.
- ❖ Take care not to ask leading questions. Ask open-ended "what" and "how" questions, such as "What happened next?" or "How did that make you feel?" rather than "Did your father yell at you then?" and "Did that make you scared?"
- ❖ Maintain balance by remaining in contact with both parents and by addressing issues with regard to both homes.
- ❖ Have some toys in the office that lend themselves to expressive play on the part of the child — puppets, dolls, art materials, sand box. If possible, have *two* dollhouses.

Chapter Eight Key Points

* ❖ Know that it is normal for children to have problems during divorce.
* ❖ Communicate this to the parents.
* ❖ Coach parents to keep children out of the middle.
* ❖ Coach parents to manage transitions in ways that meet the children's needs.
* ❖ Tailor parenting plans to children's developmental needs.
* ❖ If counseling children, maintain contact with both parents.
* ❖ Ensure children's confidentiality and sense of safety in therapy.
* ❖ Help children develop mastery and coping skills.
* ❖ Avoid repeated questioning for information about specific incidents

10 ❖

The Legal Process and the Players

To strengthen your credibility and efficacy with clients, it is helpful to know something about the life terrain they are navigating. In the case of divorcing clients, this terrain includes the legal arena. The more you know about the legal process of divorce and its players, the more the client will feel able to rely on you to provide meaningful, informed, and practical support. In terms of your own understanding, too, the more you know about it, the better you can anticipate the roadblocks and challenges the client is likely to face and help her prepare for these.

Basic knowledge about this process can help us better understand why the client might be experiencing heightened stress or helplessness during certain periods and can enable us to spot Critical Entry Points for lending support. Wiser decisions can then be made and potential disasters averted. Perhaps, for example, it is not a sound idea for a client to confront an ex-spouse over visitation issues two days before a hearing on a motion for modification of child support. By having some awareness about the legal hot spots ourselves, we are better able to spot possible red flags for the client.

Knowledge can be helpful, too, when it comes to supporting the client in planning the kind of divorce process that will work best for him. The more you know about the options that exist, the better you can help the client intelligently evaluate choices and make the kinds of practical decisions that will cause the least pain and frustration. Knowing, for example, that Attorney A is highly litigious while Attorney B has a reputation for conciliation can be extremely beneficial. Knowing what *collaborative law* means and which lawyers in the area practice it allows us to present a viable alternative to litigation for the client to consider.

This does not mean, of course, that we give legal advice; only an attorney may do that. Nor does it mean that we should tell the client what to do. But we *can* offer alternatives for consideration, direct the client toward sources of additional information, and help the client thoroughly evaluate all options. To do that, some minimal knowledge is useful.

Divorce law varies greatly from state to state and technicalities abound. It is wise to become familiar with the key precedents, statutes, procedures, and legal tendencies within your own state. This chapter offers only a basic primer to allow helpers to better "talk the talk" — a starting point from which to make further inquiries. This presentation may feel a bit elementary at times; it seems preferable to assume too little knowledge than too much.

❖ *The Process*

Traditionally, our legal system has been adversarial and therefore not best suited to helping families adapt to the trauma of divorce. As divorce has become more commonplace, modifications and alternatives to the traditional divorce process have emerged. Nevertheless, the legal divorce process usually involves two *litigants*, or legal contestants, each seeking the most advantageous possible settlement for themselves. In many cases, each party is represented by an attorney whose duty it is to advocate for the client's interests. (Individuals may opt not to use an attorney. In the case where clients choose to represent themselves, they are considered to be "*pro se*.") When negotiated in an adversarial manner, the divorce process often involves a certain amount of posturing. Both parties may feel compelled to ask for more than they believe they will really get or make accusations about the other so as to give themselves an advantage in negotiations.

A divorce is initiated by the filing of a divorce petition or complaint by one party or the other. In the complaint the *grounds* for seeking the divorce are customarily stated. The reasons for requesting the divorce must be in line with legally established grounds that are recognized in the couple's state. The party who files the complaint, known as the *plaintiff*, has the legal burden of proving that the claimed grounds are valid. The divorce complaint may also specify what sort of recourse the plaintiff is seeking — custody of the children, division of the assets, etc.

A divorce complaint is generally served *by* the plaintiff *on* the defendant, or *respondent*. Legal papers are typically hand delivered to the spouse by a legal authority or designee thereof. The respondent then usually answers the complaint by agreeing with it in full, denying its allegations in full or in part, and/or filing a countercomplaint.

Since the late 1970s/early 1980s, many states have adopted provisions for "*no-fault*" divorce, in which neither party is legally identified as the cause for the dissolution of the marriage. To file for a no-fault divorce, both parties must agree to this approach. In such cases *irretrievable breakdown of the marriage* is considered to be the grounds for divorce. As mentioned in an earlier chapter, the no-fault provision has certainly made divorce easier and less painful and, by so doing, has likely played a role in the increase in the total number of annual divorces in the United States.

A divorce may be *contested* or *uncontested*. A contested divorce means that one or more open areas of disagreement exist between the parties. Uncontested means that both parties have come to a complete agreement on the terms of the divorce before entering the courtroom. In the case of a contested divorce, there is generally a court proceeding, or trial, in which the attorneys present their respective cases and the judge makes a ruling. Contested cases generally take longer to schedule before a court than uncontested cases, which tend to be more routine.

Even when the agreement is uncontested, the parties must appear before a judge. In such cases, however, the judge usually "rubber stamps" whatever agreement the parties and their attorneys have ironed out on their own. Only if the judge has reason to question any aspects of the agreement will she generally challenge the provisions. For example, if one party has few assets and little income but elects to waive alimony and child support payments, the judge might rightfully consider this arrangement suspect and question it. Is some form of coercion being used by one party over the other? Have all the facts been presented truthfully? In cases where the agreement is *largely* uncontested — both parties agree on most provisions — but one or two areas remain contested, the judge will usually hear arguments only on the contested points.

Many divorces begin as contested cases but end up being uncontested by the time they go before the judge, because the parties reach an agreement. It is almost always preferable for parties to come to an agreement on their own if possible rather than try their case in court, as a trial can be a time-consuming and expensive process. In addition, whenever a case is taken to trial, unpredictable things can happen and clients run the risk of being blindsided. It is not uncommon for parties to reach a compromise agreement on the steps of the courthouse to avoid trial. Litigious cases tend to become increasingly hostile as negotiations fail to achieve resolution and a case nears trial.

Negotiations during the divorce process, whether contested or uncontested, are aimed toward arriving at a *separation agreement* or divorce agreement. This is a binding document that spells out such provisions as the terms of legal and physical custody of the children, the division of the marital assets, and the payment of alimony and/or child support. In some states, a couple is considered to be *legally separated* after the separation agreement is approved but before the divorce is finalized. In other states, separation is not recognized as a distinct legal status — the couple merely remains married and living apart until the divorce is finalized. In many states, even when the divorce is uncontested and the judge has granted the divorce, a waiting period must elapse before the divorce is final.

Early in the divorce process, one of the parties may file a motion requesting *temporary orders for relief.* Relief here refers to the correcting of any conditions that urgently need addressing: which spouse will live in the house for now, where the children will stay and how they will be cared for, who will pay what to whom. The court will then issue orders calling for a temporary parenting plan or child support payment. Sometimes the two parties will jockey energetically to obtain temporary orders that are favorable. Why? Because "temporary" orders have a tendency to remain in place far longer than anticipated, often for months or even years.

The court system is notoriously torpid — repeated postponements and continuances occur, new motions and countermotions are filed, cases drag on. Arrangements established via the temporary orders, which judges may be reluctant to challenge, can often acquire their own inertia. The children, for example, can grow comfortable with a certain visitation schedule that may or may not be fair to both parents but that becomes entrenched by force of habit and then becomes "permanent."

In general, the less able the parties are to reach agreement, the longer the divorce process will go on. Cases sometimes drag on for years, only to end up being settled by trial. In such instances, the temporary orders usually remain in place for a very long time, and by the time the case gets scheduled for a trial, one or both of the parties have become seriously disenchanted with the arrangements. Emotions run high, anger soars, accusations fly. This is often a time at which clients seek counseling from professionals; in fact, this can be the primary Critical Entry Point — our first encounter with a new client. Waiting periods for trials tend to be substantially longer than those for simpler uncontested proceedings because trials consume a great deal more court and attorney time. So temporary orders tend to remain in place longer when the divorce is contested, adding heat to what is already a pressured situation.

During a divorce trial, both sides present witnesses and are able to cross-examine the other party's witnesses. The process varies from jurisdiction to jurisdiction. In most cases, a divorce trial is heard and ruled upon by a single judge. Judges can be quite idiosyncratic in their rules of procedure and judgments, which, again, is why wisdom urges that the two sides come to an agreement before setting foot in the courtroom. The outcome of any litigated case is far from certain. It is important for helpers to keep in mind that clients often feel out of control when they are approaching trial. They may sense, and with good justification, that their entire fate hangs on the whims of one person. Tensions run high and conflict within the family system generally increases as trial approaches. Arguments and confrontational incidents outside the courtroom often occur, seemingly unbidden, during this time.

When a helping professional hears reports of emotional blowups or increased sniping between the spouses, it is generally useful to ask what is happening on the legal front. Quite often, confrontational incidents coincide with court appearances. Once helpers recognize where the *real* source of tension lies, they help the client cope with the core issues and strategize more effectively.

❖ *Special Terms Relative to the Divorce Process*

The following situations, actions, and procedures may be encountered as clients proceed toward trial. These may have a strong effect on the client's mental/emotional status.

Discovery. Parties in divorce are entitled to disclosure of one another's financial status and any other information relevant to contested issues. To establish this, they usually go through a process called *discovery*. In discovery, both parties provide full statements of their finances — earnings, property, stock holdings, detailed budget, etc. — to each other. Preparing the financial statement is daunting work and can make clients feel quite helpless, panicky, and vulnerable. Issues of trust often come up, as the client must try to verify that the spouse is reporting his or her own financial situation honestly and accurately. The process of discovery can be a sobering revelation, especially if one's finances are more precarious (or salutary) than one thought. It can open a variety of psychological "cans of worms."

Interrogatories. As part of the discovery process, each party may provide a set of written questions for the other to answer regarding issues that could affect the divorce settlement. Spouses and/or their attorneys can sometimes use these interrogatories as devices whereby to attack, harass, or embarrass the ex or to seek inappropriately private information. As with many divorce tactics, the more probing and hostile one side's behavior, the more likely that the other side will respond in kind, sharpening the conflict and deepening the mistrust. Is this what the client really wants? Or would a more respectful approach be better for the emotional health of the whole family? We may wish to explore this with the client.

Deposition. A deposition is a formal meeting, usually held in an attorney's office, for the purpose of collecting sworn testimony before trial. Attorneys may depose witnesses and the parties to get an idea of what kind of testimony that person might provide should the case go to trial. The client may often choose whether or not to be present at the spouse's deposition. Sometimes clients who may be very eager to sit in at a spouse's deposition "so I can watch him squirm," can end up regretting their attendance. Helpers might want to explore such decisions with clients. It can be surprisingly difficult, emotionally, to watch one's spouse endure the focused grilling of a skilled attorney. Also, the client may learn things she does not wish to know about the spouse or may unintentionally exhibit emotional reactions. Are genuinely productive goals going to be achieved by the client's attendance? It is advisable to ask the question.

Pretrial conference. Prior to trial — usually fairly close to the trial date — a conference is often held in which both clients and their attorneys (if the clients have attorneys) meet with the judge to discuss disputed issues and to determine which issues need to be addressed at trial. Often the judge or a court officer will attempt to mediate the areas of disagreement. The judge may also offer suggestions or hint at his inclinations as to possible rulings. Anxiety and hostility between the parties may increase to a new level as a pre-trial conference approaches during the time period between the pretrial conference and the trial itself.

Subpoena. This is a legal request to produce information or to appear in person to provide testimony. A subpoena is usually served by a legal authority. *How* a subpoena is served — often by a sheriff, police officer, or constable — can alone produce great anxiety in its recipient. Either litigant, the plaintiff or the respondent, may subpoena the other spouse to a deposition or to the courtroom as a witness. Records may also be subpoenaed for the other side to view. Helping professionals need to be aware that they themselves and/or their client records may be subpoenaed to a deposition or trial. We will discuss this further in chapter 10.

Order to vacate the marital home. When neither spouse is willing to move out of the home after a divorce action has been initiated, one party may ask the court to order the other to vacate. Sometime the order to vacate is served on a party with no warning. This kind of "surprise attack" can lead to what Johnston and Campbell (1988) call "traumatic separation." Being ordered unexpectedly (often by an armed officer) to abandon one's home has a primal emotional effect on almost any human being and provokes enormous resentment, defensiveness, and desire for counterattack. Whether the client is the cause or recipient of such an action, it is bound to create shock waves in the family that we will need to deal with in our practice.

Restraining orders. A restraining order is an order of the court that legally restrains a party from taking a specific action, such as using marital assets or taking the children out of state. When lay people refer to restraining orders, they usually mean one particular type, the *abuse prevention order* or *stay away order*. In most states, an allegedly abused party can ask the court to issue an order demanding that the alleged abuser vacate the marital home and remain a certain distance away from her and/or the marital home.

Abuse prevention orders are usually issued temporarily, pending a court hearing. However, in some states — and this is important — the usual rules of evidence do not apply at the hearing. Orders may be extended, or prolonged indefinitely, without a full investigation of a case. This means that, while abuse prevention orders can be an indispensable tool for the abused, they can also be misused. Stay away orders can be issued based on spurious accusations or one-time/minor incidents that do not represent a genuine danger to the family. Often such orders prevent the restrained parent from having any contact whatsoever with the children. The orders can remain in effect for months, causing the children to become estranged from that parent and to internalize feelings of fear about the parent that may be unjustified. While this may seem to be a victory of sorts to the parent who remains in the home, this kind of situation can be extremely damaging to the children in the long run as it hinders their maintaining relationships with both parents. Helpers can ask clients whether it serves their children to institutionalize such estrangement via a restraining order.

In some cases, restraining orders can be modified in court to allow for some level of parental contact. Here a little research on the helper's part may provide useful information to the client. In some states, for example, both the district court and the family court can issue restraining orders, but only the latter can issue *modified* restraining orders that allow for some kind of ongoing contact between the children and the vacated parent.

Contempt of court actions. *Contempt of court* refers to the deliberate interference with court procedures or the refusal to obey a court order. It is mentioned here because contempt of court charges often become the weapon of choice for ex-spouses in high-conflict divorces. Either before or after the divorce decree has been granted, one party may bring a contempt action against the other when he believes that the other has disobeyed a court order. The contempt action becomes a lever to get the case back into court to request modifications to or enforcement of the separation agreement. High-conflict cases often involve mutual ongoing contempt actions.

The above events and processes occur commonly during adversarial divorces and can bring a great deal of stress into clients' lives. Fortunately, there are alternatives to litigation that are slowly gaining acceptance and popularity.

❖ *Alternatives to Litigated Divorce*

Alternative dispute resolution, sometimes called ADR, tends to generate less conflict and, accordingly, less expense than litigation. When ADR is employed, clients are generally happier with the outcome and more likely to comply with the agreements (Kelly, 1996). Not surprisingly, people feel more ownership of agreements that they helped author themselves than those imposed upon them by outside authorities. Research also indicates that both parents are more likely to remain actively involved with their children in divorces that are settled without litigation. When cooperative divorce strategies are used, there is far less alienation of one parent by another through hostile or retaliatory actions.

There are three main avenues for resolving divorce issues without litigation. These are Mediation, Arbitration, and Collaborative Law.

Mediation

Divorce Mediation is a process by which a neutral third-party professional (the mediator) works with both spouses in negotiating a divorce agreement, also known as a *marital separation agreement.* Mediation is usually a voluntary process, although some jurisdictions have mandatory mediation policies by which couples are required to sit down with a court officer or court-appointed mediator to try to reach settlement before proceeding with litigation.

The mediator is generally trained in divorce mediation and may be a lawyer, mental health professional, or lay person. If engaging in voluntary mediation, it is important that spouses choose a trained mediator who has good credentials and a substantial amount of experience specifically in *divorce* mediation. Some states award certification to mediators; others do not. In states where government certification does not exist, there may be a local association that sets up its own criteria for professionalism and awards its own certificates or endorsements.

Mediation is not therapy, although the process can have beneficial effects. Both parties tend to benefit by communicating with one another in a safe, neutral setting with an informed and neutral third party. Sometimes mediation can permit couples to confront their anger and pain and grow accustomed to conducting a business-like relationship with one another. Mediators can, and often do, suggest that their clients try therapeutic counseling to work through their more complex feelings and to separate their emotions from the business of the divorce.

Good candidates for mediation work are clients who are high functioning and reasonably mentally healthy, with no major personality issues. Articulate, mature, and empowered people are best able to participate fairly and effectively in the process. Mediation is *not* appropriate for couples in which there is an extreme power or intellectual imbalance. Clients who cannot advocate well for themselves or articulate their thoughts clearly will probably not have their needs met through mediation.

This has led many mental health professionals to conclude that mediation is inappropriate, as a rule, in cases where domestic violence has occurred. I do not necessarily agree; I recommend a case-by-case approach. Certainly if there has been domestic violence, it is crucial that the client feel safe and empowered in the mediation setting. The client must be ensured that safeguards will be in place such that she does not feel pressured to accept a settlement that is undesirable. If in doubt, the client may be better served by another process. The main issue is empowerment: can both parties feel fully empowered in the same room together? Some types of domestic abuse, as we have seen, involve a systematic disempowerment of one spouse by another. In such cases mediation would be inappropriate. Other forms of abuse, as we have also seen, may be minor or one-time flare-ups that do not compromise the efficacy of the client.

Mediators often advise their clients to retain their own legal counsel on the sidelines. In this way, another trained observer is available to provide advice, help evaluate alternatives, and assess whether an appropriate settlement has been reached.

Arbitration

Mediation and *arbitration* are terms that are sometimes confused. Mediators differ from arbitrators in that the former work in an open, cooperative manner with the two disputing parties, assisting them with finding agreement on their own. An arbitrator listens to both sides of a case and then issues a decision (arbitrament). Arbitration, as well as mediation, can sometimes be used in divorce cases. Couples may agree to submit certain aspects of their separation agreement to arbitration when they are unable to reach consensus but still wish to avoid a costly and bitter court trial. Typically arbitration is used to settle financial disputes but not to resolve child custody matters.

Collaborative law

Collaborative Law is a relatively new practice that represents a potential paradigm shift in the legal handling of divorce. Attorneys for both parties, rather than a single mediator, are hired as negotiators, but the very first agreement that the parties make is that they will not litigate. Rather, the terms of the divorce will be reached by a cooperative, respectful out-of-court process. All four parties — the two clients and their two lawyers — sit down together to negotiate. Neutral experts such as accountants, appraisers, and child mental health specialists may be brought in as consultants to both parties.

The engine that drives collaborative law is the contract between the attorneys and their respective clients that states that the attorneys will withdraw from the case should the parties fail to reach an agreement. Thus, if litigation becomes necessary, all work done by the lawyers during the collaborative process — all testimony, all correspondence — becomes inadmissible in court and new attorneys must be hired. This means that neither collaborative lawyer has a built-in conflict of interest. Neither has anything to gain by allowing the case to devolve into litigation; rather, both have something to lose. This unique operating position gives the lawyers a strong incentive to negotiate a resolution.

Another purported advantage of collaborative law is that it encourages lawyers to use skills that are not usually maximized in the litigation arena. Solving problems through logical reasoning, offering creative financial options, and analyzing the future consequences of decisions are just a few of these skills. Proponents of collaborative law are quick to point out, as noted earlier, that the vast majority of divorce cases — some ninety-five to ninety-seven percent — never reach the trial stage. But in a great many of the cases that are settled out of court, the negotiated agreement comes only after protracted months of legal posturing and wrangling that drains its participants both financially and emotionally. Collaborative law aims to bypass the "warfare" stage while maintaining strong legal advocacy for each client. When handled well, the collaborative law process is a classic "win/win" situation in which clients retain their emotional well-being and come away with an agreement that serves all members of the family.

The marital separation agreement

Whether the ex-partners elect to work cooperatively through the divorce process or travel a more litigious route, the goal of all of the legal maneuvering is, once again, to arrive at a *marital separation agreement*, also known as a *divorce agreement* or *settlement agreement* that spells out the rules by which the ex-couple will live in the future. Specifically, these rules revolve around the care and custody of the children and the allocation of the financial assets. In many jurisdictions the agreement may serve as the basis for a legal separation and subsequently a divorce. In others, couples do not generally obtain a legal separation, but the marital separation agreement, once it is established, becomes the basis for the couple's interactions until such a time as it becomes part of the divorce decree. If a couple does not agree on the marital separation agreement, the parties will need to go to trial and have the court determine the parameters of the divorce judgment. Some of the main concepts encountered in marital separation agreements are

Custody. This term refers to the care and guardianship of the children following the divorce. There are two types of custody:

* Legal custody — The legal authority to make decisions for the children. It includes the right to access all relevant records and documents.
* Physical custody — The primary day-to-day care and housing of the children.

It is important to know which of the above types of custody is being discussed in any instance where the term is used. The same parent can have both legal and physical custody, but in many cases legal and physical custody arrangements differ. Either kind of custody can be sole (resting with one parent) or joint (resting with both). In the case of joint physical custody, the time allotment for each parent approaches relative equality but is not necessarily a 50/50 split in time.

Legal *presumptions* as to the awarding of custody have evolved over time, as noted in an earlier chapter, and vary somewhat from one jurisdiction to another. In most cases there is a presumption, or established legal tendency, toward awarding joint *legal* custody to both parents, with primary *physical* custody being awarded to the parent who has thus far assumed the dominant parenting role. This is a "rebuttable" presumption, i.e., subject to arguments for or against it from either side. In recent years, a few states have modified their statutes toward a presumption of joint physical custody. Fathers' rights groups in the United States and several other countries are lobbying for widespread establishment of this precedent.

Parenting plan. Described in chapter 7 (Parenting and Divorce), this is a written schedule of which parent has the children at which times that is generally included in the marital separation agreement. It includes provisions for vacations, holidays, and special events and frequently includes provisions of expense sharing, medical and educational decisions, and other issues that are bound to come up in the lives of the children. The higher the level of conflict between the parents, the greater the need for specificity in the plan.

Child support. Child support is money paid by one parent to the other specifically to the support the children. There has been a tendency in recent years toward standardization; however, child support guidelines and policies vary widely from state to state. In some states an "income shares" model is used. The incomes of both parents are weighed and a table is then applied to determine child support. In other states only the income of the party *paying* child support is considered.

An important point to remember is that the amount of child support is usually linked to the custody arrangement. In most cases, money is paid to the primary physical custodian by the noncustodial parent. In the case of shared physical custody, the parent with substantially greater income typically pays money to the other parent to create a more equitable distribution of support funds. And so, parents' competition for primary physical custody of the children is often inextricably tied to the financial negotiations. A counselor needs to be aware of this conundrum to better help parents sort out what is best for the children.

Spousal support. *Spousal support*, or *alimony*, is money paid by one partner to the other for adult living support. It is distinct and separate from child support. Usually the ex-partner with greater income pays money to the ex-partner with less. The awarding of alimony has not been standardized and is still largely in the hands of individual courts. A variety of factors may be weighed by a judge: the ability of each spouse to earn money; the duration of the marriage; the age and health of the ex-partners; the behavior of the spouses (e.g., infidelity, abuse, etc.); the previous "dependency" of one spouse on the other. As with most matters of divorce law, the awarding of alimony varies substantially from state to state. In some states alimony is ordered for a limited period of time; in other states it can go on indefinitely.

Helping professionals who wish to get a true sense of their clients' financial status after divorce should be aware that alimony and child support are reported differently on the recipient's tax return. Alimony is generally *taxable income* for the recipient, but *tax deductible* for the payer. Child support, on the other hand, is nontaxable for the recipient and nondeductible for the payer. As tax law has a way of changing with the political winds, it is helpful for clients to consult a tax professional for current information regarding state and federal law. There is often a great deal of negotiating between divorcing partners as to how much money will be paid as child support and how much as alimony. How the money is allocated in the separation agreement can make a substantial difference in actual dollars in hand. When a client complains about how much she pays or how little she receives in child support, it can be enlightening to ask how much the alimony payment is.

Frequently, both ex-partners feel cheated in the postdivorce financial arrangements and, to a certain extent, both are probably justified in their feelings. After all, income that was previously consolidated in one household is now being spread out to support two. The math speaks for itself.

❖ Parenting Disputes

Disputes between divorcing parents can be very difficult to resolve, especially when emotions are at an all-time high because of the trauma of the separation and the vicissitudes of negotiating the separation agreement. For some, the controversy centers around the parenting plan; for others, controversies arise as the parents need to communicate about various smaller issues regarding the children. In high-conflict divorces, parents may have difficulty in both arenas. The following professionals may assist parents to resolve their disputes.

Child custody evaluator, custody investigator, guardian **ad litem,** *or law guardian.* When custody is disputed, the judge will often appoint a special third party to evaluate the situation and, in some cases, make recommendations to the court. The title, qualifications, and precise responsibilities of this appointed individual vary from state to state. In general, the role is one of evaluating and reporting to the court what is best for the child, in keeping with the so-called "best interest standard." Unfortunately, this "standard" is far from standardized and is subject to a wide range of interpretations. There is ever-evolving *legal precedent* in various jurisdictions as to what constitutes the best interest of children. The report of the child custody evaluator may or may not contain recommendations regarding custody and parenting plan arrangements. While undergoing a custody evaluation, it is common for parents to feel that their life is under a microscope. Clients will often become anxious and may need coaching about how to respond to a custody evaluator. It is also not uncommon for conflicts between divorcing couples to heighten during a custody dispute. Helpers can support their clients to manage their anxiety and their anger so as to respond appropriately to their ex-spouses and their children.

Parenting coordinator (PC). This role is relatively new and goes by various names in various locations, i.e., *special master, custody commissioner, parenting referee,* and in one jurisdiction, *wise person.* The parenting coordinator is a trained professional — sometimes an attorney, often a mental health professional — who assists parents to resolve ongoing disputes about parenting. The PC generally plays a mediation/arbitration role and attempts to mediate disputes but also has the power to render decisions that are binding upon the parties, subject to revision by the court. A parenting coordinator may be appointed by the court or may be hired voluntarily by the parents. The appointment of the PC can be a Critical Entry Point in a family's divorce drama. A PC essentially helps both parents manage ongoing disputes such as where the children will spend summers and holidays and monitors the implementation of the parenting plan. The PC may also do the following, depending on the parameters of the PC's appointment and contract:

- ❖ Teach basic anger management, communication, coping, and negotiation skills as related to parenting.
- ❖ Educate parents about the impact of conflict on the children.
- ❖ Monitor potential counseling needs of all family members and make referrals as necessary.
- ❖ Identify communication impasses and devise strategies for resolving same.
- ❖ Identify signs of parental alienation and intervene as needed.
- ❖ Monitor potential negative impact of parental behaviors, such as substance abuse or sexual promiscuity, on the children.
- ❖ Assess, at least informally, the emotional and physical needs of each child.
- ❖ Monitor visitation arrangements and modify these as necessary.
- ❖ Observe parental effectiveness and teach new parenting skills (or make referrals for this purpose) as needed.

Voluntary use of a parenting coordinator can greatly reduce conflict and financial expense for ex-partners who might otherwise tend to engage in ongoing litigation to resolve parenting issues. For the practicing helping professional, the PC role offers a new and challenging way to play a vital role with divorcing families. We must be careful about stepping into this role, however, if we already have a relationship with any of the players. We will discuss this type of potential conflict more in the next chapter.

Divorce coach. As divorces have become increasingly common, so too has another new role for helping professionals — divorce coaching. Divorce coaches are helping professionals who specialize in assisting clients and/or their lawyers to navigate the divorce process and to reach settlements. Divorce coaches are sometimes employed as consultants to the parties in the process of a collaborative law negotiation. In other cases, the coach may be employed by individuals who want assistance managing their divorce. Issues for the divorce coach may include many of the topics included in this book, such as helping clients to

- ❖ learn positive parenting skills
- ❖ deal with their ex-partners
- ❖ cope with difficult litigation
- ❖ manage anger, grief, and frustration
- ❖ find a balance between engaging in the divorce process and getting on with life
- ❖ prepare for a custody evaluation
- ❖ maintain emotional balance through the divorce process.

❖ *Some General Principles*

When working with clients as they manage the various legal aspects of divorce, here are a few helpful points to keep in mind.

Discourage "surprise attacks." One the greatest avoidable triggers of conflict in divorce proceedings is the "surprise attack," the serving of legal papers without warning or preparation. When a person receives divorce papers, a restraining order (in the absence of abuse), or an order to vacate the home out of the blue, her first reaction is usually shock, fear, and extreme defensiveness. There is a strong tendency to launch a counterattack on the party responsible. In the vast majority of cases, unwelcome surprises escalate the level of conflict and have a harmful effect, if only indirectly, on the children. We are wise to work with our clients to fully consider (1) whether the proposed legal action is indeed necessary, and (2) whether and how the spouse should be informed of the legal action beforehand. Sometimes serving papers without warning is absolutely appropriate, as in the case where a dangerous abuser is dominating the household or there is reason to believe that the spouse will hide joint assets. But in many cases, the client has not fully thought out the consequences of a "surprise attack" or is deliberately trying to commit a provocative act.

Help the client evaluate the pros and cons of both litigious and nonlitigious approaches to divorce resolution. Often a client heads down a particular path, such as hiring a "shark" lawyer, because he is not fully aware of the alternatives. At such a Critical Entry Point, mediation and collaborative law can offer viable alternatives to the inimical divorce process. The more we know as helpers about the legal resources in our community and the reputations and styles of the local players, the better range of meaningful options we can discuss with the client.

Know what is happening in the client's particular legal process and be aware of how this can impact her emotional life. A sudden increase in interspousal conflict, depression, or anxiety can often signal an upcoming court date. By being aware of the timetable of events in the legal process, we can help the client prepare for emotionally trying times and avoid unnecessary blowups. We can help the client to time actions in a way that is most propitious. Calling the ex-husband to talk about Johnny's grades, for example, may not be well advised on the eve of a court hearing.

Become aware of the legal processes and procedures in your jurisdiction. As we have seen, divorce proceedings can vary not only from state to state but from courthouse to courthouse. The more we know about the legal system in our area, the more credible support we can offer the client. One excellent way to learn more about the process and its players is to sit in on divorce court. In many jurisdictions, divorce court is open to the public. A great deal can be learned just by sitting in and observing divorce proceedings for an hour or two per week.

Empower the client in his or her dealings with the other players in the divorce process. Divorce is a demoralizing process that can sap a person's self-esteem and leave him vulnerable to being led in unwanted directions by a powerful personality or to behaving in self-defeating ways. For instance, clients often go along with a lawyer's recommendations simply because "he's the expert." We can try to bolster the client's sense of empowerment and remind him that he has the right to ask questions and to ask the attorney to advocate for his needs. In cases when a client is dealing with a guardian *ad litem* or a parenting coordinator, we can help him assess how to most productively interact with these individuals.

Chapter Nine Key Points

- ❖ Get to know the legal process in your jurisdiction.
- ❖ Become familiar with the local "players."
- ❖ Note the interplay between a client's emotional life and legal events.
- ❖ Discourage overly aggressive legal actions and "surprise attacks."
- ❖ Be aware of the alternatives to a litigated divorce.
- ❖ Encourage assertive interactions with the legal system and players.

11

Avoiding the Traps

Most of the book has dealt with how to help *clients;* this chapter is dedicated to helping the working professional. Many intelligent, well-meaning and otherwise conscientious practitioners find themselves in legal and ethical hot water due to common traps that emerge when dealing with divorcing clients. Divorce, especially high-conflict divorce, tends to create more danger zones for therapists and other counseling professionals than most other therapeutic situations. There are many reasons for this, some of which we have touched on before:

- ❖ **Divorce is an adversarial arena.** The parties with whom you're dealing have something vitally important to gain or lose, such as the custody of their children, child support, or their home. Because of they have intimate knowledge about one or more members of the family, helping professionals are often perceived - and often *rightfully* so — as possessing valuable information and/or insights that could sway decisions one way or another. Attorneys and/or their clients may believe they have something to gain from various helpers — information, recommendations, allegiance, etc. — and may try to pressure or manipulate a professional to take their side.
- ❖ **Clients are extremely needy during divorce.** Divorcing clients are in life crisis and have often regressed to abnormal states of dependency. They frequently seize upon a professional to offer a helping hand. Once they discover helpers to be trustworthy and competent, clients often begin to depend upon us to advocate for them. Clients can

play into helpers' vulnerabilities and seduce the
professional into stepping out of the boundaries dictated
by professional ethics.

❖ **Professionals can easily buy into the drama and lose
objectivity.** When abuse, neglect and infidelity accusations
fly, our personal and political "hot buttons" may be
pushed. Helpers may reflexively leap to a client's aid and
defense without sufficiently probing into the facts. Too
often, professionals become protective advocates and lose
objectivity.

❖ **Other professionals often do not know the rules of
ethical conduct which guide the various helping
professions.** Lawyers or court personnel can pressure us
to divulge information and provide opinions because they
may not understand (or respect) particular profession's
rules of confidentiality and privilege. When helpers
themselves are not completely clear about these matters, it
is easy for them to default to the opinions or the requests
of others and violate ethical obligations.

❖ **Professional courtesy becomes overextended.** Divorce
proceedings often bring helpling professionals into contact
with many outside professionals. These may be respected
colleagues — lawyers, child custody evaluators, court
personnel, fellow counselors — with whom we have
frequent dealings and form peer relationships or friendships.
When professional favors and courtesies are exchanged, it
is surprisingly easy to "leak" a piece of confidential
information in the interest of being a helpful colleague, or
to readjust one's professional objectivity to accommodate
the case or viewpoint of a friendly professional peer.

❖ **Family constellations change during divorce.** Sometimes
professional relationships need to change along with changing
family structures. For example, a therapist may have been
seeing a couple for counseling and is suddenly asked to see
one or both clients as individuals. Or perhaps a client seen
in individual counseling now asks the therapist to do some
family work. Changing roles pose inherent conflicts.

It is assumed that everyone reading this book already knows the general ethical and legal rules of his/her profession. This chapter will focus on those areas in which *divorce* counseling, in particular, can get the helping professional in trouble. The intent here is to help avoid common traps rather than provide an encyclopedia of professional ethics. I hope that at least some of the advice offered here is new. However, to the extent that the chapter restates information that is familiar, please just consider it a refresher course, a helpful reminder to stay sharp and to stay in bounds. Certain cautions are emphasized because, in my decades of experience dealing with professionals in the divorce field, I have seen professionals repeatedly commit certain types of gaffes.

What Hat Are You Wearing?

One of the most common and fundamental mistakes that helping professionals make when working with divorcing clients is role ambiguity. It is easy to lose sight of who your client is and what role you are committed to playing with that client. This can happen if you are coaxed into seeing more than one member of the family or into playing additional official roles, such as parenting coordinator or child custody evaluator, which are inappropriate given your previous role. In other cases — and perhaps this is where the greatest danger lies — professionals may be lulled into playing new roles, but in an unofficial or unacknowledged way.

Clients, especially in high-conflict divorces, are feeling desperate and can pull at helping professionals in a multitude of ways. They latch onto you as trusted allies, tell you how indispensable you are to them, shower you with their needs, and then start to ask more and more from you. Many helpers are vulnerable to such requests; perhaps you entered your chosen profession because it is your nature (and/or neurotic need — but that's another topic) to help people. When clients open up and proclaim their need, you may feel flattered and gratified on some level. Helpers generally enjoy being trusted confidants, protectors and rescuers. Most clients, however, do not fully understand professional boundaries, and so they often ask for help, such as legal advice, that are not within your purview.

It falls upon the professional to point out when a client attempts to cross a boundary line. But it can be difficult to enforce boundaries when a client's life is in turmoil and s/he is feeling extremely vulnerable and wounded.

It is important to be *very* cautious whenever you stray from the role you initially agreed to play with the client. Switching from a therapeutic role to an advisor, mediator, evaluator or parenting coordinator requires the forming of a new sort of relationship with the client, in which one provides an entirely different kind of feedback and is alert to a different set of concerns. In the vast majority of cases, switching hats is ill-advised because changing your role with a client is irreversible. Once you start playing the new role, there is no going back to the old one.

When you are asked to wear a new hat, it is an opportunity to reflect carefully on the nature of the *relationship* with the client. With divorcing clients, it is especially important not to proceed unconsciously or armed only with good intentions. If doing therapy with a client, for example, then *empowering* the client is a major component of that relationship. Switching to a new role which involves making recommendations or stating evaluative findings can destroy the therapeutic alliance with a client and weaken the original goal of aiding empowerment. Or, if you have played a role in which you have been evaluating (i.e. passing judgment on) family members, it can be tricky to then become a therapist to one of the clients, a role that calls for non-judgmental listening. In both cases, it would be impossible to resume the original role once you accepted the new one.

Helping professionals make mistakes in these matters with surprising frequency. Eager to help, they accept reframed roles without adequately anticipating the consequences. That is why ethical guidelines for most helping professions spell out clear rules regarding engaging in **dual relationships** with clients and engaging in new *types* of relationship with former clients. In general, the rule of thumb is to avoid doing so. Wear only one hat at a time and, in most cases, wear only one hat. This is a relatively easy call when it comes to entering business, personal or sexual relationships with a client. Most professionals know enough not to do this. But there is "wiggle room" in many divorce cases. Some roles that are closely related to one another or lie within the same professional arena may not be clearly classified as dual roles. Switching from an individual to a couple therapist or from a family therapist to a parenting coordinator, for example, would probably not be expressly forbidden in any ethical guidelines. Choosing to accept such a role change remains a judgment call. The easiest answer is usually to "just say no."

If a helping professional decides to consider accepting a new role relative to the client, the following steps can be taken:

1. **Personally evaluate the decision.** Before speaking to the client, carefully and personally weigh the pros and cons of accepting the new role, particularly insofar as it may affect your ongoing primary relationship with the client. What are the risks and benefits? Where are the ethical potholes? Getting advice from a supervisor or trusted colleague is a good idea. Before giving the client an answer or even discussing it with him/her, strive to be internally clear about what the potential treatment hazards might be.

2. **Discuss the risks and drawbacks candidly and clearly with the client.** Ensure that the client is fully aware of the potential downsides — including therapeutic implications — of your playing the new role. Clearly state your desire to be the best possible support you can be to the client. It is advisable to "bend over backwards" to explain the risks, because the client may marginalize or dismiss our admonitions. When unwanted circumstances develop later, the client may not recall having been fully apprised of the risks.

3. **If you decide to accept a new role, it is wise to:**
   ❖ **Seek and document professional consultation.**
   Seeking the advice of a knowledgeable senior professional helps to clarify the decision and demonstrates for the record that due diligence was employed as you undertook the new role.

❖ **Ask the client to sign a letter of consent and understanding.** Spell out in writing the risks and expectations (for both yourself and the client) involved in your accepting the new role, and provide a consent form for the client to sign.

❖ **Carefully document the decision.** Record in writing your reasons for making the decision, including why you think serious adverse effects for the client are unlikely or have been minimized, and what any benefits might be.

❖ **Monitor the situation.** For your own protection as well as the client's, you may wish to put your treatment concerns in writing and regularly note the status of these concerns.

Helping professionals are often asked to assume a new role because of their particular, intimate knowledge of the client and/or her family. A family therapist, for example, might seem like the most likely and most natural candidate to serve as a parenting coordinator. (Of course, this is not sufficient reason to accept a new role.) Many types of role switch can potentially occur. Here are a few to consider:

❖ **Couple to individual therapist.** In order to make this switch, you will need to acknowledge that seeing one party individually will most likely compromise your ability to maintain neutrality were you to then work with the couple again. An individual counselor will be likely to view the situation more fully through the lens of one party. Thus, you will want to terminate your role as couple therapist when individual work commences. If you decide to accept the new role, it is wise to obtain the permission of *both parties*, not just the individual you will be seeing.

❖ **Individual to couple therapist.** If you have been working with an individual and then agree to see the couple as a unit, you may lose the ability to provide vigorous support for your individual client. If your "client" is going to be the couple as a unit, does your current client fully understand what she is giving up as she agrees to go into couples work? Do you recognize the potential compromise of your ability to maintain neutrality? Also, it will take some catching up and alliance building with the other party in order to understand both parties' perspective and develop a neutral stance with regard to the couple. Not all couple consultations require helpers to alter their alliances. For example, a therapist may see the client and her spouse together for a few sessions with the stated purpose of helping her negotiate with her spouse. However, it becomes more complicated if the counselor agrees to continue to see the couple and the original client then requests an individual meeting. In such case, it would be useful to meet with both partners individually so as to maintain neutrality and the balance of power in the therapeutic relationship with the couple.

❖ **Individual or couple therapist to child custody evaluator.** This is clearly a dual role and thus a violation of the professional ethics of most mental health professions. As a therapist, you will have received confidential information from one or both parties. It is not possible to move into a role which requires you to be a neutral third party. In addition, as a child custody evaluator, there is the strong possibility of being called as a witness. Thus, the evaluator might be placed in the position of having to reveal intimate details of the clients' lives in court that would not normally be revealed as part of a custody evaluation. Finally, the evaluator's job is to render advice to the court as to what is in the best interest of the children, which may contradict the perceived best interest of the former client or clients. Such a possibility puts the professional at risk for an ethics board complaint by an angry disenfranchised client. Ethical implications aside, it is unlikely to be in any client's interest to experience a breach of trust with a therapist and may inhibit the client's willingness to seek needed help in the future.

❖ **Child custody evaluator to therapist.** Doing the reverse of the above does not introduce as many ethical dilemmas, but also tends to be ill-advised. In most cases, a client would probably not *want* you to switch from child custody evaluator to therapist unless you have viewed him favorably in your evaluation. However, if one or both ex-spouses did wish the professional to assume this new role, it would be necessary to build trust in order to assure your new client(s) that you are no longer playing the role of judgmental evaluator, but are now playing one of open and impartial listener. Switching from evaluator to therapist is another unidirectional move. Once you have elicited confidential information, you cannot then go back and use this information as the basis for further recommendations to the court. Thus, were the family in need of a child custody evaluator to re-enter a case at key points in the future, they would need to find a new person to assume the role.

❖ **Couple therapist to parenting coordinator (PC).** Can such a shift be made? Possibly, but, again, not without cost. Since the PC often makes decisions about how and where the children will spend their time, he/she will frequently present at least the *appearance* of choosing one parent over another, arousing anger and distrust in one or both clients. The clients also lose the benefit of having the therapist help them process the feedback of the PC in a non-judgmental way.

This is far from an exhaustive list of possible role changes, but it provides a taste of the types of concerns professionals need to examine. Anytime you shift from a therapeutic role to a role that requires impartiality, our knowledge of the underlying dynamics of the relationship can, and probably will, color that impartiality. If the new role involves making recommendations or rendering decisions, the professional's alliance with the client(s) is likely to be compromised. When the shift occurs in the opposite direction — from a decision-making role to a neutral-listening role — then establishing a trusting, non-judgmental, therapeutic environment often becomes a challenge.

Whenever professionals are asked to perform a new role on an official basis, we have the formal opportunity to assess the impact that role will have on our professional ethics and on ongoing relationship with the client(s). However, the toughest role challenges often occur *unofficially*. No one asks us to assume a new title or role; rather they ask the helper to provide services that involve switching roles on a *de facto* basis. An attorney asks for an "off the record" evaluation of a client as a parent. A client asks us to provide an opinion letter to the court, to act as a go-between with the ex-spouse, or to provide advice or professional referrals. In these cases, and many similar cases, our *actual* role with the client shifts, even though our title does not. Here is where caution is especially needed and where mistakes are often made. When we are eager to be good helpers, it is easy to step in and provide services that put us at risk professionally.

When requests to provide questionable services arise, it is often helpful to say something to this effect: "I want to be the best support I can possibly be to you as a therapist. How will [proving new service *x*] affect my ability to do that?" The professional then weighs the pros and cons, the risks and benefits, along with the client. In some cases, it is up to the helping professional alone to consider the implications of taking a specific action. If the client requests, for example, the name of a good divorce attorney, it probably does not make sense to simply provide a referral. If we decide to help with this request, it is far better to present the client with a *list* of attorneys. We can then take the opportunity to discuss each of the lawyers' unique approaches and reputations, with an eye toward letting the client decide which style of attorney best suits his/her needs. *Supporting the client in choosing*, rather than making the choice for them, is the key.

It is not uncommon for clients to ask for our testimony or for a written letter of opinion. Helping professionals can be clear with clients about the possible adverse consequences of this. For example, once we render an opinion, we may be subpoenaed and cross-examined by the opposing attorney, in which case all information learned through the therapeutic relationship might be introduced (see more on this below). Anytime we feel that we are doing something *for* the client, we are well advised to step back and take a fresh look.

❖ *Confidentiality and Privilege*

A crucial aspect of staying out of professional trouble is knowing our rights and responsibilities regarding confidentiality and privilege. Confidentiality and Privilege are closely-related terms that are often confused.

Confidentiality refers to the privacy with which we are required to treat all patient/client communications. **Privilege** is the legal analog of confidentiality and refers to the release of confidential information to the court or an agent of the court. For most helping professionals, the sharing of any information about a client must be approved by the client. This includes even acknowledging the fact that there is a professional relationship with that particular client. Any oral or written information pertaining to the client and his/her treatment is kept private, except under a few very specific conditions, which vary from state to state and from profession to profession. These conditions may include the need to report suspicions of child or elder abuse, the need to take action if the client is potentially harming him/herself, and the "duty to warn" if the client poses a risk to others.

The matter of privilege may be subject to different rules, particularly with regard to issues relating to child custody. It is important for professionals to be familiar with the laws that apply in their jurisdiction. In many states, a judge may order a mental health professional to testify in a custody hearing if s/he has information relevant to the competence of one or both parent. Jurisdictions may also vary with regard to protection of therapeutic information obtained from a child. Whereas, a custodial parent can normally release confidential information about a child, s/he may not be able to waive the child's therapeutic privilege. In Massachusetts, for instance, current case law requires the appointment of a guardian *ad litem* for the child to determine if it is in the child's interest to allow therapeutic information to be revealed in court or to a child custody evaluator who is considered an agent of the court.

When it comes to client information, a helping professional's default attitude is one of protectiveness and privacy. Assume that anyone asking for information is *not* entitled to it, unless and until the clients sign the appropriate release forms or unless the information is ordered to be released to the court. When treating adults or children of divorce, you may be approached by attorneys or others for confidential information. You are permitted neither to confirm nor to deny knowledge of the client nor provide information without the appropriate release forms signed by your client, or the custodial parent(s) if the client is a minor. If you have served as a couple or family therapist, you may not provide information about any of the parties without the permission of *all parties* or the court. Any information that arose during couple therapy is confidential information for both spouses. Of course, in adversarial cases, permission to divulge information may not be readily given by both parties.

As mentioned in chapter 8, when working with a child, it is good policy to be clear about who has legal custody of the child and to obtain a copy of the separation agreement if the custody status is unclear. It is safe practice to have both custodial parents (if indeed both are legal custodians) sign all releases of information pertaining to their children. This also maintains a sense of empowerment for both parents.

When third parties such as attorneys or child custody evalators pressure helpers to cross the lines of confidentiality and privilege, often we can educate them regarding your ethical rules and be firm about the importance of complying with these rules. In this way, we can maintain our clients' trust and preserve a safe and inviolate place for them to discuss their intimate life issues.

Anytime you have questions about divulging confidential/privileged information, you have the option of consulting a legal adviser who specializes in these matters. Most professional organizations have attorneys available for consultations.

Common Ways Helpers Interact with the Legal System

Because divorce is both a therapeutic and a legal matter, there are many "opportunities" for helpers to become ensnared in the legal proceedings. Some common examples of interface with the legal system are:

Requests by attorneys for information, consultation or records. Attorneys for clients sometimes wish to speak with professionals and seek opinions. It is often tempting to accede to these requests as a professional courtesy or service to the client. The safest route, however, is to recommend that the client communicate with the attorney directly. Our role with the client — to provide support in a safe and trusting environment — remains the primary consideration. By speaking to an attorney, even with the client's permission, professional helpers run the risk of losing the alliance with the client; your words may be misinterpreted or inappropriately relayed back to the client. In addition, you run the risk of placing yourself in a potential role conflict if you offer "advice" to the attorney about how to manage the client. If a client requests that the helper speak to his/her attorney, it may be useful to discuss with the client the purpose of the consultation, its pros and cons, and what is appropriate to communicate.

Requests for Written Opinions. Rendering written opinions is a dangerous and ill-advised practice for any helping professional. It is easy to lose perspective in the name of "helping" clients. Clients who ask for written opinions frequently do so because they are embroiled in conflict and want a helper to step in on their behalf. Seemingly competent professionals sometimes write the most egregiously biased letters on behalf of their clients. Whenever you write an opinion or recommendation letter, citing your professional title as the basis of your expertise, you run the risk of having the letter used in legal proceedings and/or of being subpoenaed to testify in court. If you feel it is appropriate to write a letter and have obtained the appropriate signed permission from your client, it is safest to state in writing only the facts you know first-hand, based on direct contact with the client. In addition, it is important to note that it is unethical to render opinions about individuals whom you have never met, or to render opinions about an individual that you are not professionally qualified to make.

In one case, mentioned in chapter 1, a pediatrician wrote a letter on behalf of a divorcing mother, whose children were his patients. Its message (not quoted directly) was similar to this:

I have been the pediatrician for the D. children. During the past two years the children have been seen for a variety of symptoms related to post traumatic stress disorder. I believe that Mrs. D is an abused woman and the children have been emotionally abused by their father. It would be in their interest to terminate contact with him.

A more appropriate letter, should there be good reason to write one at all, might read more like this:

I am the pediatrician for the D. children. I have seen the children for yearly check ups and sick visits over the last two years. The children have been accompanied to all visits by their mother. In July and August, 2005, Ms. D. brought the children to my office on eight occasions, due to difficulty sleeping, bad dreams, fatigue, and stomach aches. She reported to me that Mr. D. hit her on numerous occasions in front of the children. I am aware that Mr. and Mrs. D. are divorcing and I have referred the family for counseling.

In the case of the first letter above, three glaring errors have occurred: 1) the doctor was not a psychotherapist, thus not qualified to make a judgment about whether the children have post traumatic stress disorder, 2) the doctor had never met or spoken to the father, and 3) there was more than one possible explanation for the children's symptoms. The pediatrician soon came to regret his literary venture, as he was verbally dissected in court by the father's skilled attorney.

Whenever we supply *content* (facts, opinions, recommendations) to the court, we invite adversarial challenges and open the door for unpredictable and damaging actions that may affect our clients and their family members. We also open the door for ethical charges to be brought against us by an aggrieved party.

Subpoenas and testimony. Whenever a helper receives a subpoena — a written order directing him or her to appear in court or at a deposition hearing, or to surrender evidence such as a client's records — proceeding with caution is advisable. Failure to appear as directed by a subpoena may be considered contempt of court. However, a subpoena can only order a person to *appear;* it cannot compel the individual to provide testimony or information that violates the rules of confidentiality and privilege. A subpoena does not trump legal principles of confidentiality and privilege. If subpoenaed, you should first verify that the subpoena is valid and that it has been served in a legally appropriate fashion. Here again, knowing state laws and/or seeking legal consultation is useful.

Once subpoenaed, professionals may wish to contact the issuing attorney to discuss the situation. It is useful to emphasize that when you testify in court you are open to cross-examination and refutation by the opposing attorney(s). This can often be damaging to the client. In addition, you can explain the limits of confidentiality as well as your restriction to testifying only to what you have observed or heard from your client. Often when the limits of the testimony are carefully explained, the attorney will decide that the appearance is not necessary.

One of the first things you may wish to ask the attorney is whether you are being asked to appear as a *lay (fact)* witness or an *expert* witness. When appearing as a lay witness, professionals must stick only to observable, quantifiable facts. In such a case you should make it clear that all you can do is state that you saw the client, the dates on which those sessions occurred (assuming that the appropriate release has been signed by the client), what the client said and/or what you observed. If asked to render an *opinion,* as a professional you should point out that you will now be appearing as an expert witness, that is, one whose specialized experience and training qualifies one to render an opinion about the facts. In this case, you are entitled to compensation, since providing expert testimony is a paid professional service.

In general it is advisable for mental health professionals to avoid confusion about compensation by including a statement about being paid for time at deposition or in court in the written fee agreements given to clients at the beginning of treatment. When attorneys understand that compensation is due to the professional according to contract, they sometimes back off. At the very least, if the professional is asked to testify, compensation can be collected for court preparation time as well as time in court. The following wording may be useful in professional service contracts with divorcing clients or family members:

> *If you become involved in legal proceedings that require my participation, you will be expected to pay for all of my professional time, including preparation and transportation costs, even if I am called to testify by another party. Because of the complexity of legal involvement, I charge $XXX per hour for preparation for and attendance at any legal proceeding.*

Helping professionals may be subpoenaed to appear either: 1) in court or 2) at a sworn deposition hearing. The latter usually takes place in an attorney's office. Its purpose is to discover what kind of testimony an individual might provide at trial and to put the testimony on record in case it differs at trial. In either setting, you may be questioned by attorneys about your background, training and experience. This is done with the intention of bolstering, or detracting from, your credibility. It may feel like a hostile exercise and you would do well to be prepared for such. It is usually best to answer briefly and concretely and to respond only to what is asked. It can also be useful to be accompanied by your own counsel.

As a general rule, whenever asked to testify, render written opinions, or share confidential information with the court, an attorney, a GAL or anyone else, the helper may want to discuss with the client what will likely be said during such testimony. The professional who is asked by a *client* to provide information should not assume that the client fully understands the possible ramifications of such a request. In the vast majority of cases, it is not in the best interest of the therapeutic relationship for the helper to provide testimony or expert opinions. Helpers can point out to clients the potential risks to the relationship that can occur via testimony. The overriding focus needs to be preserving a safe and trusting relationship with the client.

❖ *Tips for Staying out of Trouble*

Well intentioned professionals can dig substantial holes for themselves. Potential trouble can be avoided by observing the following simple practices, adapted from Berkowitz (1993). Some of these have been mentioned previously but bear repeating.

❖ **Maintain a Mixed Record.** If you are seeing, or have seen, more than one member of a family or couple, keep all of their records together in the same file, listed under *all* of their names. The simple step of creating a mixed record makes it much more difficult for either party alone, or any outside parties, to gain unwanted access to the files. The record now belongs not only to Client X but also to Client Y. Both parties, or in some cases three or more parties, must now give permission for anyone to access the records. In a custody dispute, for example, one parent cannot release a record involving more that one party to an attorney or waive the privilege for a mixed record to be reviewed in court.

❖ **Avoid legal alliances.** It is rarely wise to ally with attorneys. Though in broad strokes, you may both be "on the client's side" (or not), the client's therapeutic interests and legal interests may, in the end, be at odds with one another. Unless you have been hired by an attorney as a consultant whose job is to provide expert testimony or evaluative services, you should probably question why you are talking to an attorney at all. It is best to refer the attorney to the client directly or to meet jointly with the client and the attorney if you and your client agree that this is in the client's interest.

❖ **Avoid providing legal advice.** Even in situations where you have considerable knowledge of the law or extensive experience with a particular legal issue, do not fall into the trap of providing feedback that might be construed as legal advice. Refer clients to an attorney and take the added step of documenting the client's request for legal advice and your refusal to provide it.

❖ **Insist upon signed releases.** Again, always operate under the assumption that *anyone* requesting client information is *not* entitled to it. In this way you will not accidentally breach confidentiality. "Loose lips" not only sink ships, they sink careers. In order to communicate about the client with any third party, including court personnel and state social service agencies, first ask the client to sign a release of information form specific to that party. Make sure that the release of information is in writing to avoid later controversy about whether or not the client gave consent.

❖ **Do not write letters of opinion.** It is not usually your role, as a helping professional, to make recommendations in matters of custody and visitation. There are set procedures for conducting custody evaluations and specific professionals who are trained to do this job. In most cases, you do not have the whole picture and thus are not in a position to give fully informed opinions. Writing letters that recommend a particular custody arrangement may well be a violation of your professional code of ethics. Above all, *never* render an opinion about someone you have not met.

❖ **Clearly outline the limits of your knowledge and remain within those limits.** If you choose to provide testimony or cannot avoid doing so, be very explicit about the limits within which you can testify. Stick to the empirical data available to you directly and do not offer conjecture or supposition. If you have seen only the mother as a client, for example, you cannot testify about other family members. You may make statements such as, "I have only seen the mother and cannot comment on the daughter," or, "The mother has maintained [x] about the father, but I have not met the father nor have I directly observed him with the children."

❖ **Be cautious with acquired client records.** When records of past treatment, casework and/or hospitalization become part of your client record, they are best handled with caution. In some cases, the information contained therein may not be shared with the client. Usually, if this is the case, a warning is stamped on the paperwork, but extreme caution should be used in sharing material in any inherited records. It is also inadvisable to accept as fact anything that appears in a past record. With alarming frequency, hearsay information and gross inaccuracies make their way into clients' records and, from there, into courtrooms. If there is ever cause to reveal information from past records, always make sure it is legally permissible for you to do so and that you have attributed the information to the source from which you received it, i.e. "According to records from Glendale State Hospital, [client] served in the U.S. Army from 1987-89."

❖ **Seek legal consultation.** Whenever you are unsure about providing any kind of information to anyone about the client, get a legal stamp of approval and then document that you have done so in the client record.

Chapter Ten Key Points

- ❖ Be clear as to what role you are playing with the client.
- ❖ Play only one role.
- ❖ Be wary about switching roles.
- ❖ Protect the client relationship whenever possible.
- ❖ Know the rules about confidentiality and privilege in your jurisdiction.
- ❖ Be wary of rendering opinions when you do not have all the facts.
- ❖ Be cautious about speaking with clients' attorneys.
- ❖ Observe the boundaries of your professional ethics.
- ❖ Seek legal consultation when unsure how to handle a situation.

A Final Word

Divorce is a province in which pain can be caused by lack of awareness. Clients who do not know all of their available options or who have not been helped to see the likely consequences of their actions can make disastrous decisions. Helpers who know too little about the legal and emotional processes of divorce or about related issues such as domestic abuse, parenting, and child custody can miss opportunities to provide a simple intervention that might steer the entire divorce process in a healthy direction. When it comes to divorce, a single ill-informed decision — hiring the wrong attorney, serving divorce papers in a careless manner, filing a questionable restraining order — can trigger years of unnecessary conflict and acrimony. Attacks beget bigger counterattacks, and the entire process can degenerate into an unseemly contest in which the biggest losers are the children. *Divorce doesn't have to be that way.*

This book is a plea for greater awareness. I believe that, armed with the proper information and insight, most helpers and most clients will make the right choices. If we can effectively communicate to divorcing parents, for example, that conflict is the most damaging factor for children in the postdivorce environment, the majority will try to avert stress for their children. If we can discuss the painful consequences of hostile and retaliatory actions, many of our clients will reconsider. We have the opportunity and privilege as counseling professionals to expand clients' awareness, to help them consider their actions and their options.

Of course, to accomplish these goals, we must expand our own awareness. While we may not need to know how to fly a plane to work with a client who is an airline pilot, we do need some knowledge about the ins and outs of divorce to work with divorcing clients. The more we know about the legal system and its players, parenting plans, domestic abuse, community support resources, child care options, parenting skills, alternatives to litigation, and the dozens of other related subjects that affect the lives and choices of divorcing clients, the more we can make wise interventions at Critical Entry Points.

We can also expand our awareness regarding our own skills. There are a few key approaches that helpers can learn, which, if practiced consistently, will aid our clients' long-term success and avert negative outcomes. We have talked about these, but they bear repeating. One of these is to take the big picture approach, as opposed to blindly advocating for our client. Stepping back and looking at the needs of the entire family system will ultimately benefit both the client and the family. The solution that promotes the greatest level of peace for the greatest number of people is usually the best one, though it is not necessarily the solution that feels the most emotionally gratifying in the moment. A shortsighted, win-the-battle perspective often prolongs the war or results in unforeseen casualties.

Another vital approach is to focus on the client's mental and emotional health *at the present moment.* Clients are often devastated by divorce and are at the lowest point in their emotional lives. And yet this is a time at which they must make some of life's most crucial decisions. Clients frequently come to us contemplating a major move of some kind — leaving the home, kicking out the spouse, filing divorce papers, — but their judgment is compromised because of their emotional state. When Critical Entry Points arise, we can be the trained and compassionate voice that argues for the clients' well-being above all, making sure that they become healthy *first* and make life-shaping decisions *later.*

We cannot become experts overnight on the panoply of skills that the perfect divorce counselor should possess. But increasing our awareness by just a small degree about good boundaries, coping skills, confidentiality concerns, the grieving process, empowerment, child development, and communications skills will *vastly* improve our effectiveness with clients. Every small increase in awareness has potential payoffs for the individuals and families in our practices.

Divorce can be a minefield. We cannot hope to cross it safely, nor help our clients to cross it, unless we have some idea where the mines lie.

I hope this book has succeeded in increasing awareness. I have kept its size and scope limited, its theory and research aspects minimal, and its language accessible so that working professionals might actually *use* its insights rather than file it on the shelf alongside more theoretical tomes. I sincerely hope that you have found the book useful or enlightening in some small way. This volume has grown out of my own practice and was not designed to be encyclopedic, academic, or definitive; it is an invitation to further learning and exploration.

And further learning is indeed sorely needed, for all of us, at all levels of the helping professions — therapists, nurses, guidance counselors, clergy, social workers, mental health workers, pediatricians. Divorce affects about half of all marriages in the United States. If we were to survey a typical high school classroom today, we might find that the statistics were even starker — children who come from single, intact, two-parent families seem to be in the distinct minority in many communities. Divorce is all around us; it is not a "fringe" phenomenon but a mainstream concern. Families in virtually every neighborhood in America are being hurt emotionally as the result of divorce decisions that could have been handled more thoughtfully.

Divorce is painful under the best of circumstances, but when added suffering is caused by lack of information and understanding on the part of helpers, that is truly tragic. We in the helping professions can take the lead in broadening awareness, not only in ourselves and our clients but in our culture at large. We can advance a new model for the divorce process, one that puts the needs of the whole family first, one that is respectful, growth oriented, peaceful, intelligent, and, dare I say, *kind*.

I hope this book will play a small role in that evolution.

Bibliography

Alberti, R.E. & Emmons, M.L. (2001). *Your perfect right: Assertiveness and equality in your life and relationships* (eighth edition). Atascadero, CA: Impact Publishers.

Ahrons, Constance (1994). *The good divorce*. New York: Harper Collins.

American Bar Association Commission on Domestic Violence. Available at www.abanet.org/domviol/stats.

American Psychological Association (1996). *Report of the American Psychological Association Presidential Task Force on Violence and the Family*. Washington, D.C.: American Psychological Association.

American Psychiatric Association (2000). *Diagnostic and statistical manual of mental disorders 4th edition: DSM-IV-TR*. Washington, D.C.: American Psychiatric Association.

Arizona Supreme Court (2001). *Model parenting time plans for parent/child access*.

Bankcroft, R.L. (2002). The batterer as a parent. *Synergy* (Newsletter of the National Council of Juvenile and Family Court Judges), 6(1), 6–8.

Baumrind, D. (1991). The influence of parenting style on adolescent competence and substance use. *Journal of Early Adolescence, 11*(1), 56–95.

Beck, A.T. (1976). *Cognitive therapy and the emotional disorders*. New York: International Universities Press.

Beck, A.T., Freeman, A., et al. (1990). *Cognitive therapy of personality disorders*. New York: The Guilford Press.

Belenky, M., Clinchy, B., Goldberger, N., & Tarule, J. (1986). *Women's ways of knowing: The development of self, voice, and mind*. New York: Basic Books.

Benjamin, R. D. (2003). "Managing the natural energy of conflict: Mediators, tricksters, and the constructive uses of deception. In Bowling, D. & Hoffman, D. (eds.), *Bringing peace into the room*. San Francisco: Jossey-Bass.

Berkowitz, S.R. (1993). The role of the psychologist in a divorce case. *MPA Quarterly*, 37:1.

Bly, R. (1990). *Iron John: A Book About Men*. New York: Addison-Wesley.

Bogolub, E.B. (1995). *Helping families through divorce: An eclectic approach*. New York: Springer.

Bowen, M.(1976). Theory in the practice of psychotherapy. In Guerin, P.J. (Ed.), *Family therapy*. New York: Gardner Press.

Bower, S.A., & Bower, G.H. (1991). *Asserting yourself: A practical guide for positive change*. Reading, MA: Perseus Books.

Bowlby, J. (1969). *Attachment and loss: Loss (vol. 1): Attachment*. New York: Basic Books.

Bowlby, J. (1980). *Attachment and loss: Loss (vol. 3): Loss, sadness, and depression.* New York: Basic Books.

Bragg, H.L. (2003). *Child protection in families experiencing domestic violence.* Washington, D.C.: National Clearinghouse on Child Abuse and Neglect Information.

Braver, S.L. & O'Connell, D. (1998). *Divorced dads: Shattering the myths.* New York: Penguin.

Carnes, C.N. (2002). *Forensic evaluation of children when sexual abuse is suspected,* Fourth edition. Huntsville, AL: The National Children's Advocacy Center.

Ceci, S.J. & Bruck, M. (1995). *Jeopardy in the courtroom: A scientific analysis of children's testimony.* Washington, DC: American Psychological Association.

Ceci. S.J., Loftus, E.F., Leichtman, M.D., & Bruck, M. (1994). The possible role of source misattributions in the creation of false beliefs among preschoolsers. *International Journal of Clinical and Experimental Hypnosis, 42,* 304–320.

Choca, J.P., Shanley, L.A., & Van Denburg, E. (1992). *Interpretative guide to the Millon Clinical Multiaxial Inventory.* Washington, D.C.: American Psychological Association.

Chodorow, N. (1978). *The reproduction of mothering.* Berkeley: University of California Press.

Clawar S.S., Rivlin BV (1991). *Children held hostage: Dealing with programmed and brainwashed children.* Chicago, American Bar Association.

Cloke, K. (2001). *Mediating dangerously: The frontiers of conflict resolution.* New York: Jossey-Bass.

Cloke, K. (2005). *Into the heart of conflict: Techniques for family mediators.* Presented at the Family Mediation Institute. Wellesley, MA: Massachusetts Council on Family Mediation.

Darnell, D. (1998). *Divorce casualties: Protecting your children from parental alienation.* Lanham, MD: Taylor.

Drozd, L.M. & Olesen, N.W. (2004). Is it abuse, alienation, and/or estrangement? A decision tree. *Journal of Child Custody, 1*(3), 65–106.

Dryden, W. (1990). *Dealing with anger problems: Rational-emotive therapeutic interventions.* Sarasota, FL: Professional Resource Exchange.

Dutton, D.G. & Painter, S. (1993). The battered woman syndrome: effects of severity and intermittency of abuse. *American Journal of Orthopsychiatry, 63,* 614–622.

Einstein, E. & Albert, L. (2005). *Strengthening your stepfamily.* Atascadero, CA: Impact Publishers.

Ellis, A.E. & Lange, A. (1994). *How to keep people from pushing your buttons.* New York: Birch Lane Press.

Ellis, A.E. & MacLaren, C. (2005). *Rational emotive behavior therapy: A therapist's guide* (second edition). Atascadero, CA: Impact Publishers.

Ellis, A.E. & Powers, M.G. (2000). *The secret of overcoming verbal abuse.* North Hollywood, CA: Wilshire.

Eddy, B.(2005). *High-conflict people in legal disputes.* Calgary: Janis Publications.

Emery, R.E. (1994). *Renegotiating family relationships.* New York: Guilford.

Emery, R.E. (2004). *The truth about children and divorce.* New York: Viking.

Emery, R.E., Laumann-Billings, L., Waldron, M., Sbarra, D.A., & Dillon, P. (2001). Twelve-year follow-up of mediated and litigated child custody disputes. *Journal of Consulting and Clinical Psychology, 69,* 323–32.

Enright, R.D.(2001). *Forgiveness is a choice: A step-by-step process for resolving anger and restoring hope.* Washington, D.C.: American Psychological Association.

Fazzone, P.A., Holton, J.K., Reed, B.G. & Center for Substance Abuse Treatment (2001). *Substance abuse treatment and domestic violence.* Rockville, MD: Dept of Health and Human Services, Public Health Service, Substance Abuse and Mental Health Services Administration, Center for Substance Abuse Treatment. HV 6626 .F49 2001

Fisher, B. & Alberti, R.E. (2000). *Rebuilding: When your relationship ends.* Atascadero, CA: Impact Publishers.

Ford, D. (2001). *Spiritual divorce; Divorce as a catalyst for an extraordinary life.* San Francisco: Harper.

Fuhrmann, G., & McGill, J. (1995). *Parents Apart,* Worcester, MA., University of Massachusetts Medical School.

Furstenberg, F.F. & Cherlin, A.J. (1991). *Divided families: What happens to children when parents part.* Harvard University Press, Cambridge.

Garber, B. (2005). The tools and weapons of affiliation: Attachment, alignment and alienation in developmental perspective. Presented at conference entitled *Attachment Theory: Implications for Probate & Juvenile Courts.* Massachusetts Association of Guardians ad Litem, Regis College, Weston, MA.

Garber, B. (2004). Parental alienation in light of attachment theory: Consideration of the broader implications for child development, clinical practice and forensic process. *Journal of Child Custody, 1*(4), 49–76.

Gardner, R.A. (2002). Parental alienation syndrome vs. parental alienation: Which diagnosis should evaluators use in child-custody disputes? *American Journal of Family Therapy,* 30:93–115.

Gardner, R.A.(1999). Family therapy of the moderate type of parental alienation syndrome. *The American Journal of Family Therapy,* 27: 195–212.

Gardner, R.A.(1989). *Parent alienation syndrome.* Cresskill, NJ: Creative Therapeutics.

Gelcer, E., McCabe, A.E., & Smith-Resnick, C. (1990). *Milan family therapy; Variant and invariant methods.* New York: Jason Aronson.

Gilligan, C. (1982). *In a different voice: Psychological theory and women's development.* Cambridge, MA Harvard University Press.

Gondolf, E.W., & Fisher, E.R. (1988). *Battered women as survivors: An alternative to treating learned helplessness.* Lexington, MA: Lexington Books.

Gottman, J. (1994). *What predicts divorce.* Hillsdale, N.J.: Erlbaum.

Gray, J. (1992). *Men are from mars, women are from venus: The classic guide to understanding the opposite sex.* New York: Harper Collins.

Harway, M. & Hansen, M. (1993, 2004). *Spouse abuse; Assessing & treating battered women, batterers, & their children.* Sarasota, FL: Professional Resource Press.

Hawkins, D.R. (1995). *Power vs. force: The hidden determinants of human behavior.* Carlsbad, CA: Hay House.

Haynes, J. (1988), Power Balancing. In J. Folberg and A. Mitro (eds), *Divorce mediation: Theory and practice.* New York: Guilford Press.

Herman, J. (1992). *Trauma and recovery.* New York: Basic Books.

Hetherington, E.M. (1999). The adjustment of children with divorced parents: A risk and resiliency perspective. *Journal of Child Psychology and Psychiatry,* 40, 129–40.

Hetherington, E.M. & Kelly, J. (2002). *For better or for worse: Divorce reconsidered.* W.W. Norton.

Johnson, M.P. (1995). Patriarchal terrorism and common couple violence: Two forms of violence against women. *Journal of Marriage and the Family* 57:283–294.

Johnson, M.P. (2001). Conflict and control: Symmetry and asymmetry in domestic violence. In A. Booth, A.C. Crouter, & M. Clements (Eds.), *Couples in conflict* (pp. 95–104). Mahwah, NJ: Lawrence Erlbaum.

Johnson, M.P. (2005). Apples and oranges in child custody disputes: Intimate terrorism vs. situational couple violence. *Journal of Child Custody,* 2:43–52.

Johnston J.R (1993): Children of divorce who refuse visitation. In Depner C.E. Bray J.H. (Eds.). *Nonresidential parenting: New vistas in family living.* London: Sage Publications.

Johnston, J.R. & Campbell, L.E.G. (1988). *Impasses of divorce; The dynamics and resolution of family conflict.* New York: The Free Press.

Johnston, J.R. & Campbell, L.E.G. (1993). Parent-child relationships in domestic violence families disputing custody. *Family and Conciliation Courts Review, 37*(4), 422–428.

Johnston, J.R., Campbell, L.E.G., & Tall, M.C. (1985). Impasses to the resolution of custody and visitation disputes. *American Journal of Orthopsychiatry,* 55:112–119.

Johnston, J.R. & Roseby, V. (1997). *In the name of the child: A developmental approach to understanding and helping children of conflicted and violent divorce*. New York: The Free Press.

Johnston, J.R., Soyoung, L., & Olesen, N.W. (2005). Allegations and substantiations of abuse in custody-disputing families. *Family Court Review*, 43:283–294.

Kabat-Zinn, J. (1990). *Full catastrophe living: Using the wisdom of your body and mind to face stress, pain, and illness*. New York: Dell.

Kabat-Zinn, J. (2005). *Coming to our sense: Healing ourselves and the world through mindfulness*. New York: Hyperion.

Kaslow, F.W. & Schwartz, L.L. (1987). *The dynamics of divorce: A life cycle perspective*. New York: Brunner/Mazel.

Kassinove, H. & Trafrate, R.C. (2002). *Anger management: The complete treatment guidebook for practitioners*. Atascadero, CA: Impact Publishers.

Kelly, J.B. (1995). Power imbalance in divorce and interpersonal mediation: assessment and intervention. *Mediation Quarterly, 13*(2), 85–98.

Kelly, J.B. (1996). A decade of divorce mediation research. *Family and Conciliation Courts Review, 34*(3), 373-385.

Kelly, J.B. (2000). Children's adjustment in conflicted marriage and divorce: A decade review of research. *Journal of the American Academy of Child & Adolescent Psychiatry*, 39, 963–973.

Kelly, J.B. & Johnston, J.R. (2001). A reformulation of parental alienation syndrome. *Family Court Review*, 39:249–266.

Kelly, J.B. & Lamb, Michael E. (2000). Using child development research to make appropriate custody and access decisions for young children, *Family and Conciliation Courts Review, 38*(3), 297–311.

Kerr, M.E., Bowen, M. (1988). *Family evaluation*. New York: W.W. Norton.

Kessler, S. (1975). *The American way of divorce: Prescriptions for change*. Chicago: Nelson Hall.

Kübler-Ross, E. (1969). *On death and dying*. New York: Touchstone.

Kuehnle, K. (2002). Child sexual abuse evaluations. In A.M. Goldstein & I.B. Weiner (Eds.), *Comprehensive handbook of psychology, Volume eleven: Forensic psychology* (pp. 437–460). New York: Wiley & Sons.

Lamb, M.E., ed. (1986). *The father's role: Applied perspectives*. New York: John Wiley & Sons.

Lamb, M.E., ed. (1997). *The role of the father in child development*. New York: John Wiley & Sons.

Lamb, M.E. & Kelly, J.B. (2001). Using the empirical literature to guide the development of parenting plans for young children. *Family Court Review*, 39, 365–371.

Linehan, M. (1995). *Cognitive-behavioral treatment of borderline personality disorder*. New York: The Guilford Press.

Long, N. & Forehand, R. (2002). *Making divorce easier on your child; 50 effective ways to help children adjust.* New York: Contemporary Books.

Maccoby, E.E., & Mnookin, R.H. (1992). *Dividing the child: Social & legal dilemmas of custody.* Cambridge, MA: Harvard University Press.

Maslow, A. (1970). *Motivation and personality,* 2nd ed. New York: Harper & Row.

Massachusetts Association of Family and Conciliation Courts (2004). *Planning for shared parenting: A guide for parents living apart.*

Macfarlane, J. (2005) *The emerging phenomenon of collaborative family law (CFL): A qualitative study of CFL cases.* Department of Justice Canada.

MacGregor (2005). *Jigsaw puzzle family.* Atascadero, CA: Impact Publishers.

MacGregor, C. (2004). *The divorce helpbook for teens.* Atascadero, CA: Impact Publishers.

MacGregor, C. (2001). *The divorce helpbook for kids.* Atascadero, CA: Impact Publishers.

McGill, H.C., Deutsch, R.M., & Zibbell, R.A. (1999). Visitation and domestic violence: A clinical model of family assessment and treatment planning, *Family and Conciliation Courts Review, 37*(3), 315–334.

McGoldrick, M., Gordano, J., & Garcia-Preto, N. (2005). *Ethnicity and family therapy* (third edition). New York: Guilford.

McKay, M., Rogers, P.D., & McKay, J. (2003). *When anger hurts: Quieting the storm within* (second edition). Oakland, CA: New Harbinger.

Mid-Valley Women's Crisis Service (2003). *Domestic violence.* Salem Oregon. Available at www.wmwcs.com/cycledomesticviolence.

Miller, J.B. (1976). *Toward a new psychology of women.* Boston: Beacon Press.

Millon, T. Millon, C., & Davis, R. (1996). *Millon Clinical Multiaxial Inventory-III.* Bloomington, MN: Pearson Assessments.

Millon, T. (1990). *Toward a new personology: An evolutionary model.* New York: John Wiley & Sons.

Minuchin, S., Rosman, B. L., and Baker, L. (1978). *Psychosomatic families: Anorexia nervosa in context.* Cambridge, MA: Harvard University Press.

Moore, C.W. (1996). *The mediation process: Practical strategies for resolving conflict.* San Francisco: Jossey-Bass.

Neumann (1992). How Mediation Can Effectively Address the Male-Female Power Imbalance in Divorce. *Mediation Quarterly, 9*(3), 227–239.

Nichols, M., & Schwartz, R. (2004). *Family therapy: Concepts and methods* (6th ed.). New York: Allyn & Bacon.

North, J. (1987). Wrongdoing and forgiveness. *Philosophy,* 62: 499-508.

O'Hanlon, B. (1994). The third wave. *Family Therapy Networker, 18*(6), 18–26, 28–29.

O'Leary, K.D. (1993). Through a psychological lens: Personality traits, personality disorders, and levels of violence. In R. Gelles & D. Loseke (Eds.), *Current controversies on family violence*. Newbury Park, CA: Sage.

O'Leary, K.D. (2001). Psychological abuse: A variable deserving critical attention in domestic violence. In O'Leary, K. D., & Maiuro, RD (Eds.). *Psychological abuse in violent domestic relations*. New York: Springer.

Oregon Judicial Department State Family Law Advisory Committee & Office of the State Court Administrator (2003). *Basic parenting plan guide for parents*.

Papernow, P.L (1993). *Becoming a stepfamily: Patterns of development in remarried families*. New York: Jossey-Bass.

Potter-Efron, R. (2001). *Stop the anger now: A workbook for the prevention, containment, and resolution of anger*. Oakland, CA: New Harbinger.

Pruett, M.K., Ebling, R., & Insabella, G. (2004). Critical aspects of parenting plans for young children. *Family Court Review*, 42: 39–59.

Pruett, M.K., & Pruett, K.D. (1998). Fathers, divorce and children. In K.D. Pruett & M.K. Pruett (Eds.), *Child custody issues*. New York: W.B. Saunders.

Rand, C.R. (1997). The spectrum of parental alienation syndrome (Part 1). *American Journal of Forensic Psychology, 15*(3), 23–50.

Renzetti, C.M. (1992). *Violent betrayal: Partner abuse in lesbian relationships*. Newbury Park, CA: Sage.

Renzetti, C.M. (1993). On dancing with a bear: Reflections on some of the current debates among domestic violence theorists. In Hamberger, L.K. & Renzetti, C. (Eds.). *Domestic partner abuse*. New York: Springer.

Ricci, I. (1997). *Mom's house, dad's house: Making two homes for your child*. New York: Fireside.

Rich, P. & Schwartz, L.L. (1999). The healing journey through divorce. New York: John Wiley & Sons.

Schwab, W.H. (2004). Collaborative lawyering: A closer look at an emerging practice. *Pepperdine Dispute Resolution Law Journal*, 3: 354–396.

Seligman, M.P. (1975). *Helplessness: On depression, development and death*. New York: Wiley.

Selman, R.L. (1980). *The growth of interpersonal understanding*. New York: Academic Press.

Selvini Palazzoli, M., Boscolo, L., Cecchin, G., & Prata, G. (1980). Hypothesizing-circularity-neutrality: Three guidelines for the conductor of the session. *Family Process* 19:3–12.

Shapse, S. (2005). Private conversation.

Stahl, P.M. (2000). *Parenting after divorce: A guide to resolving conflicts and meeting your children's needs*. Impact Publishers.

Strack, S. (1999). *Essentials of Millon inventories assessment*. New York: John Wiley & Sons.

Straus, M.A., Gelles, R.J. (1990), *Physical violence in American families: Risk factors and adaptations to violence in 8,145 families*. New Brunswick, NJ:Transaction Publishers.

Tannen, D. (1990). *You just don't understand: Women and men in conversation*. New York: Ballentine Books.

Tjaden, P. & Thoennes, N. (1998). *Prevalence, incidence, and consequences of violence against women: Findings from the national violence against women survey*. Washington, D.C.: National Institute of Justice.

Tillet, G. (1999). *Resolving conflict*. Oxford: Oxford University Press.

Tishelman, A. Appell, J., McLeod, S., & Nathanson, S. (2006). Discussion of the Governor's Commission on Sexual and Domestic Violence, Probate Court Issues Subcommittee. Commonwealth of Massachusetts.

Tolle, E. (1999). *The power of now: A guide to spiritual enlightenment*. Novato, CA: New World Library.

Trafford, A. (1982). *Crazy time: Surviving divorce and building a new life*. New York: Harper Collins.

Ury, W. (1991). *Getting past no: Negotiating with difficult people*. New York: Bantam Books.

U.S. Department of Justice Office of Justice Programs, Bureau of Justice Statistics (2003). *National Crime Victimization Survey*. Available at www.ojp.usdoj.gov/bjs/cvict.htm.

Walker, L. (1984). *The battered woman syndrome*. New York: Springer.

Visher, E.B. & Visher, J.S. (1996). *Therapy with stepfamilies*. New York: Brunner/Mazel.

Walker, L. (1999). *The battered woman syndrome* (2nd edition). New York: Springer.

Wallerstein, J.S., & Blakeslee, S. (2003). *What about the kids? Raising your children before, during, and after divorce*. New York: Hyperion.

Wallerstein, J.S., Lewis, J.M., & Blakeslee, S. (2000). *The unexpected legacy of divorce; A 25-year landmark study*. New York: Hyperion.

Ward, P. (2005). Family wars — In the trenches. Presented at conference entitled *Attachment Theory: Implications for Probate & Juvenile Courts*. Massachusetts Association of Guardians ad Litem, Regis College, Weston, MA.

Warshak, R.A. (2000). Blanket restrictions: Overnight contact between parents and young children. *Family & Conciliation Courts Review*, 38, 422–445.

Warshak, R.A. (2001a). Current Controversies Regarding Parental Alienation Syndrome. *American Journal of Forensic Psychology, 19*(3), 29–59.

Warshak, R.A. (2001b). *Divorce poison*. New York: Regan Books.

Warshak, R.A.(2003). Bringing sense to parental alienation: A look at the disputes and the evidence. *Family law quarterly*. 37:273–300.

Watzlawick, P., Weakland, H.H., & Fisch, R.(1974). *Change: Principles of problem formation and problem resolution.* New York: Norton.

Weeks, G.R. & L'Abate, L. (1982). *Paradoxical psychotherapy: Theory and practice with individuals, couples, and families.* New York: Brunner/Mazel.

White, M. & Epston, D. (1990). *Narrative means to therapeutic ends.* New York: W.W. Norton.

Whiting, R. (1988). *Guidelines to designing therapeutic rituals.* In Imber-Black, E., Roberts, J., & Whiting, R. Rituals in families and family therapy. New York: W.W. Norton.

Wolpe, J. & Lazarus, A. (1966). *Behavior therapy techniques: A guide to the treatment of neuroses.* New York: Pergamon Press.

Zibbell, R.A. (2004). A semi-structured initial interview for assessing the range of intimate partner violence. Presented at conference entitled *Issues of Intimate Partner Violence in Family Evaluations.* Massachusetts Association of Guardians Ad Litem, Regis College, Weston, MA.

Zibbell, R.A. (2005). Common couple aggression: Frequency and implications for child custody and access evaluations. *Family Court Review, 43*(3), 454–465.

Appendix 1

Interview Questions for Assessing Domestic Violence Adapted from Zibbell, 2004

1. **Regarding the development of the relationship:**
   a. What attracted you to your partner?
   b. Describe the things that you enjoyed doing together.
   c. Have these changed over time?
   d. How much time did you spend together early in the relationship?
   e. How did this change over time?
   f. What was the best period of the relationship? Why?

2. **Regarding outside relationships and activities:**
   a. Do you have your own friends? How often do you see them?
   b. Does your partner have friends? How often does he/she see them?
   c. What is your relationship with your family? With your partner's family?
   d. What is your partner's relationship with your family? Yours with your partner's family?
   e. Have you pursued your own interests? How has this changed over the course of the relationship?
   f. Have either of you stood in the way of the other seeing friends or family?
   g. Have either of you prohibited the other from pursuing outside interests or activities?
   h. Does your partner follow you to "check up" on you or check the mileage on your car? If so, how often?
   i. Do you ever follow your spouse to check up on where s/he is going?) If so, how often?
   j. Does your partner telephone you a lot while you are at work or at home? If so, how often?
   k. How often do you telephone your partner during the course of a typical day?

3. **About decision making in the relationship:**
   a. Regarding money?
      i. Who pays the bills?
      ii. Who makes more money?
      iii. Do you have joint bank accounts and/or separate bank accounts?
      iv. Who keeps the bank records of joint accounts, of your accounts, and of your partner's accounts?
      v. Who made major purchases?
      vi. Do you own a home? In whose name is it?
      vii. What amount of money could you or your partner spend without first checking with the other?
   b. Regarding work and education?
      i. Has either of you stood in the way of the other's job or education?
   c. Family chores?
      i. What household tasks do you do?
      ii. What household tasks does your partner do?
      iii. How are decisions made about who will do a particular task?
   d. Regarding children?
      i. How do you handle discipline?
      ii. How does your partner handle discipline?
      iii. Do either of you use physical punishment?
      iv. Have either you or your partner ever hurt the children physically?
      v. Do you or your partner yell at the children?
      vi. Do you and your partner generally agree about how to handle the children?
      vii. Is there one child about whom you tend to disagree most?
      viii. What happens when you and your partner do not agree on how to handle a situation with one of your children?

4. **About the dynamics of conflict in the relationship:**
   a. How often did you and your spouse argue?
   b. What issues did you generally fight about?
   c. Describe a typical fight that you have had with your partner.
      i. If I were a fly on the wall, what would I have heard?
      ii. Who initiated the fight?
      iii. What happened next?
      iv. Then what?
      v. How would the fight end?
      vi. Did you or your partner raise your voices?

    vii. Did your partner insult you?
        1. How often?
        2. What kinds of words did s/he use?
    viii. Has your partner ever blamed you or said you were at "fault" for family problems
    ix. Did you insult your partner?
        1. How often?
        2. What kinds of words did you use?
    x. Have you ever blamed your partner for causing problems in the family?
    xi. Have either of you put the other down in public?
  d. Have either of you ever threatened suicide in an argument? How did the other respond?
  e. Have either of you ever threatened divorce in an argument? How did the other respond?
  f. Have either of you ever threatened to take the children away or get them from the other in a custody battle?
  g. Were you ever afraid of your partner? Are you now?
  h. Has your partner ever been afraid of you? Is s/he now?

5. **About physical violence:**
  a. Have fights ever gone beyond words or yelling? If yes, describe.
  b. Have either of you ever:
    i. Thrown things?
    ii. Broken things?
    iii. Punched or kicked walls?
    iv. Slammed doors?
    v. Locked the other in or out of somewhere?
    vi. Driven the other to a place and forced the other out of the car?
    vii. Confiscated the other's car keys?
    viii. Kept the other up at night to "talk" so that the other was not able to sleep?
    ix. Threatened to hurt you?
    x. Has your partner ever been aggressive physically with you? Describe.
    xi. Have you ever gotten "physical" with your partner? Describe.
    xii. How often have there been physical incidents?
    xiii. Have you or your partner ever called the police on one another?
    xiv. Have either of you ever requested protection via an abuse order?

6. **About the violent incident(s):**
   a. When was the first incident? Describe
      i. What happened first?
      ii. What happened next?
      iii. Then what? Etc.
      iv. What triggered the incident?
      v. How did the incident end?
   b. When was the most recent incident? Describe in detail — first, then, etc.
   c. Describe the worst incident in detail — first, then, etc.
   d. How did the incident(s) affect you?
   e. How did the incident(s) affect your partner?
   f. Have either of you ever been injured as the result of a violent incident between you? Describe the injuries.
   g. Did a doctor or hospital treat the injuries?

7. **About weapons:**
   a. Have you or your partner ever possessed or used a weapon?
   b. Are there weapons in your home?
   c. Where are they kept and who has access?
   d. Has either of you threatened the other with a weapon?

8. **About substance use:**
   a. Do you drink or use drugs? If yes, how often?
   b. Does your spouse drink or use drugs? If yes, how often?
   c. Was either of you drinking or using drugs during the violent incidents you mentioned?

9. **About your sexual relationship:**
   a. Did you have the ability to initiate sexual relations?
   b. Were you able to decline sexual relations if the other initiated it?
   c. Has your partner ever forced you into sexual activity you did not want? Describe.
   d. Has your partner humiliated or embarrassed you in public with comments or criticisms about your sexual abilities or the sexual relationship? Describe.

10. **About pets:**
    a. Do you have pets?
    b. How are they treated?
    c. Have they ever been mistreated by a family member?

11. About the children:

    a. Have arguments taken place in front of the children?

    b. Where were the children when the incidents described above happened?

    c. What do you think that the children have seen and/or heard?

    d. Have the children ever said anything about your arguments?

    e. Have you ever talked with the children about them?

    f. Are any of the children afraid of you or your partner?

    g. Do any of the children lose their temper?

        i. In what way?

        ii. How often?

    h. Do the children hit one another?

    i. Do any of the children get in frequent fights with peers?

    j. Do any of the children ever try to hurt you or your partner?

    k. If yes, how has this affected your parenting of them? Your partner's parenting?

    l. What consequences have there been for the children physically hurting someone?

    m. Has the department of family or social services been involved with your family?

Appendix 2

Interview Questions for Assessing Domestic Violence Child Protocol

When interviewing children of divorce about abuse, the general principles and the interview protocol below can be used to question children about domestic abuse. This protocol uses methods contained in Bragg (2003), Carnes (2002), and Faller (2003), and Kuehnle (2002), Tishelman, Appell, McLeod, & Nathanson (2006).

General Principles

It is useful to follow these guiding principles to help the child feel comfortable and to avoid unduly influencing the child's perceptions:

- Be clear about your role with the child and the limits of confidentiality.
- Build an initial rapport with the child by addressing neutral topics such as school, hobbies or activities.
- Word questions appropriately for the child's developmental level.
- Review the child's ability to distinguish between truth and lies. Encourage the truth. Older children can often define truth and lie and younger children will often be able to distinguish between the truth and a lie with examples. Eg. " I am a boy. Is that a truth or a lie?" If the child tells stories that sound questionable, the interviewer can ask if it is a truth or a lie.
- Give children permission to answer questions in whatever way they want. Give them permission to say: "I don't want to talk about it," "I don't understand the question", "I don't remember" or "I don't know." Rehearse these responses by giving them neutral questions that can be answered in these ways.
- Progress slowly from general questions to questions that more specifically address the management of conflict in the family. Eg.

"Tell me about your family" to "Tell me about your [mother/father]," to ... "Do people in your family get angry at one another?" Focused questions can involve *places (locations), persons, actions or events.* However, it is best not to ask combination questions. In other words, one can ask, "tell me about yelling," and "Tell me about your dad," but it is less recommended to ask a child to "tell me about when your dad yells" as the latter tends to be suggestive.

❖ Use open-ended questions, followed by requests for elaboration.

❖ Be careful not to use leading questions, especially questions that contain the suggestion of an answer embedded in the question (e.g., Your dad tickles you a lot, doesn't he?)

❖ If the child mentions a specific incident that may have happened, indicate that you understand something may have occurred and ask the child to tell you what happened from beginning to middle to end.

❖ For some children, especially younger ones, drawing the place and/or the event can be useful.

❖ If a child provides a response that requires elaboration, ask for additional elaboration. For instance, if the child says, "Mommy is mean," ask, "Can you tell me more about that?" or "Can you tell more about how she is mean?"

❖ It may be useful to follow a child's general response with a multiple choice question that helps to refine the response without leading the child to respond with a preordained answer. For instance, if a child indicates that daddy hit mommy: "Were you inside your house or outside when daddy hit her, or somewhere else?" Make sure you leave options for all answers in multiple choice questions but do not include too many choices.

❖ Attempt to get the full sequence of events from beginning to end whenever possible, using such prompts as "what happened before (or after) that?" With young children, this may not be possible.

❖ In order to evaluate children's responses, determine whether they understand time concepts such as before and after or the length of time between events by asking such questions as "When do you have breakfast?," "When do you have lunch?," "Which one is before the other one?" "How much time is it between breakfast and lunch?" "What do you usually do after lunch?," etc.

❖ Attempt to recruit information about place, location, actions, persons, and sensory information.

❖ Attempt to determine the child's feelings and the feelings of others during or after events that the child describes. It can be useful for young children for the examiner to present pictures of heads with angry, sad, scared, confused, nervous and happy faces that are drawn by the examiner or contained on a feelings poster to which the child points.

❖ *Specific Interview Questions*

1. **About the possible influence by a parent or other on the child's statements:**
   a. Do you have any worries about talking to me?
   b. Has anyone told you what you should tell me? Who?
   c. What are you supposed to tell me?
   d. Is there anything you're not supposed to tell me?
   e. What do you think will happen if you tell me something different from what you were supposed to say?

2. **General questions about the family:**
   a. Tell me who is in your family.
   b. Tell me about your [father, mother, sister, brother].
   c. What is [father, mother, sister, brother] like?
   d. Is there anyone in your family that you like to spend time with?
   e. Do you talk to anyone in your family if you are upset?

3. **About the nature and frequency of exposure to domestic violence:**
   a. Most people get angry sometimes. Do people at your house get angry with one another?
   b. How can you tell when [your mom, dad, sister, brother, etc.] are angry?
   c. What does [your mom, dad, sister, brother, etc.] do when they are angry?
   d. Do people in your family fight? Who fights with who?
   e. What do they do when they fight?
   f. Do your parents fight with one another?
   g. How do you know when they are fighting?
   h. Have you seen the fights? Heard the fights?
   i. Where are you when they fight?
   j. What kinds of things do your parents fight about?
   k. What kinds of things do (your sister, brother, other) fight about?
   l. What happens when they argue?
   m. Does anything bad or scary happen when they fight?

n. Do they ever hurt one another? If so, describe what happens.

o. How does the [bad thing] usually start?

p. How often do your mom and dad (or other) argue? (For young child, did this happen just once or more than once?)

q. Have the police ever come to your home? Why?

r. Have you ever seen people in your family hurt one another?

s. Can you remember one particular fight? Tell me what happened.
   * What happened first?
   * What happened next?
   * And then, etc.?

t. How did the fighting make you feel?

4. About safety risks to children:

a. What happens to you when mom and dad fight?

b. Do others in your family ever get involved when mom and dad fight? Who?

c. Tell me about it. Can you tell me about one time you another family member/you got involved during a fight?

d. How do fights between your parent's end?

e. What do you do when your parent's fight?

f. Has anything scary or bad ever happened to you during a fight between your parents?

g. Have you ever been hit or hurt when mom and dad (or other) are fighting?

h. Has your brother or sister ever been hit or hurt during a fight?

i. What do you do when they start arguing or when someone starts hitting?

j. Has either your mom or dad hurt your pet? Has anyone else in your house?

k. Does anyone in your family have a gun or knife? Who?
   * What can you tell me about the [gun or knife]?
   * Do you know where it is kept?
   * Have you ever played with it?

5. About substance use and abuse:

a. What do your parents like to eat and drink?

b. Does anyone in your house drink alcohhol [grown up drinks that children are not allowed to drink]?

c. What do they drink?

d. How often do they drink? [Do they drink every day, less than that, more than that, etc.?]

e. How much do they drink? [Do they drink a glass, several glasses, a bottle, etc.?]
f. Does anyone in your family smoke cigarettes?
g. How often do they smoke cigarettes?
h. Does anyone in your family smoke anything else?
i. Describe what they smoke.
j. How often do they smoke it?
k. Does anyone in your family take medicine or pills?
l. What do they take it for?
m. How often do they take it?
n. Does anyone in your family give [him/herself shots]
o. Why does [s/he] do that for?
p. How often does [s/he] do that?
q. What happens after [s/he] [drinks, smokes, takes medicine, or has a shot]?
r. How do other people in the family react?
s. How do you feel when [s/he] [drinks, smokes, takes medicine, or has a shot]?
t. Do people in your family ever get very angry after they have [had a drink, taken medicine, etc.]?
u. Tell me about what happens.

6. **About the impact of exposure to domestic violence:**
   a. Do you think about mom and dad (or others in home) fighting/arguing? —-How much do you think about mom and dad fighting/arguing (once a month, once a week, once a day, once an hour, etc)
   b. When do you think about mom and dad fighting/arguing?
      ❖ Do you think about it when you are at school?
      ❖ While you're playing?
      ❖ When you're by yourself?
   c. How does the fighting/arguing make you feel?
   d. Do you ever have trouble sleeping at night?
   e. Do you ever have good dreams? Tell me about one good dream.
   f. Do you ever have bad dreams? If so, what are they about?
   g. Do you tell anyone about the dreams? What would you like [your mother, father]to do to make you feel better?
   h. Are you ever afraid at home? Tell me about when you are afraid at home.
   i. Are you ever afraid to leave home?
   j. What or who makes you afraid?
   k. Do you think it's okay to hit when you're angry?
   l. When is it okay to hit someone?

7. **About protective factors.**
   a. What do you do when mom and dad (or other) are fighting?
      If the child has difficulty responding to an open-ended
      question, the interviewer can ask if the child has:
      ❖ Stayed in the room
      ❖ Left or hidden
      ❖ Gotten help
      ❖ Gone to an older sibling
      ❖ Asked parents to stop
      ❖ Tried to stop the fighting
   b. Have you ever called someone to help when your parents are
      fighting?
   c. Have you ever talked to anyone about your parent's fighting?
   d. Is there an adult you can talk to about what's happening at
      home?
   e. What makes you feel better when you think about your parent's
      fighting?
   f. Who takes care of you when you are upset about the fighting?
   g. How do they take care of you?
   h. Are there things you like about how they do this? Tell me about
      them.
   i. Are there things you don't like about how they do this?
   j. Tell me about them.

8. **About facts or reported facts that the examiner may have (if
   not previously addressed by the child):**
   a. I understand that . . . or X told me that . . . (Y happened.)
   b. Can you tell me about that?
   c. Did you see what happened?
   d. Did you hear it when it happened?
   e. What were you told about what happened? By whom?

Appendix 3

Developmental Issues and Parenting Plan Guidelines for Children of Divorce

The following is a brief summary of major issues and considerations for children at various ages. It offers some guidelines for the development of parenting plans. These guidelines are based on information from the Massachusetts Association of Family and Conciliation Courts (2004), Arizona Supreme Court (2001) and the Oregon Judicial Department (2003). Parenting plan guidelines from these organizations are available at www.afccnet.org. The latter two sources provide detailed parenting plan alternatives for children of different ages and parents with different parenting styles.

Be aware that there is no definitive research as to what constitutes the best parenting plan. Multiple factors should be considered when developing a plan, including:

- ❖ the child's temperament and/or special needs,
- ❖ strength of the child's attachment to each parent,
- ❖ relationship with siblings and extended family,
- ❖ geographic distance between households,
- ❖ flexibility of parents' schedules,
- ❖ childcare needs,
- ❖ cultural and religious practices,
- ❖ parents' ability to meet the needs of the child,
- ❖ level of conflict between the parents, and
- ❖ parents' ability to communicate with one another.

Parenting plans need to change as the developmental needs of the child change and as family circumstances change.

❖ *Infants/Babies (0–18 months)*

Developmental Tasks

- ❖ Developing a sense of trust in the environment and significant others
- ❖ Forming secure attachments — multiple attachments can be formed
- ❖ Acquiring new skills rapidly

Psychological Issues

- ❖ Need for predictability and consistency
- ❖ Sensitivity to environment, parental moods
- ❖ Recognition of caregivers by age of six months
- ❖ Stranger anxiety more common as baby gets older

Parenting Plan Considerations

- ❖ Allow frequent contact with both parents.
- ❖ Minimize time of separation from primary caregiver(s). Daytime visits may gradually extend to one or two nonconsecutive overnights for older infants.
- ❖ Maintain feeding and sleeping routines from day to day and between households.
- ❖ Facilitate communication between parents. A communication log is a useful tool.
- ❖ Minimize conflict during transitions between parents.

❖ *Toddlers (18–36 months)*

Developmental Tasks

- ❖ Separation-Individuation
- ❖ Mastery of speech and mobility
- ❖ Learning self-control

Psychological Issues

- ❖ Separation anxiety and fears not unusual
- ❖ Internalized representation of primary caretakers is formed
- ❖ Need for limits and structure
- ❖ Regression common when child is stressed
- ❖ Temper tantrums common

Parenting Plan Considerations

- ❖ Maintain predictable schedules between households.

- Avoid separation from either parent for more than to two or three days, except during occasional vacation periods.
- Arrange three daytime contacts per week with non-residential parent. May include one or two nonconsecutive overnights, working toward two consecutive overnights for older toddlers.
- Use transitional objects (picture of parent, toy that goes back and forth, etc.).
- Maintain daily phone contact with other parent.

Pre-schoolers (3–5 years)

Developmental Tasks
- Defining one's role in the family
- Management of emotions and impulses
- Development of socialization skills
- Sex role identification

Psychological Issues
- Egocentric view of world (sees self as center of the universe)
- May blame self for the divorce
- May say what parent wants to hear
- May misunderstand and misrepresent facts
- Bad dreams common
- Need for consistency and predictability
- Need for structured time with other children
- Awareness of holiday celebrations

Parenting Plan Considerations
- Avoid separating child from either parent for more than three days as a general rule. Two or three overnights with non-residential parent okay.
- If both parents have been highly involved, separations from one parent for up to five days can be implemented as long as the child is comfortable with this and contact with other parent is maintained.
- Maintain daily telephone contact.
- Use transitional objects.
- Incorporate holiday plans and birthday celebrations into parenting plan.
- Occasional vacations of up to a week with one parent may be arranged, as long as regular overnights have been established and regular telephone contact with other parent is maintained.

❖ School Age (6–9 years)

Developmental Tasks

* Development of personal, social and academic skills
* Development of peer and community relationships
* Growth of empathy
* Development of morality
* Concrete (black and white) thinking

Psychological Issues

* Greater independence
* Comprehension of time
* Can adjust to different parenting styles
* Desire for parental reunification a common theme
* Conflicting loyalties possible
* Family as emotional anchor

Parenting Plan Considerations

* If both parents are highly involved, children can generally adjust to visits of up to four nights with non-residential parent. Plan in which each parent retains the same two consecutive weeknights consistently (M, T or W, Th) and alternates three-day weekends (F, S, S) can be implemented if child is able to accommodate to a 5, 5, 2, 2 schedule over fourteen days.
* If there is one primary parent, one to three overnights may be possible with non-residential parent so that non-residential parent can participate in schooling.
* Maintain regular phone contact with other parent, preferably daily.
* Use calendar as a tool for helping children track visits or changes in residence.
* Inform school of divorce and parenting plan.
* Occasional vacations of up to one week with one parent can be implemented as long as telephone contact is maintained with other parent.

❖ Pre-teens (10–13 years)

Developmental Tasks

* Development of self-esteem
* Emergence of values and beliefs
* Forging of connections with school and peers

Psychological Issues

* Greater ability to balance differing parental practices
* Can be rule-bound
* May align themselves with one parent
* May blame one parent for divorce
* Increased attachment to friends
* Need to balance family time with outside activities
* Need for open communication with parents
* Privacy increasingly important
* Need for structure

Parenting Plan Considerations

* Children can accommodate to a variety of parenting plans. Regular contact with both parents should be maintained.
* Children's preferences should be considered, with parents making the final decision.
* Accommodate child's social activities and commitments.
* Vacation periods may extend to two or more weeks if there is periodic telephone contact with other parent.
* Allow privacy for telephone contact with other parent.

Adolescents (14–17 years)

Developmental Tasks

* Development of separate identity from parents
* Development of moral values
* Incorporation of positive role models

Psychological Issues

* Desire for a say in parenting plan
* May express resistance and rebelliousness
* Ambivalence around dependence and independence
* Tendency to be self-centered
* Increasing awareness of sexuality and relationship issues
* Increased ability for abstract thinking
* Easily shamed and/or embarrassed
* May be overly influenced (positively or negatively) by peers
* Need permission to have less family involvement
* Need appropriate structure and limits

Parenting Plan Considerations

* Expect some resistance to a well-defined schedule.

❖ Be as flexible as possible.

❖ Know that adolescents may have difficulty with midweek visits or overnights due to demands of homework or other activities

❖ Expect that adolescents may want to try different plans or change home bases for periods of time.

❖ Young Adults/College Students (18–21 years)

Most parent guides do not include guidelines for young adults, as they are considered able to make their own decisions. However, the following guidelines are offered:

Developmental Tasks

❖ Establishment of adult independence
❖ Acquisition and maintenance of adult self-care skills
❖ Consolidation of moral values
❖ Consolidation of self-identity

Psychological Issues

❖ Need to touch base with parents as independence grows
❖ Can still be deeply saddened by loss of home base if divorce occurs after leaving home
❖ May experience loyalty conflicts when deciding how to visit "home"
❖ May attempt to play confidant to parent.

Parenting Plan Considerations

❖ Be flexible.
❖ Avoid trapping young adult in loyalty conflict.
❖ Maintain one or more home bases, with available bedrooms and privacy, etc., to which young adult can return.
❖ Be open to preferences of young adult.
❖ Provide structure for helping young adult deal with significant events and holidays if he/she is unable to state preferences.
❖ Maintain regular contact and encourage contact with other parent.

Index

The Practical Therapist Series®

Books in *The Practical Therapist Series®* are designed to answer the troubling "what-do-I-do-now-and-how-do-I-do-it?" questions often confronted in the practice of psychotherapy. Written in plain language, technically innovative, theoretically integrative, filled with case examples, *The Practical Therapist Series®* brings the wisdom and experience of expert mentors to the desk of every therapist.

Rational Emotive Behavior Therapy
A Therapist's Guide (Second Edition)
Albert Ellis, Ph.D. and Catharine MacLaren, M.S.W., CEAP
Hardcover: $24.95   176 pages   ISBN: 1-886230-61-7
Up-to-date guidebook by the innovator of Rational Emotive Behavior Therapy. Includes thorough description of REBT theory and procedures, case examples, exercises.

Metaphor in Psychotherapy
Clinical Applications of Stories and Allegories
Henry T. Close, Th.M.
Hardcover: $29.95   320 pages   ISBN: 1-886230-10-2
Creative collection of stories and allegories, and how to use them as teaching tools in psychotherapy, including metaphors for children.

Integrative Brief Therapy: Cognitive, Psycho-dynamic, Humanistic & Neurobehavioral Approaches
John Preston, Psy.D.
Softcover: $27.95   272 pages   ISBN: 1-886230-09-9
Answers the perennial therapist question, "What do I do now?" Integrates proven elements of therapeutic efficacy from diverse theoretical viewpoints.

Anger Management: The Complete Treatment Guidebook for Practitioners
Howard Kassinove, Ph.D. and R. Chip Tafrate, Ph.D.
Softcover: $27.95   320 pages   ISBN: 1-886230-45-5
Research-based and empirically validated "anger episode model" presented in a desktop manual for practitioners. Offers a comprehensive state-of-the-art program that can be implemented almost immediately in any practice setting.
Also available on 2-DVD set, approx. 150 min., $69.95.

Please see the following page for more books.

The Practical Therapist Series®

The Soul of Counseling: A New Model for Understanding Human Experience
Dwight Webb, Ph.D.
Softcover: $24.95   192 pages   ISBN: 1-886230-59-5
Practical, down-to-earth aids to integrate into professional psychotherapy practice to help deal with clients' issues of the human spirit.

Meditative Therapy
Facilitating Inner-Directed Healing
Michael L. Emmons, Ph.D. and Janet Emmons, M.S.
Softcover: $27.95   230 pages   ISBN: 1-886230-11-0
Guide to creating the conditions for natural healing and recovery. Help clients harness their inner resources for emotional, physical, and spiritual growth.

Creative Therapy with Children and Adolescents
Angela Hobday, M.Sc. and Kate Ollier, M.Psych.
Hardcover: $21.95   192 pages   ISBN: 1-886230-19-6
Over 100 activities for therapeutic work with children, adolescents, and families. Simple ideas, fun games, fresh innovations to use as tools to supplement a variety of therapeutic interventions.

How to Fail as a Therapist
Bernard Schwartz, Ph.D. and John V. Flowers, Ph.D.
Hardcover: $22.95   160 pages   ISBN: 1-886230-70-6
Well-researched strategies reduce dropout rates and increase positive treatment outcomes. This book details the 50 most common errors therapists make, and how to avoid them. Practical, helpful steps for avoiding not recognizing one's limitations, performing incomplete assessments, ignoring science, ruining the client relationship, much more.

Ask your local or online bookseller, or call 1-800-246-7228 to order direct.

Impact 📖 Publishers®
POST OFFICE BOX 6016 • ATASCADERO, CALIFORNIA 93423-6016
Visit us on the Internet at WWW.impactpublishers.com • Write for our free catalog.

Since 1970 — Psychology you can use, from professionals you can trust